Praise for *So That All May Flourish*

"This is an essential read for anyone who wonders about the value of Lutheran higher education in the 21st century. The selections offer a necessary combination of descriptive, prescriptive, and critical analysis to the field that each author tills as an educator or administrator. The goal of the book, which is one and the same with the goal of Lutheran higher education, is summed in the title: that *all* may flourish. Not just Lutherans, or just Christians, or even just people, but that all creatures may thrive. Toward such a lofty goal, each contributor delivers a deep, timely, and sacred reflection."
—Drew Tucker, university pastor and director of the Center for Faith and Learning, Capital University

"This book shows, more clearly than any other document, why and how the Lutheran tradition with its special vocabulary of vocation and neighbor-love, its commitment to musical intelligence, its integral connection from the beginning to free and open inquiry, and its care for creation, has been so specially impressive in strengthening higher education amid all the opportunities that pluralism and diversity offer to colleges and universities today. In many respects the NECU schools celebrated here are more like their Roman Catholic counterparts than they are like other Protestant schools; they are indeed 'rooted and open.'"
—Mark R. Schwehn, professor of humanities, Christ College; project director, Lilly Fellows Program, Valparaiso University

"As a long-time president of one of our NECU institutions, I firmly believe that our Lutheran intellectual and theological traditions provide a durable foundation for higher education in the 21st century. Our 'third way,' between sectarian and secular extremes, offers our students and faculty an education that is rooted and open, faithful and relevant. In this important volume, some of our leading scholars plumb the depths of our Lutheran tradition to offer us a roadmap to that education, exploring its theological roots, its curricular and pedagogical priorities, and its relevance for some of our most pressing social issues. I commend this volume to all of us who care deeply about the future of Lutheran higher education in the 21st century."

—Paul C. Pribbenow, president, Augsburg University

"*So That All May Flourish* is both the title of this book and the *telos* of all Lutheran higher education. Fifteen authors, each of them teachers as well as scholars, eschew today's binary of education as public good or private benefit in favor of embracing the core commitments, signature strengths, and contemporary callings that make education of the whole person for the sake of the whole world possible. Lutheran institutions of higher education engage today's issues and explore tomorrow's methods because they are Lutheran, which is to say: always reforming, ever widening access, steadfast in love of neighbor. Every vocation of every neighbor is needed so that all may flourish."

—Colleen Windham-Hughes, professor of religion and Wilbert & Darlene Carlson Endowed Chair in Youth & Family Ministry, California Lutheran University

"Call them the Lutheran Brain Trust: these fifteen contributors represent some of the finest theological thinking and cultural reflection on Lutheran higher education today. Each one of them is also a skilled practitioner of the pedagogies and perspectives that they describe. Their reflections on the inheritance, challenges, and opportunities at Lutheran colleges and universities are essential reading—not only within the denomination, but for everyone working to help independent higher education fulfill its promising future."

—David S. Cunningham, professor of theology, Aquinas College; director, Network for Vocation in Undergraduate Education (NetVUE)

So That All May Flourish

So That All May Flourish

The Aims of Lutheran Higher Education

Edited by
Marcia J. Bunge, Jason A. Mahn, and Martha E. Stortz

Fortress Press
Minneapolis

SO THAT ALL MAY FLOURISH
The Aims of Lutheran Higher Education

Cover design and illustration: Soupiset Design

Print ISBN: 978-1-5064-8089-3
eBook ISBN: 978-1-5064-8090-9

Contents

Foreword

Mark Wilhelm, Executive Director, Network of ELCA Colleges and Universities

Lutheran higher education is an intellectual and educational tradition that matters. It sparked a radical commitment to universal education in the sixteenth century and has played a major role in the development of western higher education. This tradition also prompted the creation of a host of colleges and universities here and abroad, including the twenty-seven institutions in the Network of ELCA Colleges and Universities (NECU). These institutions provide students today with a holistic, liberal arts education that fosters lifelong learning and equips them for service and leadership in the world. The Lutheran intellectual and educational tradition matters in the history of education and for students and society today. Amidst rapid changes in and even widespread misconceptions of higher education today, it is important to pause, name, and celebrate the influence, contributions, and characteristics of this distinctive tradition.

Remember that the Lutheran Reformation was not only about the reform of the church but also about the reform of society, including the reform of education. Those reforms included commitments such as an insistence on the critical study of sources, education for the community as a whole instead elites only, and education imbued with the breadth of liberal studies. These and other educational ideals forged in the Lutheran Reformation have continued to influence western higher education to the present day.

The common heuristic categories used to label higher education
in the western world—character education (liberal arts colleges) and
knowledge-creation education (research universities)—have roots in
the Lutheran tradition. Education for character development (sometimes called "educating the whole person") was shaped directly by the
sixteenth-century Lutheran Reformation. Knowledge-creation education has its origins in the founding of the University of Berlin in 1809
and developed within the Lutheran milieu in early nineteenth-century
Germany. No straight line exists between the Lutheran educational
reform in these earlier centuries and the existence of today's liberal arts
colleges and research universities. Nonetheless, the western tradition
of higher education is profoundly indebted to and connected with the
Lutheran intellectual and educational tradition.

Despite the importance of the Lutheran tradition for western
higher education, many educators and students—Lutheran and
non-Lutheran alike—at Lutheran colleges and universities are
unaware of and do not understand how the Lutheran tradition has
shaped the educational culture in which they live, work, teach, and
study. This reality has multiple sources, but two will be named here.

First, Lutheran higher education in the United States and Canada
certainly began as an educational culture shaped by Lutheran values for higher education. Nonetheless, those values, although fully
appropriated, were often not publicly articulated because the culture
of Lutheran higher education simply assumed them well into the late
twentieth century.

Second, contemporary attitudes about religion and higher education in the United States and Canada have mitigated against addressing the received culture of unarticulated values and their sources in
the Lutheran Reformation. To the modern mind, Lutheran educational ideals, such as opening education to the entire community, are
secular rather than religious. Accordingly, no reason exists to locate
a commitment to these educational values in a college's Lutheran
heritage. For the Lutheran tradition, however, its educational ideals
are religious because they are an implication of the gospel of Jesus
Christ. They stem from a religious motivation and purpose, even
though their outward expression appears secular. They are religious

for the Lutheran tradition even as the Lutheran tradition considers a shoemaker to be a Christian shoemaker because the shoemaker makes good shoes, not good shoes studded with gold crosses. This perspective befuddles the many people who associate church-related higher education's continued religious identity only with serving the parochial interests of the sponsoring church or churches, not with a church-related school's core educational mission.

NECU institutions have significantly reversed this situation in recent years through active conversations on most campuses about the aims and ideals of Lutheran higher education. The publication of *Rooted and Open: The Common Calling of the Network of ELCA Colleges and Universities* in 2018 was a major step forward to articulate and reaffirm the distinctive strengths of Lutheran higher education. This publication and the urgent needs of students and the world are helping many campus leaders to prompt more active and intentional conversations on their campuses about the Lutheran Reformation's sources for the ideals of Lutheran higher education.

Rooted and Open has also increased an awareness that NECU colleges and universities should remember the rich resources of the Lutheran intellectual and educational tradition for addressing new educational challenges. *Rooted and Open*'s description, for example, of Lutheran higher education's openness to others, to hospitality and humility before others and their ideas, and to a profound commitment to diversity has reminded NECU institutions that they have resources available beyond secular concerns for socioeconomic and political rights when expanding their efforts to embrace racial justice and diversity, equity, and inclusion. Lutheran foundations for moving toward what Martin Luther King, Jr. called the beloved community provide a strong basis for sustaining such work.

So That All May Flourish is part of a larger effort by NECU to encourage its institutions to overtly reclaim and articulate the shared educational identity of their diverse missions within the larger academy. The Lutheran intellectual and educational tradition is a heritage of which NECU institutions should be proud. It is a heritage that should redefine "historically related" to mean "contemporarily relevant." It is a heritage deserving to be recognized, understood, appreciated, and claimed by NECU institutions as the cultural foundation for what we do.

Actively reclaiming and embracing our founding tradition is also our best protection against the forces that all too often encourage shifting our cherished educational mission to seemingly attractive, survival-based educational schemes. The deeper an educational culture is established, the easier it is to sustain.

For these reasons and more, Lutheran higher education is a tradition that matters. It matters because educating the whole person matters, free inquiry matters, and all the other particular commitments, strengths, and aims of this tradition matter. It matters because culture cannot be easily invented, but it can be recognized, understood, reclaimed, and embraced. It matters because the flourishing of all matters, institutionally and individually.

Welcome to *So That All May Flourish* and its revealing tour through the core commitments, distinctive strengths, and challenging new callings in the culture of Lutheran higher education.

Introduction

Marcia J. Bunge, Jason A. Mahn, and Martha E. Stortz

"If I go to study or work at a Lutheran institution, will I need to sign a statement of faith?"

"If this is a church-affiliated school, why is there so much interfaith work going on?"

"Are professors free to teach and pursue research without restrictions?"

"Does the institution's Lutheran affiliation really matter to anyone but Lutherans?"

Maybe you've heard or raised some of these questions. Maybe you've tried to answer them. Whoever you are—member of the faculty, staff, administration, alumni council, or board of trustees, or a student or prospective student—if you have questions about the value of Lutheran higher education or simply want to know more, this book is for you. Individuals from diverse backgrounds and traditions learn and work together at Lutheran colleges and universities, and this book sheds light on how and why the "Lutheran-ness" of these schools matters for them and for the flourishing of individuals, communities, and the planet.

Lutheran educational institutions are found worldwide, and this book focuses on the central aims and practices of twenty-seven institutions in North America that make up the Network of ELCA Colleges and Universities (NECU). Chapters highlight the core values and distinctive pursuits of these institutions, reflect on their contemporary challenges, and explore how they seek to live out their values with integrity. In this way, the chapters speak to the character of NECU institutions and reflect the reforming spirit of the Lutheran intellectual tradition. Sparked by the Reformation and rooted in specific theological principles, this tradition values universal education, the liberal arts, and service to the world. While these and other key values have withstood the test of time, ways of living them out are always in the process of being reformed in order to meet the challenges of the present moment.

This introduction invites you into the distinctive and compelling work of these twenty-seven institutions by examining their unique place in the landscape of higher education, highlighting their common aims, and introducing the volume's three-part structure.

All colleges and universities in North America have a particular history and heritage, and many of them were founded by religious leaders or organizations. For example, among the twenty-five oldest universities in the United States, Harvard and Yale were established by Puritans, Georgetown by Jesuits, and Princeton by Presbyterians. Emory University was later founded by Methodists, Notre Dame by Roman Catholic priests from France, and Brandeis by Jews. Although some educational institutions have formally severed ties to their religious roots, approximately one thousand colleges and universities in the United States are still "religiously affiliated." Of course, their relationships to the religious bodies that founded them vary greatly, from loose affiliation to close and intimate ties.

Of the twenty-seven NECU institutions, twenty-six affiliate with the Evangelical Lutheran Church in America (ELCA) and one with the Evangelical Lutheran Church in Canada (ELCIC).[1] Although these two branches of Lutheranism both use the word "evangelical" in their names, they do not align with groups that identify as fundamentalist or "born again." Rather, like other Lutherans worldwide, they return to the original meaning of the Greek word εὐαγγέλιον, which simply means "gospel" or "good news," and they emphasize

---

1 Together these institutions represent the major expression of Lutheran higher education in North America. The ELCA and ELCIC comprise two branches of Lutheranism, and Lutherans make up about 70 million of approximately 2.2 billion Christians worldwide. Lutheran churches have close historical and contemporary ties to the Roman Catholic Church; in studies of global Christianity, Lutherans are generally grouped with other so-called "mainline Protestants," such as Episcopalians and Methodists.

responding freely and joyfully to this gospel through compassionate and just actions in the world.

NECU institutions span the coasts of North America, from California Lutheran University and Pacific Lutheran University in the West; to Gettysburg College and Muhlenberg College in the East; to Luther College in Regina, Saskatchewan in the North; and twenty-two in between. These institutions were primarily founded by German or Scandinavian immigrants who valued Lutheran commitments to universal education, the liberal arts, and the task of equipping students to contribute to the common good. Finlandia University was established by Finns; Grand View University by Danes; Augustana College (Rock Island, IL), Gustavus Adolphus College, and Bethany College by Swedes; and the rest by Germans and Norwegians.

While these twenty-seven institutions began with few resources and initially mainly served their immigrant communities, their commitment to universal education compelled most of them to be coeducational from the start and to open their doors to any students wishing to apply. Today, all twenty-seven institutions welcome students, staff, and faculty from diverse ethnic, racial, religious, secular, and national backgrounds and offer a range of academic and professional programs. Because of their immigrant beginnings, these institutions have been particularly welcoming to immigrant and first-generation college students. Given their commitments to contributing to the common good, today they also reckon with systemic racism and with the unceded land on which their campuses stand.

Although these institutions have distinctive histories and signature strengths, they are grounded in a shared mission. Institutional mission statements draw on the past to navigate the future, and in 2018, the twenty-seven NECU schools produced a vision for the network itself entitled *Rooted and Open: The Common Calling of the Network of ELCA Colleges and Universities*.[2] NECU presidents,

---

2 NECU, *Rooted and Open: The Common Calling of the Network of ELCA Colleges and Universities*, https://download.elca.org/ELCA%20Resource%20 Repository/Rooted_and_Open.pdf.

sitting as its Board of Directors, formally approved *Rooted and Open* along with the central mission statement therein:

Together, these educational communities equip graduates who are:

Called and empowered
To serve the neighbor
So that all may flourish.

This statement articulates the common calling or vocation of the network as a whole. Individual schools deliver on that promise differently, drawing on their distinctive resources and strengths, but all schools share in this common mission.

The statement casts a three-dimensional vision for graduates from any one of its member institutions, a vision that highlights what is distinctive about NECU institutions and informs their educational priorities. First, NECU institutions will equip graduates who are "called and empowered," and they are therefore committed to academic and pedagogical excellence, freedom of inquiry, and intellectual humility. Second, they will equip graduates "to serve the neighbor." *Neighbor* here means all creatures, human and nonhuman, and service includes justice. NECU institutions train students to see the world as *neighbor*, rather than threat, stranger, or enemy, and to cultivate a commitment to work against injustice and suffering. Finally, the purpose of the entire educational endeavor is "so that all may flourish." Here *all* is understood to include all people, all other creatures, and the planet they all populate. Rather than connoting an extra note in music or an unnecessary rhetorical flourish, *flourishing* means thriving, experiencing abundant and interdependent life, and becoming what we are created to be.[3] In line with this dimension of the vision, NECU institutions pursue radical hospitality, social and environmental responsibility, and holistic education of body, mind, and spirit.

---

3 See also the reflections on flourishing by Mindy Makant, "Called to Flourish: An Ethic of Care," *Intersections* 52 (Fall 2020): 30–33.

NECU institutions ground these educational priorities in robust theological principles. For example, "called and empowered" is anchored in a spirited theological understanding of freedom that emphasizes freedom *from* fears of unworthiness and freedom *for* service and justice. Such a notion of freedom casts off fundamentalisms of left and right and fosters a healthy sense of human limit coupled with bold confidence in divine generosity. "Service to the neighbor" is grounded in a theological understanding of vocation as a response to divine generosity, while the presence of neighbors and a neighborhood invites people out of the isolation of sin into community. Furthermore, a Lutheran "theology of the cross" discloses a God in solidarity with those who suffer. Undergirding the hope that "all may flourish" is a response to a God whose own radical hospitality pulses beneath the skin of ordinary life.

One subtle but important characteristic of *Rooted and Open* is this distinction between the three central educational priorities on the one hand, and the core Lutheran theological values that undergird them on the other. To distinguish without separating the two means that NECU institutions do not move immediately from Christian commitments to missions and institutional vocations; their central aim is decidedly *not* to Christianize and catechize students, faculty, and staff. At the same time, the fact that these institutions *do* deeply root their central missions, strategic plans, and central institutional vocations in rich theological soil also distinguishes them from so-called secular schools, for whom the educational priorities and mission statements often have shallower sources.

A Lutheran college or university might seem to occupy a mild and safe middle ground, a "sort-of Christian, but not *too* Christian" institution. However, the institutions comprising NECU and affirming *Rooted and Open* think differently. For NECU, to have deep theological roots *and* to have an educational mission that is widely inclusive of, and dependent on, the diverse members of the institution means that all can flourish on our campuses—and flourish as they are—while also being invited to appreciate and critically examine the Lutheran theological tradition that allows for such flourishing.[4] Together, this threefold vision along with the theological principles that grounds it make Lutheran education "a joyful undertaking with serious purpose. Called and empowered to understand the world and to help transform it, students of NECU institutions go into that world with wisdom, humility and a sense of hope."[5]

In confessing the common calling of twenty-seven diverse institutions and in offering this bold vision to their graduates, NECU institutions telegraphed the contours of Lutheran higher education through *Rooted and Open*. When its readers asked for more depth, a group of teaching theologians from across the network tagged the topics that begged for further elaboration and identified authors with expertise to write on them. This volume is the result of that effort.

Intended as a "primer," this book seeks to cultivate a knowledge of Lutheran higher education that is both appreciative and critical. The book includes fifteen chapters written by scholars from various NECU institutions. Three sections explore the core commitments, signature strengths, and common challenges of Lutheran higher education at this moment in the twenty-first century. Each chapter highlights a distinctive commitment or educational priority of NECU, explores its theological groundings, and offers examples of how it is embodied on NECU campuses.

Part 1 digs deeply into some of the most central and abiding values, or "core commitments," that characterize NECU institutions. In "Vocation and the Dynamics of Discernment," Marcia J. Bunge (Gustavus Adolphus College) introduces the robust concept of vocation that shapes the aims of NECU institutions. Bunge clarifies that vocation refers not just to professions and passions but

---

4 In the words of *Rooted and Open*: "Because NECU institutions are both rooted in the Lutheran tradition and open to others, they are distinctive in higher education in the United States. Neither sectarian nor secular, NECU colleges and universities take a third path of being rooted in the Lutheran intellectual and educational traditions while being open to others." NECU, *Rooted and Open*, 4. For further analysis, see the essays by Darrell Jodock, Jason A. Mahn, Martha E. Stortz, and Colleen Windham-Hughes in *Intersections* 49 (Spring 2019): 10–12; 19–22; 24–26; and 27–30, respectively.
5 NECU, *Rooted and Open*, 5.

rather to the many ways individuals are called to use their gifts and strengths to contribute to the common good, and she describes how and why NECU institutions offer plenty of opportunities for vocational discernment. In "Freedom of Inquiry and Academic Excellence," Samuel Torvend (Pacific Lutheran University) demonstrates how NECU commitments to academic freedom and educating citizens for thoughtful and principled leadership in the world have roots in the Lutheran Reformation. In line with these commitments, NECU institutions promote critical conversations between learning and faith, advance knowledge through research, and cultivate the countercultural aims of the liberal ("liberating") arts. Mindy Makant (Lenoir-Rhyne University) explores the central Christian calling toward loving the neighbor in her chapter, "Service, Justice, and Love of Neighbor." Although justice and service are deeply intertwined in Lutheran theology, Makant recognizes that some forms of service can become paternalistic or self-serving. She articulates a full-bodied notion of service and highlights approaches to community engagement at Lutheran institutions that emphasize mutuality and strive toward justice. In her chapter, "Why Religion Matters in a Diverse and Divisive Society," Martha E. Stortz (Augsburg University) unpacks Lutheranism's unique approach to the study of religion and shows how an approach that is simultaneously personal/appreciative and academic/critical helps students develop the knowledge, skills, and sensibilities needed for life in an increasingly religiously diverse world. Finally, in "Educating Whole Persons for Wholeness," Jason A. Mahn (Augustana College, Rock Island, IL) traces NECU's commitments to holistic learning in mind, body, and spirit back to Luther's "incarnational realism," an understanding that resists separating mind from body and each from spirit, and so undergirds contemporary practices that lead to the flourishing of whole people within whole communities and ecosystems.

Part 2 focuses on five distinctive emphases, or "signature strengths" for which Lutheran higher education is well known. Marit Trelstad (Pacific Lutheran University) in "Lutheran Values and Pedagogical Practices" finds among these signature strengths the practices of reflective, self-critical, liberative teaching and learning, which she argues can be traced back to the ethos of Lutheranism as a whole. Practicing "critical appreciation," students and educators at Lutheran institutions hold their deepest commitments as valuable while simultaneously subjecting them to analysis, critique, and study from multiple perspectives. In "Disability Accommodations and Institutional Mission," Courtney Wilder (Midland University) recounts how Christian churches and colleges have sometimes done more harm than good when it comes to the full inclusion and sense of belonging of people with disabilities. She argues that Lutheran higher education shares in these liabilities, but has assets too, including deep support of disabled students by drawing from the best of Lutheranism while also critiquing it, allowing it to develop in conversation with disability rights and other civil rights movements. In "Music, Vocation, and Transformation," Anton E. Armstrong (St. Olaf College) notes that excellence within music departments, choirs, and instrumental ensembles has marked Lutheran higher education from its inception. Far more than a co-curricular opportunity, music at NECU institutions is understood to be a powerful vehicle that can heal and renew the spirit, delight the heart and mind, create community, and deeply form—and transform—one's own voice (*vox*) and one's calling (*vocare*) toward cultivating peace and justice. Ann Milliken Pederson (Augustana University, Sioux Falls, SD), in her chapter "In the Garden of Science and Religion," emphasizes that Lutheran institutions reject "warfare" and "independence" models of the relationship between science and religion and, instead, affirm their interdependence, and she shows how drawing on both disciplines generates big questions about humanity's place in creation and strengthens our capacity to tackle contemporary challenges. Finally, in "Environmental Studies and Sustainability," James B. Martin-Schramm (Luther College, Decorah, IA), highlights interwoven and "wicked" racial, economic, and environmental problems and indicates how signature environmental studies programs and campus sustainability initiatives on NECU campuses seek to address them. He connects these efforts to Lutheran long-term commitments and summons NECU schools to respond with wisdom and hope.

Part 3, "Contemporary Callings," addresses some of the most urgent, pressing issues in higher education. To return to the botanical metaphor of *Rooted and Open*, this third part of the book moves from deep roots and solid branches to places of new growth, places that will bear good fruit only with careful tending. In "Diversity, Equity, and Inclusion in a White Supremacy Culture," Caryn D. Riswold (Wartburg College) takes on the no-less-wicked problem of white supremacy, diagnoses how predominantly white NECU institutions perpetuate this structural sin, but also lifts up several central Lutheran institutional values that move them toward self-scrutiny, equality, and justice. In "The Tragedy of Racism," Anthony Bateza (St. Olaf College) uses Lutheran understandings of humanity's "bondage to sin" to account for personal complicity in structural racism. Only by honestly coming to terms with systemic oppression, as two schools Bateza examines have, can those institutions and the people within them hear and heed the call toward racial reckoning. Krista E. Hughes (Newberry College), in her chapter, "Lutheran Institutions on Unceded Indigenous and Former Slaveholding Lands," grapples with the historic legacy of white colonialism and slavery, and how Lutheran institutions often materially benefit from, and are thus complicit in, these historic wrongs. Along with digging up these sins of the past, Hughes excavates the central Christian/Lutheran practice of repentance, employing it as she imagines what reparations, repatriations, and "rematriations" might look like today. In "Race, Climate, and Decolonizing Liberal Arts Education," Vic Thasiah (California Lutheran University) challenges the stated aims of liberal arts colleges themselves, critiquing them for ignoring climate justice, even as they address work, life, and democracy. For Thasiah and the Lutheran resources from which he draws, only by pairing matters of social justice with climate justice can Lutheran higher education benefit the vulnerable human and nonhuman communities disproportionately affected by climate change. Deanna A. Thompson (St. Olaf College) writes the final chapter of the book, entitled "Vocation, Deep Sadness, and Hope in a Virtual Real World." Building on insights gained amidst the twin pandemics of COVID-19 and racial violence, Thompson suggests that people's deep sadness, and not only their gladness, should be included in their vocational stories, and she recommends ways that digital technologies can be used to see and hold one another's pain, bearing witness to healing love.

While we trust some readers have found this book on their own, we hope others are reading and discussing it alongside friends, colleagues, or classmates. We think it will be helpful within programs for faculty, staff, administrators, or board members at Lutheran and other church-related institutions; in faculty and staff workshops or retreats; in ELCA and other congregations or social-service agencies who want to understand how Lutheranism is lived out in sister colleges and universities; or even within college classes or among prospective college students who want to know if and how studying at a Lutheran college will make a difference in their lives and the lives of those they serve. Whatever your starting place or companions on the way, we invite you here to explore an intellectual and educational tradition that still shapes the mission of Lutheran higher education, even as it is always in the process of reforming to better display its core commitments, witness to its strengths, confess its own short-sightedness, and meet what Rev. Dr. Martin Luther King, Jr. called "the fierce urgency of now"—so that all may flourish.

Part 1
Core Commitments

1

Vocation and the Dynamics of Discernment

Marcia J. Bunge, Gustavus Adolphus College

As students at ELCA-affiliated colleges and universities pursue their studies and participate in campus activities, they are offered many opportunities to explore their identity and deeper sense of purpose. Both inside and outside the classroom, they are invited to consider some of life's big questions: What are my strengths and passions? What core values guide my decisions? What grounds me and gives me joy? What adversities and injustices break my heart? How can I make a difference? Exploring such foundational questions serves students now and for a lifetime, equipping them to navigate life's challenges more confidently and to contribute more fully to professional and public life.

The emphasis that institutions in the Network of ELCA Colleges and Universities (NECU) place on academic excellence as well as exploring larger questions of meaning and purpose is grounded in a particular understanding of calling or vocation. At NECU institutions, vocation means more than personal passions or career goals. NECU institutions speak about vocation as the many ways in which *all are called to use their unique gifts and strengths to love others, seek justice, and contribute to the common good in various spheres of life—whether at home, at work, or in civic life.* Thus, discerning one's vocation is not limited to decisions about an academic major or career. Rather, vocational discernment is a dynamic, ongoing, and life-giving process that involves recognizing one's strengths and passions, paying attention to the needs of the world, balancing multiple responsibilities, and cultivating the creativity, courage, and collaborative skills to address injustices and make a difference.

Although the twenty-seven NECU institutions have unique histories and strengths, this full-bodied notion of vocation informs their shared aims and educational priorities.[1] This chapter introduces the concept of vocation and illustrates its significance for faculty, staff, and students today. After outlining the beginnings of this robust concept of vocation in the work of the sixteenth-century reformer, Martin Luther, this chapter highlights essential features of vocation and its foundational principles and provides an overview of how NECU institutions today seek to help all students strengthen their academic skills while also exploring their sense of vocation.

Although this rich concept of vocation is anchored in the Lutheran intellectual tradition, it provides a powerful springboard for people from diverse backgrounds and worldviews to reflect on questions of meaning and purpose and discover ways to use their skills and talents to help individuals, societies, and the planet flourish. Indeed, attention to vocation is growing across disciplines and academic institutions for a host of reasons. For example, many faculty and staff value how elements of the concept of vocation intersect with social scientific research on resilience, grit, and happiness. Those engaged in career and academic advising appreciate how the dynamics of vocational discernment resonate with insightful theories of student development, life design, and self-advocacy. Many also find that by prompting reflection on injustices and one's core values and beliefs, vocation enriches ethical debates and interreligious understanding. In these and other ways, the concept of vocation provides a fruitful resource for NECU institutions and all those seeking deeper self-awareness and a life-giving sense of purpose.

1 For shared priorities, see NECU, *Rooted and Open: The Common Calling of the Network of ELCA Colleges and Universities*, https://download.elca.org/ELCA%20Resource%20Repository/Rooted_and_Open.pdf.

Vocation and Lutheran Higher Education

The term "vocation" comes from the Latin word, *vocatio*, meaning calling, and over the centuries it has been used in various ways. For example, in Luther's time and for some people today, "calling" narrowly refers to those entering the monastic life, the priesthood, or other forms of ministry. Others today might speak about their job or a personal passion as a vocation, and popular books refer to various professions, from teaching to business, as callings.

However, Luther's notion of vocation is more comprehensive. For Luther, vocation embraces far more than the adult world of paid work, pastoral ministries, or personal fulfillment. Rather, vocation addresses a sense of purpose that applies to all ages and diverse spheres of life. He and other leading Protestant reformers stated that all people have a "vocation" or "calling" in two senses.[2] On the one hand, they are all called to love God and to love and serve the neighbor, especially those in need. This is their common vocation or calling: it is, as some Protestants have said, a "general" or "spiritual" vocation. On the other hand, people are also called to particular vocations: to specific "offices," "stations," or "places of responsibility" in which they use their gifts and talents to serve the well-being of others, whether at home, at work, or in civic life. They serve others in particular ways, for example, as siblings and parents; students and teachers; doctors and lawyers; or politicians and soldiers. This is sometimes called their "particular" or "external" vocation. For Luther, these various and specific callings are ways in which people of all ages love and serve others. The many duties and responsibilities we carry out in our families, our professions, and in civic life are ways in which we use our gifts to address the world's needs.

Luther emphasized a conviction that all work that benefits the community holds equal ethical and spiritual value. Luther firmly rejected the idea, popular in his time, that people who enter the priesthood or who become monks and nuns are more pleasing to God or have a "higher calling" than shoemakers, parents, or others

---

2 William C. Placher, ed., *Callings: Twenty Centuries of Christian Wisdom on Vocation* (Grand Rapids, MI: Eerdmans, 2005), 206.

immersed in affairs of the world. All roles and positions that serve the neighbor and benefit the community are equally sacred and worthy callings. As he states in his treatise, "To the Christian Nobility": "Everyone must benefit and serve every other by means of his own work or office so that in this way many kinds of work may be done for the bodily and spiritual welfare of the community, just as all the members of the body serve one another."[3]

Just as viral pandemics and other global challenges have reminded us today, Luther recognized in his time that various roles, including many that go unnoticed, serve the common good and should be honored. During the height of the COVID-19 pandemic, for example, we saw more clearly how those who grow, deliver, package, or sell our food play a larger role in individual and communal well-being than we often realize. We witnessed how all members of hospital teams and larger networks of medical researchers and health professionals, some who are publicly celebrated yet many who work behind the scenes, play a vital role in human health. We also vividly saw how many young people creatively and courageously stand up against healthcare disparities and other forms of injustice, whether racial, environmental, or socioeconomic, and are powerful activists and voices of conscience.

In addition to honoring the many ways all people—old and young, at home and in public life—contribute to the common good, Luther's robust notion of vocation also galvanized his radical support of universal education. At a time when formal education was viewed as unnecessary for most children and educational opportunities were limited primarily to the nobility, boys, or those entering monasteries, Luther and his followers recommended that all children, including girls and the poor, be given a basic education. Luther ardently supported education and encouraged parents to educate their children because he was convinced that well-educated citizens would serve both church and society. For him, excellent schools ensure all young people can read and gain the skills and knowledge

---

3 Martin Luther, "To the Christian Nobility of the German Nation (1520)," in *Luther's Works*, ed. Jaroslav Pelikan and Helmut Lehmann (St. Louis: Concordia Publishing House, 1955–1986), 44:129–30.

necessary to live out their vocations and take up roles or responsibilities that serve others. As he stated in his appeal to city governments to establish schools, "A city's best and greatest welfare, safety, and strength consist in its having many able, learned, wise, honorable, and well-educated citizens."[4] Luther relied on his friend and colleague, Philipp Melanchthon, to help carry forward a strong public effort to advance universal schooling, the liberal arts, and educational reform, which continued after Luther's death.

Essential Insights for Discerning Vocations Today

Martin Luther's notion of vocation has inspired Lutherans worldwide to establish schools and colleges, and NECU institutions today find that although Luther's concept of vocation springs from a Christian worldview, many elements of this concept speak meaningfully to people from diverse secular and religious backgrounds. Since NECU institutions today hire and serve individuals of all creeds and convictions, and since the concept of vocation is new to many of them, campus leaders seek to clarify its depth and distinctiveness by emphasizing at least four essential points.

First, callings are lived out in multiple spheres of life. They are not limited to paid work but extend to every sphere of life, including family, educational settings, and civic life. Thus in Lutheran higher education, vocation is not equated with personal passions or future careers, and students are reminded of the ways that they already have responsibilities or are summoned to serve others in their families, the classroom, places of employment, or public life.

Second, vocation is lifelong. Vocation is not limited by age or paid activities. At every stage of life, and even amidst our changing physical condition or external circumstances, we can use our existing strengths and capacities to love and serve others in large and small ways. As Rev. Dr. Martin Luther King, Jr. stated, "Everybody can be great because everybody can serve . . . You only need a heart full of

---

4 "To the Councilmen of All Cities in Germany That They Establish and Maintain Christian Schools (1524)," in *Luther's Works*, ed. Jaroslav Pelikan and Helmut Lehmann (St. Louis: Concordia Publishing House, 1955–86), 45:356.

grace, a soul generated by love."[5] Thus Lutheran colleges and universities remind students of their current and important roles and responsibilities as students and members of families and communities. They honor the contributions and agency of students and avoid speaking about one's vocation only in terms of one's future profession or what students want to be "when they grow up."

Third, discerning one's particular callings is a relational and dynamic process. Some people, including students, assume that finding their calling is a one-time "aha moment" or a set plan that follows a clear, linear path. They believe they just need to hear the call or find the path. However, vocational discernment is much more dynamic for a host of reasons: we have many gifts and skills, the urgent needs around us often summon us to take new directions, and life itself is not predictable. Furthermore, discerning our vocation is highly relational because family members, mentors, teachers, coaches, spiritual leaders, and even passing acquaintances often name our gifts, open doors to new opportunities, or call upon us to take on unexpected responsibilities. Thus, discerning our callings often requires pausing, reconsidering our situation, reevaluating our capacities, reconnecting with others, and tapping into our core values and sources of strength as we seek to chart a new path.

Fourth, the process of discernment at every stage of life is multifaceted and taps into many sources. It involves more than taking a StrengthsFinder survey or focusing on our passions. Discerning our strengths, talents, passions, and interests is, indeed, an essential element in vocational discernment. Yet the process of discernment does not stop there. Discernment involves listening carefully to what is summoning us and gathering wisdom from a range of sources. Although sources of discernment are multiple and varied, NECU institutions often point out three common wellsprings of vocational discernment in addition to recognizing our strengths and passions:

---

5 From his sermon, "The Drum Major Instinct," delivered at Ebenezer Baptist Church (February 4, 1968). See Martin Luther King, Jr., *A Testament of Hope: The Essential Writings and Speeches of Martin Luther King, Jr.*, ed. James M. Washington (New York: HarperOne; Reprint Edition 2003), 259–67. For a recording of the sermon, see https://www.youtube.com/watch?v=Mefbog-b4-4.

examining and naming our core values and beliefs; paying attention to injustices and human needs, whether in our own lives, neighborhoods, or around the world; and nurturing our spirits. NECU institutions recognize that nurturing the spirit takes many forms among the diverse members of their communities. We are renewed and inspired and find comfort and courage in a host of ways, such as through communal rituals, celebrations, and spiritual practices as well as shared stories, music, and the arts. Such practices nurture compassion both for others and ourselves. Attending to these four and other key sources of vocational discernment opens doors to a richer understanding of ourselves and the needs of the world and helps us move more compassionately and nimbly as we navigate life's joys, challenges, and transitions.

In my own experience teaching at Lutheran-affiliated colleges, those who are introduced to this broader concept of vocation and a more dynamic and multidimensional process of vocational discernment consistently report feeling more confident and empowered, even as they face challenges or adversity. They welcome the opportunity to reexamine their strengths and passions, core values and beliefs, and sources of resilience and renewal and to reflect on injustices in their own lives or around the world. They find vocational discernment also gives them space to honor the complexity of their various roles and responsibilities and the significance of self-care and care of others.

For example, I have helped lead workshops on vocation for over twenty years, and when the pandemic abruptly ended in-person learning, I also introduced a "Vocation Reflection Journal" in a course on interfaith relations. Following ethical guidelines for student journaling, I posed some common vocation questions alongside assigned readings by widely respected interfaith leaders, such as Rev. Howard Thurman, Rabbi Abraham Heschel, Diana L. Eck, and Eboo Patel. In their course evaluations, students wrote many comments about the value of the vocation journal. Amidst the pandemic, political unrest, and their own personal struggles with online learning, new responsibilities at home, and even deaths of loved ones, they appreciated how writing in the journal allowed them to pause, take a breath, and reflect on their lives and the world around them. Many wrote how they felt more confident about naming their strengths and core values and less anxious about ensuring they select "the right" major or figure out "the plan" for their life. They had the opportunity to express their grief about injustices surrounding them and their gratitude for mentors who supported them. They thought more intentionally about the values and practices that ground and guide them. Realizing that vocation is dynamic and evolving also allowed them to notice the differences, large and small, that they are already making in the world and gave them a sense of freedom to explore more fully who they are and how they want to live.

Theological Roots and Openness to the World

While this dynamic and robust understanding of vocation and vocational discernment speaks meaningfully to individuals across generations and from diverse worldviews, it has been shaped by several specific biblical and theological principles. They are the roots of a Lutheran understanding of vocation that nourish its openness to the world and attention to the needs of individuals, communities, and the planet. Although individuals at NECU institutions hold diverse worldviews, these principles shed light on the notion of vocation and reflect the shared institutional values and educational priorities of Lutheran higher education. These principles also provide a springboard for people from various backgrounds to reflect on their own values and ethical commitments.

Four of these foundational principles, among others, are loving the neighbor, honoring human dignity, seeking justice, and caring for creation. Several biblical passages express the command to "love your neighbor as yourself," and Jesus taught that love of neighbor extends to all people, including enemies.[6] Love of neighbor is deeply tied to a second principle: All human beings are made in the image of God (Gen 1:27) and are therefore equally worthy of dignity and respect. As Søren Kierkegaard (1833–55), a Danish philosopher and

---

6 See, for example, Lev 19:18; Mark 12:30–31; Matt 22:37–39; and Luke 10:23–37.

Lutheran, clarified: "One's neighbor is one's equal . . . and to love one's neighbor means equality."[7] A third biblical principle is the command to seek justice, especially for the poor and marginalized.[8] As the biblical prophet declares, "Let justice roll down like waters, and righteousness like an ever-flowing stream" (Amos 5:24). Finally, the notion of vocation also builds on biblical affirmations that creation is good, God wills its flourishing, and human beings are to care for creation.

Although Luther and his fellow reformers did not always fully live out these and other ethical mandates, from the beginning of the Reformation they articulated the breadth and depth of such mandates and creatively sought to address them. In his explanation of the Ten Commandments, for example, Luther clarifies that "stealing" means not only unjustly acquiring the property of others but also "taking advantage of our neighbors in any sort of dealings that result in loss to them." Thus, for Luther, obeying the command not to steal involves offering fair wages, charging fair prices, and generously helping the poor. He speaks not only of "petty thieves" but also of "armchair bandits" who are known as "honorable, upstanding citizens, while they rob and steal under the cloak of legality."[9] Already in 1523, Luther also helped set up what was called a "common chest" for the town of Leisnig.[10] This chest and similar initiatives pooled community resources to offer support and low-interest loans to those in need.

For Luther and Lutherans today, living out such ethical mandates and one's vocation is grounded in and motivated by a freeing and joy-filled trust in a loving and gracious God. Throughout his writings, including "The Freedom of a Christian" (1520), Luther connects works of love and justice with faith and trust in God's grace. He

---

7 Søren Kierkegaard, *Works of Love*, trans. Howard and Edna Hong (New York: HarperCollins, 1962), 72.

8 See, for example: Exod 22:22; Isa 1:17 and 58:6; Ps 82:3; Prov 31:9; and Jas 1:27.

9 Martin Luther, *The Large Catechism of Dr. Martin Luther, 1529*, The Annotated Luther Study Edition, ed. Kirsi Stjerna (Minneapolis: Fortress, 2016), 335, 337.

10 Preface to the "Ordinance of a Common Chest (1523)," in *Luther's Works*, ed. Jaroslav Pelikan and Helmut Lehmann (St. Louis: Concordia Publishing House, 1955–1986), 45:169–76.

emphasizes that faith is active in love and finds expression in serving others freely, joyfully, and lovingly.[11] His text speaks to how easy it is to become weighed down by thoughts that we are not worthy enough, whether in the eyes of God, ourselves, or others. We then spend our energies trying to measure up or put others down. Luther finds strength and comfort in the message that God is a gracious God who loves and embraces us, thereby freeing us to use our energies to love others. For Luther, God's grace frees us *from* false ideas about seeking to earn one's worthiness and *for* a life of service. He believes that grounded in God's grace, we are free to contemplate one thought alone: "to serve and benefit others in everything that may be done, having nothing else in view except the need and advantage of the neighbor."[12]

Since the Reformation, affirming the equal dignity of all people, serving those in need, seeking justice, and caring for creation have continued to be central values for Lutheran individuals and institutions worldwide. Many internationally recognized Lutherans have actively sought peace and justice, and in some cases lost their lives doing so, including Dietrich Bonhoeffer (Germany, d. 1945) and Gudina Tumsa (Ethiopia, d. 1979). More recently, Leymah Gbowee (Liberia, b. 1972) was awarded the 2011 Nobel Peace Prize for her role in engaging Muslim and Christian women in a nonviolent peace movement that helped end Liberia's civil war. Several highly respected institutions, such as Lutheran Immigration and Refugee Service and Lutheran World Relief, focus on both immediate needs and systemic injustices.

Even as Lutheran individuals and institutions worldwide have addressed contemporary injustices locally and globally, they have also sought to confess their complicity in injustices past and present. For example, in its efforts to cultivate positive relationships with diverse religious communities and Indigenous peoples, the ELCA has sought repentance for the Holocaust and Luther's statements against Jews, denounced its complicity in the evils of colonialism,

---

11 Martin Luther, *The Freedom of a Christian, 1520*, The Annotated Luther Study Edition, ed. Timothy J. Wengert (Minneapolis: Fortress, 2016), 521.
12 Luther, *Freedom of a Christian*, 520.

and repudiated the Doctrine of Discovery.[13] The ELCA has also published teaching and policy documents called "social statements" on interreligious relationships and other pressing global concerns, such as education, environmental protection, and economic and racial justice. Such statements regularly include confession of past wrongs and strategies looking forward.[14]

Rooted in such values, a Lutheran understanding of vocation demands an openness to and love for the world. Shaped by this notion of vocation, NECU colleges and universities are called to offer an excellent liberal arts education to students from all backgrounds and provide them with ample opportunities to explore and articulate their own values and sources of inspiration. Furthermore, even as they recognize that individuals on their campuses hold diverse values, NECU institutions are also called to live out their core institutional values, such as by promoting peace, social justice, and environmental responsibility and fostering interdisciplinary, interreligious, and international understanding and cooperation. These colleges and universities also acknowledge that they have a responsibility to name and address injustices, past or present, perpetuated on their own campuses and in their own communities.

Opportunities for Discerning Our Vocations

Given this understanding of vocation and its undergirding principles, the primary vocation of Lutheran higher education is to offer an excellent liberal arts education and to help all students to discern

---

13 See, for example, the "Declaration of the Evangelical Lutheran Church in America to the Jewish Community" (1994); "Guidelines for Lutheran-Jewish Relations" (1998); "Repudiation of the Doctrine of Discovery" (2016); and "Inter-religious Commitment: A Policy Statement of the Evangelical Church in America" (2019). Available at: www.elca.org. For more on Luther and the Jews, see Brooks Schramm and Kirsi I. Stjerna, eds., *Martin Luther, the Bible, and the Jewish People: A Reader* (Minneapolis: Fortress, 2012).

14 For ELCA social statements, see: www.elca.org/socialstatements. For more on environmental initiatives, see the chapter by James B. Martin-Schramm in the present volume (157–70) and the website of Lutherans Restoring Creation: www.lutheransrestoringcreation.org.

their particular vocations—to assist students as they name, claim, and cultivate their unique gifts and talents so that they can use them wisely to contribute to the common good. In other words, the vocation of Lutheran higher education is to help all students pursue their vocations.

How, then, are faculty, staff, and students from diverse worldviews and backgrounds introduced to this concept of vocation? In what ways do NECU institutions facilitate ongoing reflection on vocation? They do so by offering everyone on their campuses various opportunities to learn about the concept of vocation and to explore the four common sources for enriching vocational discernment, that is, examining one's strengths and passions, core values and beliefs, the needs of the world, and what nurtures one's spirit.

Many NECU communities intentionally take time to introduce the concept of vocation to new students and employees during orientation programs, workshops, or retreats. After orientation, NECU students, faculty, and staff can find support and additional resources for vocational discernment across campus. Many offices and programs foster reflection on vocation, for example, in their career centers, advising programs, diversity centers, chaplains' offices, or vocation-focused centers, such as The Piper Center for Vocation and Career (St. Olaf), the Muller Center (Newberry), and the Presidential Center for Faith and Learning (Augustana College). Some colleges and universities, including Gustavus, have published books for newcomers about their institution and vocation.[15] Another simple and powerful way NECU institutions introduce the concept of vocation is by hosting panels of faculty members or alumni from various professions who talk about their own vocational journeys.

Campuses also offer courses or seminars directly focused on vocation. Several offer first-year or capstone courses for students on vocation. Augsburg University, for example, requires all students to take a course entitled "Religion, Vocation, and the Search for Meaning." Augustana College offers a residential experience for

---

15 Marcia J. Bunge, ed., *Rooted in Heritage, Open to the World: Reflections on the Distinctive Character of Gustavus Adolphus College*, 2nd ed. (Minneapolis: Lutheran University Press, 2018).

second-year students called ALIVE (Augustana Leaders in Vocational Exploration). The Dovre Center for Faith and Learning at Concordia College offers several programs for faculty and staff, including a year-long mentoring program, research grants, and travel funds for vocation-related conferences. Members of all NECU institutions can also participate in national conferences, such as the NECU's annual Vocation of Lutheran Higher Education Conference and those sponsored by the Network for Vocation in Undergraduate Education (NetVUE)—a network of nearly 300 colleges and universities that foster the exploration of vocation.[16]

In addition to offering programs and courses focused *directly* on vocation, NECU institutions provide many other *indirect* yet equally powerful opportunities in nearly every corner of campus to reflect on various aspects of vocation. Perhaps most obviously but not always acknowledged, a strong liberal arts education plays a vital role in vocational discernment because it introduces students to a wide range of disciplines and sharpens their communication and critical thinking skills, thereby helping students discover their passions, interests, and strengths. Many students who begin college set on a particular major or career find themselves excelling in and excited about an area of study they had never considered.

Specific courses and activities open additional doors for reflecting on other dimensions of vocation, prompting meaningful conversations that spill over into dormitories, the cafeteria, and sports fields. For example, NECU institutions offer many opportunities for students to explore vocation by engaging ethical concerns and injustices on and off campus. Several courses and interdisciplinary programs directly explore urgent ethical challenges and injustices, such as through academic programs devoted to peace studies, race and ethnic studies, or environmental studies. Students are invited to reflect on ethical issues through many other venues, including public lectures, signature events, or opportunities to engage the arts or volunteer. For example, the annual Nobel Conference at Gustavus Adolphus College addresses global challenges, and its panelists

---

16 For more about NetVUE, see www.cic.edu/programs/netvue. For NECU, see www.elca.org/Our-Work/Leadership/Colleges-and-Universities.

include world-class ethicists and theologians as well as Nobel laureates and other experts in the sciences. Students also engage in ethical issues and cultivate leadership capacities off campus by participating in local service projects, study abroad programs, and national or international service-oriented organizations.

At NECU colleges and universities, students also broaden their ethical perspectives and deepen vocational reflection through curricular and co-curricular opportunities that strengthen religious literacy and interreligious understanding. Religious diversity is a fact and factor in the workplace and public life, and approximately 84 percent of human beings on the planet self-identify with some form of religion. Religion is also integrally related to a range of cultural, political, and ethical concerns. Given the significance of religion yet the lack of opportunities for many young people to learn about world religions in school, civic leaders and professionals in diverse fields are calling for more attention to religious literacy in educational institutions.[17] A signature strength of NECU communities is giving students opportunities to learn about diverse moral claims and religious worldviews, while exploring their own values and commitments.

Furthermore, NECU institutions foster vocational reflection by offering a variety of venues for people of all faiths or none for exploring sources of renewal, resilience, and spiritual growth. For example, campuses host events open to all, such as spiritual retreats, worship services, mindfulness programs, interreligious events, and lectures by spiritual leaders and activists. Students can also request transportation to off-campus places of worship. Some campuses also host summer programs that give high school and college students opportunities to explore faith together, such as the Gustavus Academy for Faith, Science, and Ethics. Although a growing number of young people today do not affiliate with a particular religious tradition, studies reveal that most of these so-called "nones" (or "nonaffiliated") are not atheists or "anti-religious," and they

---

17 For the growing attention to religion and ethics in higher education see, for example, Douglas and Rhonda Hustedt Jacobsen, *No Longer Invisible: Religion in University Education* (London: Oxford University Press, 2012).

appreciate exploring and discussing religious and spiritual questions, practices, and ideas when given the opportunity.[18]

Another powerful and perhaps surprising vehicle that fosters vocational reflection and nurtures the spirit is music, and NECU institutions are well-known for supporting music. Luther was a musician who believed music is a vital element of human existence and a powerful medium for promoting learning, spiritual growth, and healing. He praised the value of music in these words: "Next to the Word of God, music deserves the highest praise."[19] For these reasons and more, music is embedded in the life of Lutheran institutions. Many students, regardless of their academic majors, participate in musical ensembles, and they speak eloquently about how this experience powerfully engages their hearts and minds, refreshes their spirits, cultivates community, and enlarges their sense of purpose.

Even as NECU institutions offer these and other direct and indirect opportunities to learn about the concept of vocation and deepen vocational reflection, they must continually reaffirm their commitment to doing so because many factors can undermine their efforts. For example, given the high cultural value placed on individualism, vocation can easily be equated with professions, personal passions, or self-absorbed notions of purpose. Even service-oriented individuals can mistakenly reduce vocation to compassion for others, thereby neglecting self-compassion. Furthermore, given the role of vocation in shaping the aims of NECU institutions, some campus leaders assume vocational reflection will somehow be supported, even as they witness leaders and programs coming and going. Leaders also do not always recognize that some approaches to vocational reflection that have been meaningful in the past might not speak to all students today.

---

18 For these and other statistics on world religions and "nones," see the website of the Pew Research Center: https://www.pewresearch.org/.

19 Martin Luther, foreword to "Georg Rhau's *Symphoniae iucundae* (1538)," in *Luther's Works*, ed. Jaroslav Pelikan and Helmut Lehmann (St. Louis: Concordia Publishing House, 1955–86), 53:323. For further explication of the importance of music within Lutheran higher education, see the chapter by Anton E. Armstrong (127–41) in the present volume.

NECU institutions can address such challenges and help ensure opportunities for vocational discernment remain plentiful, robust, and meaningful for all. They can, for example, better coordinate community-wide efforts for introducing newcomers to vocation by establishing and supporting vocation-related offices or positions with clearly defined responsibilities. They can also create a variety of fresh approaches to vocational discernment by listening more carefully to and honoring the changing needs and concerns of their diverse student bodies. Rooted in Lutheran principles that inform vocation, NECU institutions can also nurture vocational reflection by continually reevaluating their own priorities, recognizing missteps, and authentically modelling institutional practices that reflect commitments to love of neighbor, justice, human dignity, and care of creation.

Conclusion

By attending to such challenges and providing various venues for vocational reflection—whether through journals, advising, orientation programs, academic courses, or co-curricular activities—NECU institutions offer a distinctive gift to students and the world. Grounded in a rich understanding of vocation, NECU institutions provide an excellent liberal arts education as well as a host of opportunities for members of their campus communities to explore their vocations. Through their emphasis on academic excellence and vocation, NECU institutions cultivate skills for future professions, civic engagement, and the dynamic and lifelong process of discerning how we all might best use our unique gifts to make a positive difference. Such life-giving skills are needed in college and throughout our lives, as we all strive to navigate personal, professional, or political transitions with integrity and are continually summoned to contribute to the flourishing of individuals, societies, and our planet.

For Further Study

Cahalan, Kathleen A. and Douglas J. Schuurman, eds. *Calling in Today's World: Voices from Eight Faith Perspectives.* Grand Rapids: Eerdmans, 2016.

Cunningham, David, ed. *At this Time and In this Place: Vocation and Higher Education.* New York: Oxford University Press, 2016.

_____. *Hearing Vocation Differently: Meaning, Purpose, and Identity in the Multi-Faith Academy.* New York: Oxford University Press, 2019.

_____. *Vocation Across the Academy: A New Vocabulary for Higher Education.* New York: Oxford University Press, 2017.

Schuurman, Douglas J. *Vocation: Discerning Our Callings in Life.* Grand Rapids: Eerdmans, 2004.

Schwehn, Kaethe and L. DeAne Lagerquist, eds. *Claiming Our Callings: Toward a New Understanding of Vocation in the Liberal Arts.* New York: Oxford University Press, 2014.

Schwehn, Mark R. and Dorothy C. Bass, eds. *Leading Lives that Matter: What We Should Do and Who We Should Be.* 2nd ed. Grand Rapids, Eerdmans, 2020.

2

Freedom of Inquiry and Academic Excellence

Samuel Torvend, Pacific Lutheran University

There are over one thousand colleges and universities in the United States and Canada sponsored by a great variety of religious communities, from American Baptists to United Methodists. Together these schools constitute a third of all four-year colleges. Among them are the colleges and universities of the Evangelical Lutheran Church in America (ELCA), a Christian body descended from Nordic and German Lutherans and distinguished by its insistence on freedom of thought and a robust tradition of higher learning. If one knew little or nothing of this spiritual community, then one might be tempted to lump the ELCA and the Network of ELCA Colleges and Universities (NECU) together with stereotypes of religion or Christianity frequently portrayed in the media: conformity of belief, a rigid sexual ethos, sharp divisions between science and religion, and school leaders who carefully watch what faculty teach.

Such is not the case in the schools connected to the ELCA, the largest Lutheran body in North America. Indeed, faculty and staff new to these schools are frequently surprised that there is no compulsory worship, no need to sign a "statement of belief," no need to leave one's training in Freudian psychology, evolutionary biology, or Muslim history, to name but a few, at the door. Rather, what clearly distinguishes these schools from a good many church-related colleges is the freedom to teach with the methods of one's discipline, the cultivation of questioning, and the absence of pressure to be "religious" or participate in religious observances. This freedom is deeply tied to the commitment across NECU institutions to academic excellence.

If freedom of inquiry and freedom to pursue methods of inquiry specific to a particular discipline are cherished and protected in ELCA colleges and universities, then those studying and working on these campuses might ask: Why is this so? What are the grounds for freedom of inquiry and academic excellence in Lutheran higher education?

In this chapter, we will consider the core values and practices that support academic excellence and the Lutheran insistence on freedom in teaching, research, and learning. This chapter begins by examining the insistence on freedom as proposed by the sixteenth-century reformers who launched what came to be called the Lutheran reform. It then explores additional marks of academic excellence and a specific understanding of the purpose of education found across ELCA colleges and universities today. This chapter also highlights some of the central themes integrally related to a robust understanding of freedom of inquiry and academic excellence in Lutheran higher education, including the critical conversation between learning and faith, advancing knowledge through research, education as formation of the whole person, promoting human and ecological flourishing, and the significance of the liberal arts.

Freedom of Inquiry

On Wednesday, October 31, 1517, Martin Luther, a monastic priest and university professor, circulated a hand-written document, known as the *Ninety-Five Theses*, to his colleagues concerning the sale of spiritual favors by church leaders, spiritual favors called indulgences. Writing theses for faculty discussion was a common way to consider a current issue in early modern universities, what we might call a faculty colloquium or forum. The focus of Luther's concern was the church-approved sale of indulgences: spiritual favors that promised the buyer release from a period of purgation in the afterlife, or so claimed their salesmen. This was a teaching and practice that flourished during the late medieval period in response to the Black Death. Luther's written consideration of the practice began with simple observations concerning the need for a sincere change of heart and the practice of forgiveness. Would anyone reading the first sentences of his document be startled by such basic Christian beliefs about repentance and forgiveness? Probably not.

However, Luther's tone changed as his theses progressed. Luther wrote that nothing done in life can follow one into death, and if nothing done in life endures beyond the moment of one's last breath, why are church authorities suggesting otherwise? The questions continued: Does this practice not unduly favor the wealthy who can purchase more spiritual favors than the poor? His questioning then expanded to include the person who approved the selling of spiritual favors for profit: Is the pope not aware, he asked, of priests who defraud the Christian people? Is this practice not a scam, one that has little to do with helping Christians and much more to do with filling the treasury of a pope who had spent all his funds on luxurious living in Rome?[1]

What we discern in Luther's famous *Ninety-Five Theses* is the questioning one expects in a university. What no one could have imagined is that such questions would lead to death threats directed at Luther. Nor could one have imagined that a handwritten document concerning a foul religious practice would lead to an educational, political, religious, and social revolution: the Protestant Reformation. Asking troubling questions about what many considered a "normal" practice or cherished belief was no small thing, no simple "academic" pursuit. Rather, Luther's claims and questions, intended to provoke discussion among his university colleagues, were the sparks that caused a firestorm of reform.

This is not to say that freedom of inquiry—asking questions without censorship—began with Luther. It had been a cherished and much-protected academic privilege for more than three hundred years before Luther wrote his controversial theses. In 1155 the Holy Roman Emperor Frederick I Barbarossa published *Privilegium scholasticum* (*Scholarly Privilege*), a law that granted immunity from

---

1 See Samuel Torvend, *Luther and the Hungry Poor: Gathered Fragments* (Eugene, OR: Wipf & Stock, 2019), 13–23.

prosecution to professors engaged in scholarly research. In 1229, Pope Gregory IX, an alumnus of the University of Paris, issued *Parens scientiarum* (*The Mother of Sciences*), a papal decree that granted independence and self-governance for the university faculty.[2]

Building on this long tradition and yet reforming it, Luther's colleague, Philip Melanchthon, led the reform of education throughout Germany and insisted that each university discipline should be free to pursue methods of research proper to the discipline itself. For example, he released the natural sciences from the control of philosophy. He recognized and championed education as a *process* that frees students from ignorance, small-minded legalisms, and outdated methods. Melanchthon was a scholar who rejected the seemingly unchanging character of late medieval scholarly study. If freedom from ignorance, religious legalism, and unhelpful methods of study were hallmarks of emerging Lutheran education, then freedom could not be constrained or censored by academics (e.g., theologians telling biologists how and what to teach), by donors uncomfortable with a new line of inquiry that questioned their money-making practices, by political leaders who were tempted to control education for the sake of their political ambitions, or by students who might be surprised by a method or proposition that expanded or rejected a dearly held belief.

Such emphasis on freedom of inquiry in ELCA schools has set them apart from those religious schools that demand conformity to a particular statement of religious belief. Yet it also sets them apart from state schools that demand conformity to a scientific perception of life that rules out any and all religious or spiritual thought and practice. The early Lutheran reformers asked that freedom of inquiry include theology (i.e., understandings of God, humankind, and the world) as well as the methods and knowledge alive in the arts and sciences of early modern universities. They were interested

---

2 For a much-needed critique of the assumption that academic freedom was established by the secular movement of the eighteenth century called the Enlightenment, see William J. Hoye, "The Religious Roots of Academic Freedom," *Theological Studies* 58 (1997): 409–28. Hoye makes clear that freedom of inquiry had its origins in the medieval Christian university.

in a *dialogue* between the rich and lively tradition of Christian learning and the complex issues of their day raised by research among university scholars. Rather than conformity to religious or scientific dogma, they were committed to conversation between religion, the arts, and sciences.

Thus *faith* and *learning* in Lutheran higher education schools are not two boxers duking it out in the ring with one bloodied winner emerging. Rather, they are partners who engage in conversation, discerning what each can offer the other as they explore the physical, intellectual, affective, and spiritual dimensions of life on this earth.[3] Indeed, in a time when state legislatures in the United States attempt to censor faculty and their assigned course readings, this Lutheran educational value becomes one of critical importance.[4]

Research, Teaching, and Collaboration

The Lutheran insistence on freedom of inquiry and questioning thus supports what rests at the heart of the university: the desire and the need to advance knowledge and understanding in every field of study, from art history to zoology. For instance, we would find it odd if biologists were teaching the biology of the Middle Ages, if nursing instructors were teaching the healthcare practices in Israel at the time of Jesus, if economists were promoting the economic colonialism and slavery of the early modern period, if an accounting professor claimed that the only tool one should use in making financial calculations is the abacus.

In other words, the university is one of the few places in society where *discomfort* is expected: where discomfort with "the way things are" leads to experimentation and research, where discomfort

---

3 See the chapter by Ann Milliken Pederson in the present volume (143–55) for a dialogical account of religion and science within Lutheran higher education.

4 At the time of writing this (2021), some state legislatures are attempting to determine what can and cannot be read in colleges by cutting budgets and speaking publicly against textbooks, course titles, and faculty research they find "inappropriate." See Duncan Agnew, "GOP Lawmakers Attempt to Ban Critical Race Theory in Texas," *Texas Tribune*, May 5, 2021, https://www.texastribune.org/2021/05/05/texas-critical-race-theory-schools-legislature/.

can lead to remarkable advances in knowledge and understanding. The very fact that Luther and his university colleagues engaged in rigorous questioning of the received traditions in biblical study, education, leadership, marriage, music, social assistance, and theology imprinted the DNA of Lutheran learning. Their questioning and their ability to see new ways of imagining life in this world advanced understanding rather than merely maintained it from one generation to the next.

Freedom of inquiry means that faculty do not live in the woefully inaccurate metaphor of an "ivory tower," but rather are actively engaged with new research and new questions unasked by previous generations. In other words, Lutheran schools do not hold vaults of unchanging theories and skills that professors simply dispense to their students. That model of education is doomed to fail. A Lutheran school vigorously supports the research and experimentation that are hallmarks of academic excellence: research that emerges not out of a retreat from but active engagement with questions, crises, tragedies, and achievements of the contemporary world.

Thus excellence in education is supported when colleges and universities provide adequate funding for faculty research. For instance, archeology, cultural ethnography, chemical analysis, musical experimentation, and restorative therapy demand time, tools, appropriate spaces, and travel. Financial support ensures that growth in understanding, a central purpose of the university or college, continues into the future.

A school committed to freedom of inquiry and academic excellence will then see teaching as the invitation to welcome students into the search for new knowledge as a lifelong process. Teaching and mentoring students are thus intended to cultivate a thirst for learning that continues long after graduation from a Lutheran school. The cultivation of lifelong learning stands in contrast to a common cultural assumption that education ends with graduation. The early Lutheran reformers of education viewed education differently. They saw advising and teaching students as the opportunity to nurture a love for learning that would influence leaders in many fields, from government to healthcare, to commerce. The same holds true for the contemporary Lutheran college or university. Rather than view-ing a school as the "marketer" of a "brand" for student "consum-ers," Lutheran education insists that higher education is a process of formation in free inquiry and learning for the whole person—body, mind, and spirit—a process led by faculty and supported by staff and administrators, a process intended to "create leaders whose lives are committed to human and ecological flourishing."[5]

The reformers who gave birth to Lutheran education did not risk their careers and lives to support an education that maintained wealth accumulation or the economic inequities of the status quo. Rather, they reformed education so that it might create a cohort of informed citizens committed to the flourishing of all life on the earth, not just some lives and not just human lives. Such support for the flourishing of all life was and is the purpose of seeking new knowledge and understanding in a Lutheran school.

It goes without saying, then, that support for teaching and learning is the *sine qua non* of Lutheran schools. Doctoral programs in North America tend to follow a German model in which a scholar must demonstrate mastery in a specialized field of study. One's doctoral dissertation or research is not a mere summary of previous research but rather a new and distinctive contribution in one's field of study that expands the landscape of one's discipline. What might surprise some is that graduate programs demand specialized study but may offer no training in teaching other than the occasional opportunity to serve as a teaching assistant who leads small discussion groups or grades the examinations required by a lecturing professor.

Thus there can be no substitute for training in pedagogy that stimulates new and long-serving faculty in a Lutheran school. Put simply, good intentions without pedagogical training do not make for good teaching, to say nothing of excellence in teaching. Where Lutheran schools support centers for teaching and learning and thus support rigorous training in the art and skill of teaching and its

---

5 See the mission of the PLU Wild Hope Center for Vocation: https://www.plu.edu/vocation/. For more on holistic education in Lutheran higher education, see the chapter by Jason A. Mahn in the present volume (73–86).

moral demands, the hard-to-define notion of "academic excellence" becomes more tangible and measurable. Consider, for instance, the Center for Faculty Enrichment at Augustana College in Rock Island, IL.[6] Here a comprehensive program supports the professional development of faculty as they improve course syllabi, methods of teaching, assessment of student learning, and the creation of new courses in light of new knowledge, current crises, and interdisciplinary learning. The center serves as a sign of the college's commitment to support and enhance the very reason for its existence: teaching by well-qualified professors who inspire engaged learning among their students.

Such learning, however, is not a one-way street, moving from professor to student. An older model of education suggested that faculty are dispensers of information gained in graduate school. In this model, their purpose is to "pass on" what they view as appropriate for undergraduate students. The old joke about the unchanging character of a professor's course syllabus from one year to the next or the final examination that has not been altered across a career supported this view of education. Perhaps that model is still alive among some faculty and appreciated by some administrators and donors. Replication of knowledge is a conservative and "safe" form of education in which critical questioning is not needed: "Just give me the information or skill I need to get a good job."

And yet another model emerged in the twentieth century that focused on collaboration between professors and students. In the late 1960s, the Massachusetts Institute of Technology established the first undergraduate research program in the United States. A decade later, the Council on Undergraduate Research was established with its headquarters in Washington, DC. These initiatives prompted faculty to welcome students into collaborative research. This model of education welcomes students to work with faculty in a variety of scholarly projects: from new musical compositions, watershed analysis, and theater production to archeological digs, art conservation, and economic modeling.

---

6 See https://www.augustana.edu/about-us/offices/academic-affairs/center-for-faculty-enrichment.

Consider the variety of collaborative learning initiatives at St. Olaf College that support research shared by faculty and students. The St. Olaf Collaborative Undergraduate Research and Inquiry (CURI) program "provides opportunities for St. Olaf students from all academic disciplines to gain an in-depth understanding of a particular subject by working closely with a St. Olaf faculty member in a research framework."[7] The attractive dimension of collaborative research at St. Olaf is that it extends to *all* academic disciplines. Collaboration between St. Olaf faculty and students has thus included researching the practices of English teachers, creating a musical composition, examining cotton fibers, identifying fossil specimens, and developing a county data index. The attractive digital presentation of every project allows students, faculty, administrators, prospective students, and donors to see clearly how collaborative learning takes place at St. Olaf and serves as a source of encouragement for future projects that extend beyond the classroom. The range of projects thus creates an atmosphere conducive to forming leaders for the future in all academic disciplines.[8]

Collaborative study, faculty research, pedagogy, student learning, and the advance of knowledge cannot take place, however, without the resources to do so. What supports academic excellence—rather than mediocre learning—is one of the oldest institutions in human history: the library. Beginning in the third millennium before the Common Era, the library is that great center where learning is cultivated.

Far from a staid book depository or mere study hall, the library is the place in which reform and revolution have been spawned. Luther's study in the library of the University of Wittenberg in the early sixteenth century gave birth to the sweeping cultural and religious changes produced by the Lutheran and Protestant Reformation. Forty-seven scholars worked in the libraries of the Universities of Oxford and Cambridge during the early seventeenth century to create one of the most celebrated texts in the English-speaking world,

7 See https://wp.stolaf.edu/curi/.

8 Information about Mentored Undergraduate Research is at https://elevator. stolaf.edu/curi.

the *King James Bible*. In the nineteenth century, Karl Marx worked on his classic study of political economy, *Das Kapital*, in the reading room of the British Museum and Library of London. The revolutionary agenda of social reform promoted by Frances Perkins, the first woman to hold a position in a United States presidential cabinet, was first worked out in the library of Columbia University in the twentieth century. To quote Jaroslav Pelikan, the distinguished scholar of Christian thought, libraries are "hospitals for the soul where men and women have recorded the pains of the heart and mind, and deposited their wisdom for its convalescence. The library is the antidote to the twin poisons of political tyranny and moral anarchy."[9]

Lutheran libraries have consistently secured past and current knowledge *without censorship* from religious or political authorities so that faculty and students will have access to viewpoints, positions, research, and experiments that might call into question or expand the current state of knowledge and its practice in the world. And today, libraries welcome digital collections that support many university disciplines—an astounding expansion of new knowledge in a global learning network. Indeed, the library—the conservator of knowledge and the incubator of reform—is indispensable in the study of the liberal arts.

The Liberating Arts

Often overlooked by contemporary North Americans who are considering college or working in one is that the modern university had its origin in the medieval Christian universities of western Europe. It was in these universities that students were formed in the liberal arts. Indeed, since the medieval period, the liberal arts have served as the center of undergraduate education in Lutheran schools. But what does that term actually mean?

Its Latin original, *liberalis*, referred to the process of becoming free, and *ars*, to principled and informed action. In other words, learning in the liberating arts was and is intended to free students from ignorance, from small-mindedness, from the uncritical acceptance of

---

9 "Hospital for the Soul," *Congressional Record* 146:66 (May 24, 2000): S4370–71.

trendy and effervescent values, conspiracy theories, misinformation, and those cultural ideologies that degrade and diminish human and ecological flourishing. The singular and significant cry of the Lutheran Reformation was for *freedom*: freedom *from* burdensome church laws, anxious religion, and ossified study, and freedom *for* serving the neighbor in need in the world, freedom *for* alleviating natural and human-made suffering.[10] The educational corollary to the gift of freedom was and is freedom for thoughtful and liberating inquiry that sustains principled action in the world: principled action informed by rigorous study in the arts and sciences.

This is where North American practicality rubs up against liberating study that aspires to free the mind and soul from the stereotypes, biases, discriminations, violence, and injustices that are ever-present in human life. Practicality or its twin, utility, asks for only one thing: "Show me how this skill will advance my chances of becoming successful in life," whatever is meant by "success." Practicality demands that learning must be immediately useful without considering the larger world in which "practical skills" are actually exercised, whether it be the practical skill of the environmental activist or the practical skill of the CEO who runs the petroleum enterprise that is fouling and thus degrading the environment. At its best, Lutheran education offers a clear "No" to the reduction of learning to technical skill. Why? The cultural impetus to focus on the acquisition of a practical skill that will advance the "success" of the individual alone overlooks the fact that "skills" change rapidly in a rapidly changing society. What is valued one day soon becomes obsolete in the next. Yet the deeper reason goes beyond pragmatics and into the heart of Lutheran liberal arts. What study in the liberal arts promises and delivers is the formation of critical thinking, asking questions, problem-solving, the ability to assess systems, an aptitude for research, high levels of written and oral communication, collaborative teamwork, and a disposition for lifelong learning.

In this regard, education in the liberal arts at a Lutheran school is at odds with the commonly held notion that education serves only

---

10 Martin Luther, "The Freedom of a Christian (1520)," in *The Annotated Luther Study Edition*, ed. Timothy J. Wengert (Minneapolis, Fortress, 2016), 1:521.

the individual and the individual's "success" in the world. Lutheran education is a *value-laden* process informed by a commitment to use one's talents, one's learning, for the good of others. One cannot afford to lose this in a culture that abides by the mantra: "Look out for yourself and no one else." The commitment to be *other-oriented* is itself a mark of excellence.

Conclusion

What makes for excellence in Lutheran education? Freedom to question the way things are without fear of censorship; an amiable conversation between faith and learning, each informing the other; the advance of knowledge through research and experimentation; financial support for faculty research and pedagogy; collaborative learning between students and professors; support for libraries and their rich resources; and the robust promotion of learning in the liberal and liberating arts and sciences. These are a few of the marks that serve as the measure of excellence in Lutheran education. There may well be more, but these are clearly *rooted* in the tradition and yet *open* to further elaboration and reform. Of course, the temptation is present to suggest that Lutheran education is really and only valuable to the degree that it supports the discernment of vocation, the pursuit of justice, or securing a well-paying job. There may well be some truth in such claims and yet none of them can serve as a substitute for the excellence in education that makes them possible and of such great value. From its beginning, Lutheran education has focused on preparing thoughtful and principled leaders in society and the world: people who have been shaped by an educational tradition that values freedom of thought and liberating learning—learning that supports human and ecological flourishing.

For Further Study

Ahlstrom, Sydney. "What's Lutheran About Higher Education? A Critique." *Papers and Proceedings of the 60th Annual Convention of the*

Lutheran Educational Conference of North America. Washington, DC: LECNA, 1974. 8–16.

Christenson, Thomas. *The Gift and Task of Lutheran Higher Education.* Minneapolis: Augsburg Fortress, 2004.

Denys, Edward P. "Philip Melanchthon's Unique Contribution to Education." PhD diss. Loyola University Chicago, 1973.

Kimball, Bruce. *Orators and Philosophers: A History of the Idea of Liberal Education.* New York: Teachers' College of Columbia University, 1986.

Nussbaum, Martha. *Cultivating Humanity: A Classical Defense of Reform in Liberal Education.* Cambridge, MA: Harvard University Press, 1997.

Torvend, Samuel. *People of Wondrous Ability: The Origins and Gifts of Lutheran Education.* Tacoma: Pacific Lutheran University Press, 2015. https://www.plu.edu/congregations/wp-content/uploads/sites/144/2021/06/people-of-wondrous-ability_compressed.pdf.

3

Service, Justice, and Love of Neighbor

Mindy Makant, Lenoir-Rhyne University

In the Lutheran theological tradition, service and justice are so intertwined that they can only be separated for heuristic purposes. In the broader Judeo-Christian tradition, justice requires right relationship; justice *is* right relationship. Right relationship requires an equality of personhood rooted in the understanding that *all* persons are created in the image of God. Service is a necessary component of justice insofar as justice without service can too easily become an abstract concept. It can become a subject of study that makes no material difference in the world. On the other hand, if service is isolated from justice, it too easily becomes paternalistic, further complicating the injustices service was intended to address. The telos of service is always justice—justice for the neighbor. As Cornel West has said, "Justice is what love looks like in public."

Love of neighbor is the theological center of Lutheran theological ethics or moral theology. That is, all Lutheran discussions of ethics begin and end with the question: Does this love the neighbor? Love of neighbor is not primarily emotive; it is manifest in concrete actions. I was recently in a conversation with a first-year student at Lenoir-Rhyne University, where I teach. The student and I were discussing the nuances between the virtues of "compassion" and "kindness." After much thought she decided that compassion was a feeling, something internal that the feeler may or may not act on; she decided that kindness, on the other hand, was action on behalf of others, whether the actor felt kind or not. She chose, she said, to be kind over compassionate as her kindness would impact the world, her compassion only herself. Now of course, I might argue that compassion as she understands it is the necessary but insufficient basis for kindness, but it is her sense that what most matters is how she conducts herself in relation to others that I want to affirm. Love of neighbor as the heart of Lutheran moral theology is both kind and compassionate. It is a disposition toward the other who is my neighbor, *and* it is concrete acts that keep my neighbor's good front and center.

In this chapter, I will show why and how, in Lutheran higher education, some (unilateral) accounts of service and service-learning need to give way to accounts of community engagement that highlight mutuality. However, I will also argue that *service* is an institutional priority and theological theme central to Lutheranism, and so is worth retrieving and reconstructing—especially as a dimension of neighbor love, this theological center of Lutheran moral theology. Service and service-learning can become self-serving, but—rightly construed—their proper end and final form is the justice of whole communities.

Justification—Grace Alone

The single most crucial and distinctive mark of Lutheranism is its understanding of God's grace as an unmerited free gift. Theology is always contextual; it does not exist in a vacuum, but grows out of the sociopolitical and economic context in which it lives. Martin Luther was a devout Catholic monk, priest, and academic. Luther wrestled with his faith and with severe doubts that he could ever be good enough or do enough good to merit God's love.

The fifteenth-century theological and political world in which Luther lived was, in many ways, quite different from our own. Church and state were wed in interesting and complicated ways that made both institutions vulnerable to corruption. One of the ways this corruption manifested itself was through the selling and purchasing of indulgences in order to earn one's salvation. Though this was not the official teaching of the Catholic Church, many people in positions of power and authority were teaching that salvation was something one had to earn—that there were quantitative qualifications for grace—and one of these was purchasing indulgences. God was often portrayed as angry and vengeful, someone who needed to be appeased, who would demand a pound of flesh. The purchase of indulgences allowed those in power to make considerable profit from the fears and insecurities of those over whom they had the power to terrorize. This was especially true when paired with the reality that literacy rates were not high and even those who read in their own language could rarely read the Latin Vulgate, the church-sanctioned translation of the Bible (which was written primarily in Hebrew and Greek). So the very people who most profited financially from the selling of indulgences were the people with the power to teach and preach what the "Bible said."

The Reformation is usually understood to have begun on October 31, 1517, when Luther nailed his *Ninety-Five Theses* on the castle church door in Wittenberg, Germany. However, Luther's argument against the need not only for indulgences but for *any* human works for the sake of salvation had been building. Based largely on Luther's reading and study of Paul's letter to the Romans, Luther had become increasingly convinced that *the* heart of the Gospel is that there is nothing we can do to earn our salvation. And that is *good* news. Because we cannot save ourselves, God in God's grace, love, and mercy, through the life, death, and resurrection of Jesus, justifies and saves us. To be justified is to be made right. We are separated from God by sin—both collective sin and our own individual sin—and we cannot, no matter how hard we try, ever make ourselves worthy of God's love. For Luther, and for Lutherans, the good news of justification by grace is that because we cannot earn God's love—God always already loves us!—we are free to stop working so hard to prove ourselves to God, to one another, and to ourselves. It is God's grace, and God's grace alone, that sets us free.

This freedom *from* self-justification actually frees us *for* service to and with the neighbor, for the sake of the world God so loves. Because we do not need to serve in order to please God, we are invited to serve the world on God's behalf. As Luther said, it is not

God who needs our good works, but our neighbor. Lutherans also understand that this same grace, which is extended to us, is extended to our neighbor. We are never in a position that makes us superior to our neighbor, even (and especially) when that neighbor is materially worse off than we. As *Rooted and Open* puts it:

> NECU institutions embrace the challenge to see all creatures as neighbor and to be a neighbor. The concept of neighbor calls students to serve others while eschewing all forms of elitism, condescension and mere charity. Seeing others as neighbor also resists all that brands them as "enemies" or "threats" or "strangers." To be a neighbor means to seek to understand and serve people, communities, and their needs. In the global and local communities in which our students move, they care for the people, space and ecology of a neighborhood; they work toward a common good.[1]

Fostering an academic environment in which students are invited into service for the sake of justice is a distinctive component of the vocation of Lutheran higher education.

Service for the Sake of Justice

In her chapter "Self, World, and the Space Between," Darby Kathleen Ray explores the shift in language from "service learning" to "community engagement" across many institutions of higher education.[2] She suggests that this shift both reflects changes in our collective understanding and drives that change. She begins by noting that service-learning programs were, of course, never intended to become inward-focused or to be *self*-centered. The objective of service-learning has always (one would hope) been that, in the practice of serving others, the disposition of love of neighbor would

---

1 NECU, *Rooted and Open: The Common Calling of the Network of ELCA Colleges and Universities*, 5. https://download.elca.org/ELCA%20Resource%20Repository/Rooted_and_Open.pdf.

2 Darby Kathleen Ray, "Self, World, and the Space Between: Community Engagement as Vocational Discernment," in *At This Time and In This Place: Vocation and Higher Education*, ed. David S. Cunningham (New York: Oxford University Press, 2016), 301–20.

be inculcated. The focus of service was always on the one being served, the other, the "least of these." This understanding of service has fit neatly within the Lutheran understanding of vocation. Vocation "is work in response to God's call to serve others; our work is a vocation if, and only if, we use it to serve our neighbor."[3]

However, a combination of the inevitable "othering" that occurs when we separate ourselves from the "least" whom we are serving and the shift from service for the sake of the neighbor to service for the sake of what *I* am learning has muddied the theological and vocational waters. In addition to the self-centered potential of "service" mentioned above, Darby recognizes that there are times— perhaps many times—when our collective institutional focus on service has done more harm than good. She speaks specifically of "service-learning days," which she refers to as "service dumps" that often overtax the resources of local agencies who are, in theory, receiving our help. Our need to provide service hours does not take into account the challenge of additional staffing and planning we are asking from those we are trying to help.

The linguistic shift from "service" to "engagement" suggests a move toward mutuality while gently nudging institutions of higher education to recognize the mutuality that is already there. Ray emphasizes that the focus on engagement requires the college or university to recognize its need for the local community. Institutions of higher education who engage the community (rather than aiming to "serve" the community) acknowledge that the relationship is mutual; the college or university has as much to learn and gain from the larger community as the reverse. Additionally, the decentering of service broadens the scope of vocational discernment to the entire college or university and the local community. In short, a focus on community engagement potentially shifts the focus from an individual who asks, "what have I learned about myself?," to community-wide discernment of who we are called to be and what we are called to do, together.

Service has often been associated with charity in the sense of unilateral gift-giving rather than in the traditional sense of *caritas* as love. Of course, there are times that the gift-giving form of charity

---

3 Ray, "Self, World, and the Space Between," 305.

is called for. Sometimes what our neighbor most needs is to have an immediate need met: a meal or a safe place to rest. But the very need for charity often (perhaps usually) reflects the reality of injustice. Thus service for the sake of the world requires advocacy for justice, advocacy for changing the material circumstances that create and sustain the need for charity.

Advocacy can be said to have two feet. One of these feet is charity or love. It is love for our neighbor that drives us to serve, to meet immediate material needs. Justice is the other foot of advocacy. Charity seeks to address the symptoms of inequities; justice seeks to address the causes. Advocacy for justice is hard work, but it is central to our vocations as colleges and universities. NECU institutions are uniquely qualified to form students to do this work and they can be wonderful laboratories for the service of advocacy. The dance of just advocacy requires an intentional focus on mutuality, on right rela- tionship with the neighbor. At the very least, just advocacy requires a focus on and movement toward better, more equitable, and sustain- able relationships. Such advocacy, in order to avoid paternalism or self-centeredness, requires a decentering of dominant voices so that the voices of "the least of these" (not an expression I love, but one Jesus gives us) can be centered.

I am not suggesting that a pedagogy of service-for-personal- growth is ever the intent of the faculty and staff charged with leading service-learning programs or projects. However, intent and outcome are not always one and the same. Without intention paired with ongoing reflection and reassessment that asks, "Whose voices are being centered?" and "What sorts of relationships are we fostering?" the intended good of service-learning can be obscured by a focus on the one doing the learning.

This surprisingly common (mis)understanding of service- learning is exactly how Martin Luther defined sin: *incurvatus in se*, turned in on the self and thus separated from the neighbor. The Lutheran theological/intellectual tradition offers a much more meaningful, healthy, and faithful understanding of service (for the individual, for the community, and for the world). Service is not a means to an end. Service is the end, the *telos*, for which we were created. Service is not about us any more than writing is about a pen and paper or than playing tennis is about the racquet. Service is about becoming more fully who we already are as we work together for the common good. When service-learning becomes meaningful engagement with and in the local community such that right relationships are formed and fostered, Lutheran higher education can— like the moral arc of the universe—bend toward justice.

Institutional Examples

All of the NECU institutions partner with the Evangelical Lutheran Church in America (ELCA).[4] The ELCA operates two community engagement opportunities for young adults: Young Adults in Global Mission (YAGM, pronounced "yag'um") and Lutheran Volunteer Corps (LVC). Both YAGM and LVC operate with an accompaniment model of ministry and mission. What this means is that young adult participants in these programs learn to live with and are fully immersed in the communities to which they are assigned. Young adults are invited to spend a semester or a gap year living in intentional community and engaging in the justice and advocacy work the community is *already* doing.

Lutheran Immigration and Refugee Services (LIRS) works closely with and through the ELCA to assist in resettling refugees, welcoming immigrants to the United States, and providing foster care for children in need. The work of LIRS is an example of the lived theology of vocation and community engagement in which the needs of the world and the needs of the individual to live a life of love of neighbor come together in rich, complex ways.

The Lutheran commitment to service and advocacy for justice is reflected in the affirmation of the baptismal promise to "strive for justice and peace in all the world." Of course, institutions do not make baptismal promises. However, NECU institutions share the vision of *Rooted and Open* that their "educational communities train graduates who are called and empowered to serve the neighbor so that all may

---

4 Or, in the case of Luther College, University of Regina (Regina, SK), with the Evangelical Lutheran Church in Canada (ELCIC).

flourish."[5] Each institution lives into this calling in ways that distinctively reflect its own history and cultural context.

Lenoir-Rhyne University

At Lenoir-Rhyne University, where I direct the Living Well Center for Vocation and Purpose, we recently began a new minor in peace and justice studies that we hope to develop into a major. This minor grew out of ongoing conversations among several faculty members from the religious studies and philosophy department about what it means to welcome non-Lutheran faculty, staff, and students on a campus where a massive statue of Martin Luther has pride of place. We were thinking in particular of new Jewish and Mennonite faculty members. The historical figure of Martin Luther, as someone who, at various times in his life, was both anti-Semitic and opposed to the Anabaptist movement, might not suggest that we would be a place where a Jewish or Mennonite person would feel at home. Asking a Mennonite to help us develop and lead a peace and justice studies program becomes one part of our response to this ongoing conversation about what it means to be ever-reforming as an institution of Lutheran higher education.

Gettysburg College

Gettysburg College has one of the oldest running service/service-learning programs among the NECU institutions. The Center for Public Service (CPS) was founded in 1991 and "engages students, community members, faculty and staff to facilitate partnerships" through which they "aim to foster social justice by promoting personal, institutional and community change."[6] The center offers numerous student leadership development opportunities. One focus of CPS is to equip students to "challenge the cultural climate" at Gettysburg and in their wider communities, particularly around issues of race and gender identity. The CPS, working with the Division of College Life, has sponsored biweekly dialogues to dismantle racial myths and confront racism. Students are equipped to engage

---

5 NECU, *Rooted and Open*, 3.
6 See https://www.gettysburg.edu/offices/center-for-public-service/.

in these conversations in ways that are serious and respectful, but also in ways that invite them into community with one another. In addition to offering students the opportunity to reflect on race and gender identity and what it means for one's own sense of self, these conversations invite students to practice multicultural skills for the sake of their neighbors.

Augsburg University

Dr. Jeremy Myers, Christensen Professor of Religion and Vocation and the executive director of the Christensen Center for Vocation,[7] says that at Augsburg they teach that service and justice work "always starts with the neighbor." Justice, he suggests, is not an adequate starting place because it is too big, too nebulous, too unachievable. But, he says, "the neighbor is real, offendable." And it is the neighbor we are called to be in relationship with, not an abstract concept. In response to this calling to be in relationship with their neighbors, Augsburg created an urban community garden. There are plots reserved for faculty and staff, plots for students and student groups, and plots for members of the community. In addition to providing a space for healthy food and an opportunity for members of an urban community to play in the dirt, it also creates a public space for personal encounters between people who might otherwise never engage with one another. The beauty of the urban garden, Myers says, is that it "creates meaningful experience with the neighbor."

In such personal encounters with the others who are our neighbors, we see injustice and are invited to respond in ways that are guided by the relationship with concrete neighbors. Myers speaks of the importance of "centering" other voices, of inviting others to teach us how to follow. Reframing service as that which decenters *us* (whoever "us" is) and centers on the voices of the neighbor invites each of us to see ourselves as embedded in community—some chosen, some not, but all important.

---

7 See https://www.augsburg.edu/ccv/.

Finlandia University

Dr. René Johnson, who serves at Finlandia University as assistant professor of religion and as the director of Vocation and Servant Leadership,[8] also uses the language of decentering. Dr. Johnson, who served as a missionary before coming to Finlandia, takes students from Finlandia's nursing program to Dar es Salaam in Tanzania. She says that she has a personal commitment to dismantle our religio-cultural mythology of "missions." She works to shift students' focus from what they might do or give to their own vulnerability and readiness to receive.

Service, Johnson says, cannot "objectify the other; the *telos* of service is justice. And justice is learning to see with the right eyes." In order to help students learn to see with the right eyes, Johnson takes nursing students to Tanzania for three weeks. The primary purpose of the trip is to "help students decenter." She tells them that friendship is the most genuine form of service. "And," she says, "I tell them, we're here for three weeks; you're twenty years old. All you have to bring to this is yourself. You have nothing else to give." Johnson says that the first thing she does when they arrive in Tanzania is take the students on a safari: "I put that at the front in part because it helps them get over the jet lag, but more importantly it helps them get over pointing and saying, 'look at that!'" After the safari she tells the students from then on that they are not to talk to one another *about* Tanzania, but to talk *with* Tanzanians. It is in talking to the people in Tanzania that the students realize that it is the host families, the people they met in the community, the everyday Tanzanian, who are their teachers. They quickly learn that it is not unilateral service (doing *for* others) that is needed, but service imbued with neighbor love—the giving and receiving of kindness, love, and compassion.

Conclusion

Community engagement as loving one's neighbor—without exception—for the sake of the common good is central to what it means to be a NECU institution. Service, when framed in this way,

---

8 See https://www.finlandia.edu/international/study-abroad/servant-leadership/.

welcomes our students, our institutions, and our communities into life-giving, ongoing conversations of vocational discernment.

For Further Study

Cunningham, David S., ed. *At This Time and In This Place: Vocation and Higher Education*. New York: Oxford University Press, 2016.

ELCA, Social Statements on "Church and Society" (1991), "Race, Ethnicity and Culture" (1993), and "Caring for Creation" (1993). https://www. elca.org/socialstatements.

———. Young Adults in Global Mission. https://www.elca.org/Our-Work/Global-Mission/Young-Adults-in-Global-Mission.

Luther, Martin. *The Freedom of a Christian*. 1520. *The Annotated Luther Study Edition*. Edited by Timothy J. Wengert. Minneapolis: Fortress, 2016.

Lutheran Volunteer Corps. http://www.lutheranvolunteercorps.org/.

Stjerna, Kirsi. *Lutheran Theology: A Grammar of Faith*. New York: T&T Clark, 2021.

4

Why Religion Matters in a Diverse and Divisive Society

Martha E. Stortz, Augsburg University

When three of their teammates hung back from lunch, a few of the football players invited them to the table. "Thanks," one of the three replied, "but it's Ramadan, and we're fasting." When the rest of the team heard why their teammates weren't eating, they decided to fast with them in solidarity, literally leveling the playing field.

An integrative learning course placed student residential advisors in weekly discussion with a residential life officer and a religion professor to explore real-life issues in the dorms, one of which was a request by a group of Jewish students to light a menorah during Hanukkah. Did the ritual violate the school's fire safety policy? As the students researched the question, they learned a lot about Judaism.

As I looked out over students in my required religion course, I knew most of them didn't want to be there. They weren't going to be majors; they feared they'd be turned into Lutherans; they were certain religion was a private matter. Over the course of the semester, as they explored Christianity, Judaism, and Islam and tracked how religion impacted art, culture, and public life, students learned to articulate their own beliefs and practices—and to respect those who believed and practiced differently. At semester's end, a senior majoring in political science approached me: "Ultimately, I want to work for the State Department, and this background will be invaluable."

As these illustrations demonstrate, religion may be deeply personal, but it is seldom private. In increasingly religiously diverse public spaces, religions rub shoulders and impact public discourse. Informed citizens need to be able to articulate their own core commitments, as well as engage those of others.

Lutheran institutions are laboratories for reflection on religion and multireligious engagement. *Because* these institutions are deeply rooted in a robust tradition, they are "boldly open to insights from other religions and secular traditions."[1] Religion matters because it is embedded in the DNA of schools committed to educating the whole person—body, mind, and spirit.

Find it on the athletic field, in the classroom, in the dorms, in campus worship spaces and ritual ceremonies. Encounters like those above provide the raw material for engaging religious traditions more deeply, offering graduates the knowledge, skills, and sensibilities they will need in a religiously diverse world, whatever their vocational calling or professional goals.[2] In this chapter, I look at the role of faith-based institutions in the landscape of higher education. Then I examine the theological and intellectual foundations for Lutheran higher education and how they are expressed in institutions within the Network of ELCA Colleges and Universities (NECU), giving examples from three schools. Finally, I identify challenges to the importance of religion on these campuses.

In the Landscape of Higher Education

Lutheran institutions of higher education have a distinctive place in higher education. They join other *faith-based* institutions (e.g., Jesuit colleges and universities, like Georgetown University or Boston College), whose very rootedness in a particular religious tradition empowers them to be open to people of other religious backgrounds— and no background at all. They stand in contrast to *faith-promoting* institutions, on one hand, and *faith-bracketing* institutions on the

---

1 NECU, *Rooted and Open: The Common Calling of the Network of ELCA Colleges and Universities*, 1. https://download.elca.org/ELCA%20Resource%20 Repository/Rooted_and_Open.pdf.

2 Director of Interfaith America, Eboo Patel, identifies the knowledge, skills, and qualities that make an interfaith leader in his book, *Interfaith Leadership: A Primer* (Boston: Beacon, 2016).

other. *Faith-promoting* schools, like Bethel University (Christian) or Hebrew Union (Reform Judaism) or Zaytuna College (Muslim), nurture a particular kind of tradition in curricular and co-curricular settings. In them, theology departments teach courses that probe deeply the faith and practices of that tradition for classrooms of practitioners.

Because of the separation between church and state, state schools are *faith-bracketing* institutions. In these institutions, religious studies departments study religion as a crucial part of culture, exploring the beliefs and practices of various traditions descriptively, not prescriptively. Religious studies departments, like that at the University of California at Santa Barbara, borrow tools from sociology, anthropology, history, and regional studies to describe the beliefs and practices of different religious traditions.

Faith-based institutions, including the NECU schools, acknowledge that religion is *both* an academic discipline (religious studies) *and* a practiced faith (theology). In these institutions, religion departments employ the descriptive and objective methodologies of religious studies while acknowledging that these great traditions have a subjective purchase on believers. They push students to understand and articulate their own religious beliefs, values, and core commitments; they help them engage with people whose beliefs differ from their own. Importantly, NECU schools help students see how their beliefs, values, and core commitments claim them, creating a horizon of meaning and purpose. This is called vocational discernment.

NECU institutions, then, do not proselytize a particular religious tradition; they rather support vocational discernment, understanding how beliefs, values, and core commitments animate people's profound desire to live a meaningful life. A Muslim student introduced me to her parents at graduation, and they spoke of their comfort in sending their daughter to a Lutheran school: "We knew you weren't going to turn Nastaran into a Lutheran. We knew you'd respect her own faith."[3] These same sentiments could have been expressed by Jewish parents at Wagner College or Hindu parents at Muhlenberg.

---

3 From the overall enrollment numbers in Fall 2021, 9.9 percent of Augsburg University students identified as Lutheran, 8.6 percent as Roman Catholic, 22.3 percent from other Christian denominations, 12.6 percent as Muslim, and

In the Lutheran Tradition

NECU institutions are deeply rooted in a tradition that demands engagement with other religious traditions. Thus Lutheran institutions have a particular purchase on religion and multireligious engagement. Arguments from both Scripture and the Lutheran tradition support that claim.

A first reason is embedded in the tradition itself. The Lutheran movement is *always in the process of reforming (semper reformanda).* From a Lutheran angle of vision, the stance of a Christian in the world is a lot like the basketball player, with one foot planted firmly in the "good news" that God became human and one foot ready to pivot into a world where God is still working. This "bilocational" stance demands that institutions be vigilant for insights that lie beyond the Lutheran or even Christian circles; they need the insights of non-Lutheran faculty, staff, and students.[4] Commitment to reform keeps Lutheran institutions flexible and nimble, alert to crosscurrents in the culture. It steers them to let form follow function and to be bold in editing out structures that stagnate or no longer pulse with mission. For these institutions, religion and religious diversity matter *because* they're Lutheran.

A second and related reason is a deeply rooted *epistemological humility.* Lutherans believe humans are both saint and sinner, a double vision that operates against absolute certainty. In fact, Lutherans should be quite certain they *don't* have all the answers. That makes them humble, open to, and dependent upon the knowledge of those outside the tent. Again, these institutions welcome religious diversity *because* they're Lutheran.

A third and final reason is the tradition's theological focus on *the neighbor.* Luther was fluent in the language of "neighbor," a theme that echoes throughout the Hebrew Bible and the New Testament (Lev 19:18; Mark 12:30–31). "Neighbor" is not the language of

---

7.1 percent as "other religions," a number that includes Hmong shamanist, secular humanist, atheist, agnostic, and no religious affiliation.

4 See, for example, George Lindbeck, "Martin Luther and the Rabbinic Mind," in *Understanding the Rabbinic Mind: Essays on the Hermeneutic of Max Kadushin,* ed. Peter Ochs (Atlanta: Scholars, 1990), 141–64.

"family," a community bound by blood; or "friends," a community bound by love and preference; or "enemy," a community bound by hatred; or even "stranger," language that erodes community altogether, creating a place where no one belongs. Regarding the other as "neighbor" describes a community bound together by place because neighbors share a common space. These institutions welcome religious diversity *because* they're Lutheran.

Luther did not always practice what he preached. He did not willingly share his sixteenth-century spaces with neighbors who were Jewish or Muslim. Luther's treatises against the Jews fit into and fueled a vicious stream of anti-Semitism. Though he urged a Latin translation of the Qur'an, even providing a preface to its publication, he railed against the "Turks."[5] The reformer left behind a rhetoric that demands reparation.[6]

The ELCA issued "A Declaration to the Jewish People" (1994) repudiating Luther's anti-Semitic writings and calling for Lutheran institutions to make amends.[7] Any conversation about Lutherans and multireligious engagement must make amends for the reformer's hate speech. Lutheran institutions intentionally engaging diverse religious traditions is part of the work of reparation. They do this, too, *because* they're Lutheran.

In the DNA of these Institutions

Religious study and multireligious engagement are part of the mission and identity of each NECU institution. Because they serve different contexts and bear different gifts, each institution lives out

---

5 See the English version of Luther's preface to the Qur'an by Sarah Henrich and James L. Boyce, "Preface to Bibliander's Edition of the Qur'an (1543)" in *Word & World* 16.2 (Spring 1996): 262–66.

6 For more on the need for concrete acts of reparation and repatriation, see Krista E. Hughes's chapter in the current volume (205–20).

7 In addition, the ELCA has called for intentional relationships with the major world religions, drawing on the language of the "neighbor" and "neighborhood" to make its point: "This is an urgent challenge since people of other faiths live next door." See the ELCA's Consultative Panel on Lutheran–Jewish Relations, https://www.elca.org/Faith/Ecumenical-and-Inter-Religious-Relations/Inter-Religious-Relations/Jewish-Relations.

mission and identity in very different ways. But all of these NECU
schools share a commitment to *see* the other as neighbor, *be* neighbor to the other, live productively in the *neighborhood*, and contribute to a *common life*.

On the ground, these commitments to neighbor and neighborhood are realized in integrated attempts to help students develop the
knowledge, skills, and *sensibilities* needed for life in an increasingly
religiously diverse world.

All of these institutions cultivate *knowledge* of the world's religious and nonreligious traditions, inviting students to develop a
high degree of multireligious literacy. For these schools, religion is
both an object of study and a matter of faith and practice. Most have
at least one religion/philosophy requirement, taught by faculty who
may be trained in Christian theology or Buddhist studies or Hindu
studies or Islam. Far from being a course in Christian catechetics
or "what it means to be Lutheran," these courses invite students to
explore and articulate their own beliefs, values, and core commitments, along with studying the world's religions. In so doing, they
gain knowledge they will need professionally and in the public realm.
For example, future doctors and nurses need to know how to interact
with religiously diverse patients. What kind of touch is appropriate,
especially across genders? Are the components of a prescribed drug,
like pork or animal products, religiously proscribed? Every professional needs multireligious literacy.

Beyond literacy, these schools seek to cultivate students' *skills* in
navigating difference, particularly interreligious difference. There's
an art to asking respectful questions, navigating conflict, and learning how to anticipate difficult situations, both in the classroom and
outside of it. For example, what happens when a religiously mixed
volleyball team is invited into a pregame huddle to pray the Lord's
Prayer by the hosting team captain at a Christian (faith-promoting)
institution? Where better to learn how to address these situations
than on a college campus, whether in a classroom, on the athletic
field, or in the residence hall?

Finally, each of these institutions aims at nurturing *sensibilities*
necessary for robust and respectful interfaith engagement: respect,

curiosity, empathy, humility, even awe. No NECU school requires chapel, something that comes as a surprise to many potential students and their parents. Yet, each offers opportunities to worship in the Lutheran Christian tradition, as well as any other traditions appropriate to the student demographic. Many NECU schools, such as Gustavus Adolphus College, offer designated interfaith worship spaces; they make available to the campus community the counsel of pastors, priests, rabbis, and imams. School calendars include non-Christian religious holidays and advice to faculty and staff on appropriate accommodation. Intentionally, both curricular and co-curricular activities put into practice the commitment to educating the whole person, mind (knowledge), body (skills), and spirit (sensibilities).[8] While every NECU school works to deliver the knowledge, skills, and sensibilities necessary to being a good neighbor in its particular neighborhood, I profile three institutions below: Concordia College in Moorhead, MN; Muhlenberg College in Allentown, PA; and Augsburg University in Minneapolis, MN.

Because Lutheran: Concordia College
Concordia College locates multireligious engagement in the Forum on Faith and Life. The center's title is a deliberate choice. The word "faith" signals a commitment to the lived practices of religion. It further signals an awareness that no religion is monolithic, but that each religion has within it a diversity in beliefs and practices. It creates space for both *inter*faith conversation between different traditions as well as *intra*faith conversation, that is, dialogue across difference within a tradition. The word "forum" signals a public space for these conversations, both within the campus community and with the religious leaders in the Fargo-Moorhead community. Locating the Forum outside campus ministry is also a deliberate choice, in order not to "reinforce Christian privilege and alienate students who don't identify as Christian and wrongly suggest that interreligious work is a subset of Christian ministry," notes founding director Jacqueline

---

8 See Jason A. Mahn's chapter in the present volume (73–86) for more on holistic education in "mind, body, and spirit."

Bussie.[9] So structured, the Forum bridges the college and the surrounding community, giving Concordia an important role in the
immediate neighborhood.

Concordia requires the religion course "Christianity and Religious Diversity" of all first-year students, including transfers. Recognizing the need for multireligious literacy in every graduate's
professional toolkit, especially prelaw, premed, or business, Concordia also offers an interfaith minor that combines coursework with an
internship/practicum and involves thirty-five faculty from thirteen
different departments.

Perhaps most significant is Concordia's Interfaith Cooperation
Statement, which states the institution's "public identity" in terms of
its interfaith commitments: "Concordia College practices interfaith
cooperation *because* of its Lutheran dedication to prepare thoughtful and informed global citizens who foster wholeness and hope,
build peace through understanding, and serve the world together."[10]
Clearly, Concordia's multireligious work grows out of its Lutheran
roots.

Finding Connection: Muhlenberg College

In terms of the composition of its student body, Muhlenberg College
moved from being predominantly Lutheran to interfaith (Lutheran
and Jewish), to multireligious, with its demographic including a
sizeable number of Jewish, Hindu, Sikh, and Muslim students. A
wildly popular baccalaureate service incorporates elements of all of
these faith traditions, even featuring a student group of Bollywood
dancers, Top Naach. Along with the freshmen candle-lighting ceremony, baccalaureate bookends the college experience of a religiously
diverse student body. As former college chaplain Rev. Kristen Glass

---

9 The founding director of the Forum was Jacqueline Bussie, who led it from
  2011–21, before she became Executive Director of the Collegeville Institute in
  Collegeville, MN in September 2021.
10 Emphasis mine. Read the full text of Concordia's Interfaith Cooperation
  Statement, as well as the work of the Forum on Faith and Life, at https://
  www.concordiacollege.edu/directories/offices-departments-directory/
  forum-on-faith-and-life/.

Perez put it: "Embracing ritual helps us figure out who we are and where we are. If we focus on that, we're a lot more connected."[11]

Although Muhlenberg does not have a religion requirement, a robust religion studies department with scholars in Judaism, Hinduism, Buddhism, and Christianity offers courses that fulfill a core humanities requirement. In addition, first-year students participate in a year-long Personal and Professional Development Seminar taught by faculty across the college, helping students explore vocational goals and community responsibility.

Muhlenberg places multireligious engagement under the direction of the campus chaplain's office. Glass Perez consciously wove that work into the college's institutional fabric, its policies and procedures, dining services, and residential life. In a reflection before every faculty meeting, she pressed the question: "Why do we do interfaith work? *Because* we're Lutheran. *Because, because, because*—I really worked the *because*." When resident advisors realized that although the college offered kosher dining, it had no halal dining for its Muslim students, dining service swiftly remedied the situation. Glass Perez also advised a "Religion in Residence" course, and the class consciously pushed beyond accommodation: "If we take seriously our rhetoric about being open, we don't simply accommodate. We make people feel at home."

As the college adjusted to its multireligious calling, there were other shifts as well. For years Muhlenberg was home to the Institute for Jewish-Christian Understanding (IJCU). In 2020 the college expanded the mission of IJCU to embrace the world's religions and created a new Institute for Religious and Cultural Understanding. Its current director has aptly stated: "Understanding the religions of the world is essential to understanding the motivations and actions of people everywhere."[12]

---

11 In the fall of 2020, Rev. Kristen Glass Perez assumed the position of University chaplain and executive director for Religious and Spiritual Life at Northwestern University in Chicago.

12 The statement is from chair of the religious studies department and institute director, William "Chip" Gruen.

Becoming Neighbors: Augsburg University

Augsburg University requires two courses from its religion/philosophy department, one of which must be "Religion, Vocation, and the Search for Meaning." Consciously designed to consider the question of vocation, the courses traditionally focused on gaining religious literacy in the Abrahamic traditions: Christianity, Judaism, and Islam. In addition to these curricular opportunities, Augsburg is exploring a vocation portfolio (vPortfolio) through its four "Centers of Commitment" (the Christensen Center for Vocation, Center for Global Education and Experience, Sabo Center for Democracy and Citizenship, and the Strommen Center for Meaningful Work). The portfolio project offers students an opportunity to reflect on how their co-curricular experience contributes to their own search for meaning.

An urban location in the Cedar-Riverside neighborhood brings multireligious engagement to the campus of Augsburg University. Adjacent neighborhoods are home to Little Earth, a vibrant Indigenous people of North America community, and one of the largest Somali Muslim communities outside of Somalia. More and more the student population reflects the demographics of its location, and today Augsburg has a larger percentage of Muslim students (12.9 percent) than Lutherans (9.9 percent).[13]

Multireligious engagement at Augsburg started by gathering scattered initiatives across campus, which began with an interfaith coordinating committee composed of faculty and staff from across the institution and now is located in Interfaith at Augsburg: An Institute to Promote Interreligious Learning and Leadership. Founding director of the Institute, Mark Hanson, explains the rationale of these developments: "Interfaith work is deeply grounded in the vocation of this institution. We strive to hold the *what* and the *why* together: what we do and why we do it."

The institute identified five dimensions of the *what*: everyday experience, moral discernment, global awareness, vocational exploration, and spiritual engagement. These five dimensions

---

13 Based on Augsburg University Fall 2021 enrollment figures. See footnote 3 above.

of interfaith work function as portals for engagement. Students moved by Zen meditation during daily chapel (spiritual engagement) would want to learn more about Buddhism in their religion classes (vocational awareness).[14]

Augsburg's Interfaith Scholars Program embodies these five different dimensions. What began as a student-led response to the 2010 earthquake in Haiti has now become a year-long, stipended course. One alumnus offered, "It's a course—but more than a course." The experience gave him the knowledge, skills, and sensibilities to be an interfaith leader.

Challenges

Similar multireligious initiatives exist across NECU, and a NECU interreligious coordinating committee periodically convenes interfaith leaders at individual schools to share strategies, programming, and granting opportunities. Yet, challenges remain to interfaith work at these predominantly white Christian institutions.[15]

"We're losing our identity!"

A troubled regent approached me at a board meeting: "I love all this interfaith work, but what about our Lutheran identity?" He saw multireligious engagement as a threat. For him—and doubtless many others—the relationship between Lutheran roots and multireligious engagement was a binary choice: interfaith *or* Lutheran. He worried his school had made the wrong one and chosen multireligious engagement over Lutheran identity.

After a longer conversation, he began to consider that a Lutheran identity might *enable, empower,* even *require* engagement with the world's religions. He began to see that his school could do multireligious work *because* it was Lutheran. Leaders will continue having

---

14 For more on four of these dimensions, see Scott Alexander, "Knowing and Loving Our Neighbor of Other Faiths," in *On Our Way,* ed. Dorothy Bass and Susan R. Briehl (Nashville: Upper Room, 2010), 149–67.

15 See the chapter by Caryn D. Riswold in the present volume (173–87) for more on the persistence of white hegemony in the cultures of NECU institutions.

to make the argument that the Lutheran identity and multireligious engagement are not in conflict, but interdependent.

"We're losing our privilege!"

Loss of privilege registers—and is often voiced—as loss of identity. No doubt, the regent above missed the familiar (at least to him) cadence of the campus pastor's prayer at the beginning of board meetings; he chafed at my "First Word," which often drew from non-Christian sacred texts and didn't always end in prayer. Meanwhile, I was trying to craft an opening reflection that spoke to all the regents in the room, not just the ones who identified as Christian, much less as Lutheran. My efforts were a breath of fresh air for some and cause for lament to others. The demographics of these NECU institutions have changed from being predominantly Lutheran to being minority Lutheran. Change often registers as loss.

A tradition that is "always in the process of reforming," that is ever-dependent on insights outside of its own, and that values the neighbor has resources to deal with change. How do these resources directly impact religious diversity?

Snapshots from the three schools above offer some resources. One is naming "Christian" privilege, as Jacqueline Bussie at Concordia did. Once identified, people could work with that privilege, analyze its contours, see where it might most effectively be used. Interfaith work did not bury or deny the Lutheran, Christian roots of the institution. It rather mined them for graduates entering a religiously diverse world.

Another resource is thinking critically about how privilege is used. Themselves in privileged positions as heads of residence halls, the Muhlenberg students used their position to identify the underlying dynamics of merely "accommodating" non-Christians in dorms and dining halls. After analyzing the host-guest relationship undergirding "accommodation," they decided to consciously move beyond accommodation. All Muhlenberg students should feel like family in their common institutional home. They used their privilege to change the frame from accommodation to family, "so that all may flourish."[16]

---

16 NECU, *Rooted and Open*, 3.

A final resource lies in vocational exploration itself, which Augsburg explicitly identifies as a component in its multireligious work. As students clarify their own core commitments and values, where they came from and how they've changed, they are better able to articulate them and engage across difference. In a section of "Religion, Vocation, and the Search for Meaning" that I taught at Augsburg, a freshman noted that "the course made me a better Lutheran" because she had to explain what it meant to be a Lutheran to classmates with no experience of Lutheranism or even Christianity. In addition, she had to be at least as articulate about her commitments as a classmate who was very well-versed in his Muslim faith and often the speaker at the campus *Jummah* or Friday prayer. Finally, all of us had to speak with respect and humility.

"But Isn't Religion Personal?"

All NECU schools have spiritual care for students, faculty, and staff, whether it is housed in campus ministry (e.g., California Lutheran University, Augsburg, Thiel College) or a center for religious life (Muhlenberg). In the eyes of some, the profound questions that a college experience evokes about meaning and purpose, faith and doubt, are best treated in a professor's office or a spiritual counselor's study. Yet, if religious conviction is treated solely as a private matter, people will be ill-prepared to engage constructively when religious difference surfaces in public spaces.

In required courses in religion or philosophy, NECU institutions can offer the academic study of different religious traditions *alongside* exploration of students' own deepest convictions. Because these schools welcome religious diversity, the classroom becomes—alongside the athletic field, the dorms, and the dining halls—a laboratory for engaging difference and the common good. In addition, at a time when political ideologies take on religious zeal, students with religious knowledge can engage in public debate with skills for navigating difference and the sensibilities of a tutored heart. This kind of engaged study of religion is needed now more than ever. The religion classroom serves as a laboratory for public life.

"It's messy."
No religion is a monolith. Each contains diverse expressions and practices. A visiting guest lecturer and Buddhist teacher demurred: "I can't tell you all about Buddhism, but I can tell you about my own practice of Zen." His upbringing as a Roman Catholic made him religiously bilingual, fluent in both the languages of Christianity and of Zen Buddhism. Increasingly, because their parents practice different faiths, students contain multiple religious expressions within their own bodies. Often they have been raised in one tradition or the other—or both. One student identified as a "Jew-Bu," Jewish and Buddhist, another as a "Mus-lick," Muslim and Catholic. College should be a place for students to deepen knowledge of these rich traditions, explore their own religious identities, and learn to speak to others with respect.

Conclusion

Because they are rooted in a rich intellectual and theological tradition, NECU institutions don't need to shy away from questions of meaning and value. Instead, these schools support multiple opportunities for engaging them. Robust departments of religion or theology combine the academic study of religion with the personal quest for meaning. Strong campus ministry programs offer students a wide range of worship and spiritual counseling. And when questions about religious practice arise on the athletic field or in the dorms, NECU institutions have ready resources for addressing them. Because they're Lutheran, these schools demonstrate that religion matters constructively for a common good.

For Further Study

Bussie, Jacqueline A. "The Vocation of Church-Related Colleges in a Multi-Faith World: Educating for Religious Pluralism." In *Hearing Vocation Differently: Meaning, Purpose, and Identity in the Multi-faith Academy,* edited by David S. Cunningham, 236–60. New York: Oxford University Press, 2019.

Cahalan, Kathleen A. and Douglas J. Schuurman, eds. *Calling in Today's World: Voices from Eight Faith Perspectives*. Grand Rapids: Eerdmans, 2016.

Cunningham, David S., ed. *Hearing Vocation Differently: Meaning, Purpose, and Identity in the Multi-faith Academy*. New York: Oxford University Press, 2019.

Mahn, Jason A. "Why Interfaith Understanding is Integral to the Lutheran Tradition." *Intersections* 40 (Fall 2014): 7–16.

Patel, Eboo. *Interfaith Leadership: A Primer*. Boston: Beacon, 2016.

Stortz, Martha E. "The 'V' Word: Different Dimensions of Vocation in a Religiously Diverse Classroom." *Intersections* 50 (Fall 2019): 29–35.

5

Educating Whole Persons for Wholeness

Jason A. Mahn, Augustana College (Rock Island, IL)

Among the mission and vision statements of the twenty-seven institutions within the Network of ELCA Colleges and Universities (NECU), it is difficult to find many that do *not* make claims to educate holistically, to enable the "whole person" to grow, "in mind, body, and spirit."

Newberry College, for example, "challenges and nurtures students for lifetimes of service and leadership through intellectual transformation, social development, a culture of physical well-being, and spiritual growth," while Luther College at the University of Regina in Canada commits to "nurturing intellectual, emotional and spiritual growth." Sometimes mention of the whole person is explicit. Wittenberg University "provides a liberal arts education dedicated to intellectual inquiry and wholeness of person within a diverse residential community," and Muhlenburg College is "committed to educating the whole person through experiences within and beyond the classroom." Wartburg College unapologetically announces its calling "to be the leading institution in education of the whole person."[1]

---

1 Other references to wholeness and holistic learning, or to "mind, body, and spirit" as a gloss for the whole, include Lenoir-Rhyne University which "seeks to liberate mind and spirit, clarify personal faith, [and] foster physical wholeness"; Grand View University's commitment "to the development of the whole person—mind, body and spirit"; Roanoke College's development of "students

Is this talk of wholeness and holistic education anything more than rhetoric that sounds good to high school students and their paying parents? Even if it goes beyond empty rhetoric and euphemisms to convey true aspirations, is it also descriptive of what we actually do? Non-Lutheran schools and nonreligiously affiliated schools have the same language in their mission statements and promotional materials. Is the Lutheran emphasis on holistic education—while not entirely unique—still distinctive? Does the theological grounding of this educational priority give it particular shape?

In this chapter, I will claim that NECU schools have useful gifts in their shared history and overlapping missions that make them vanguards in holistic education of whole persons. What is more, they educate holistically in distinctive ways, given their foundational understanding of sacramentality (broadly construed as the way God is made present in the everyday), an understanding that breaks down boundaries between what counts as body, spirit, and life of the mind.

To develop this claim, I will describe the way Lutheran holistic education is rooted in what might be called its sacramental or incarnational realism—the understanding that Spirit (or God) and "the spiritual life" (as well as deep liberal learning) are accessed not by climbing out of the material world and everyday, practical concerns, but precisely by engaging them more deeply. While education of the whole person is thus not entirely unique to Lutheran colleges and universities, Lutheran schools do bring distinctive approaches to it. They resist dualisms, overturn hierarchies, and treat persons as integral wholes who are more than the sum of their parts. Lutheran institutions have what they need to carry out their calling to educate holistically, although challenges also abound. I will end this chapter by naming some ongoing challenges related to the fragmentation of persons and the privatization of spirituality, before showcasing schools that are facing them courageously and creatively.

---

as whole persons and [preparation] for responsible lives of learning, service, and leadership"; and Augustana College's development of "the qualities of mind, spirit and body necessary for students to discern their life's calling of leadership and service in a diverse and changing world." All mission statements are found on college and university websites as of September 2021.

Resources from Luther and the Lutheran Tradition

At best, educators at NECU institutions will understand mind, body, and spirit to comprise not different parts of a person nor different dimensions targeted by different curricular and co-curricular experiences. These institutions rather strive to regard the human being as an integrated whole, which thrives in turn when integrated within whole communities. *Distinctions* between mind, body, and spirit can be helpful, but spirit is not wholly separate from the body, and neither spirit nor body is wholly separate from the mind. This nondualistic, integrated understanding of personhood comes from sensibilities deeply seated in the early Lutheran reform movement, which deconstructed the dualisms and hierarchies of that time.

Late medieval Christendom valued "spiritual life" over a "bodily/ material life," as evidenced in the way it spoke about "vocation." The "religious"—priests, nuns, monks, and clerics—alone were *called* to work in the service of God. Others—those who cooked, farmed, studied, cared for the young or old, or had countless other more material jobs and tasks—may have done *needed* and sometimes even *meaningful* work, but that work had little to no relation to God or the spiritual life. Only "the spiritual" or "the religious" had true vocations.

Martin Luther's reconception of vocation, where any and every person was called by God to do God's work in the world, democratized access to the spiritual life and to eternal life, which was previously thought to be attainable only by a select few. By proclaiming "the priesthood of all believers," Luther called all Christians, both ordained and lay, to serve as mediators between other people and God (which was a primary role of ordained priests at that time).[2] He also leveled the hierarchy of "religious" or "spiritual" over "material" or "bodily." Even today, changing dirty diapers or making a fair

---

2 That all Christians serve as "priest" does not mean that they have direct (unmediated) access to God, but rather that anyone and everyone potentially serves as a mediator for others. See Jason A. Mahn, ed., *Radical Lutherans and Lutheran Radicals* (Eugene, OR: Cascade, 2017), 18, 125. Martha E. Stortz helpfully contends that "behind the language of the universal 'priesthood of all believers' is the [universal] call to care for the poor." Stortz, "Both Priest and Beggar: Luther Among the Poor," *Intersections* 46 (Fall 2017): 24.

business deal does not seem like a particularly Christian task. But Luther insists that God works through these everyday duties as an actor works through a mask. The mask *discloses* God's presence, but also *hides* that presence. In referring to everyday, seemingly nonreligious vocations as masks of God, Luther asserts that God can be found "in, with, and under" the very ordinary undertakings of everyday people, even when they cannot see the divine presence directly.

Lutherans will recognize that phrase, "in, with, and under," as the way the Formula of Concord of 1577 describes Christ's real presence "in, with, and under" the common elements of bread and wine in Holy Communion.[3] Indeed, Lutheran understandings of vocation parallel Luther's broader sacramental realism, that is, his understanding that the physical world we see and touch is the very place God abides.

Luther argues against the sacramental theologies of other reformers (most notably, the Swiss reformer Ulrich Zwingli) precisely because they tended toward dualism and hierarchy, divorcing spirit from flesh and God from the world. Writing against Zwingli in 1528, Luther refuses to separate Christ (the second member of the Trinity) from Jesus of Nazareth, who has—or rather, *is*—a body, both before his resurrection and ascension and remaining so afterward. Access to God does not require calling down some pure spiritual presence through a ritual of remembering. Such an account, Luther believes, essentially divides Jesus the flesh-and-blood human being from Christ the Messiah, the Son of God.[4] By contrast, for him:

> Wherever you place God for me, you must also place the humanity [of Jesus] for me. They simply will not let themselves be separated and divided from each other. [Christ] has become one person and does not separate the humanity from himself as Master Jack takes off his coat and lays it aside when he goes to bed.[5]

---

3 "The Formula of Concord (1577)," Article X, in *The Book of Concord: The Confessions of the Evangelical Lutheran Church*, trans. Charles Arand, et al. (Minneapolis: Augsburg Fortress, 2000).

4 Martin Luther, "Confession Concerning Christ's Supper—From Part I (1528)," in *Martin Luther's Basic Theological Writings*, 2nd ed., ed. Timothy F. Lull (Minneapolis: Fortress, 2005), 263.

5 Luther, "Confession Concerning," 267.

According to Luther, we have God only in the form of Christ—and Christ only in the form of the bodily Jesus. Luther's sacramental, incarnational, and vocational writings here mitigate against any ultimate separation between body and spirit.

What effect does Lutheran sacramental theology have on the way Lutheran institutions consider holistic education, which aims to align the curricular and the co-curricular for deep learning? If nothing else, Luther here messes with the easiest way of doing things, the creation of a merely additive notion of holisitc education. It is rather easy, for example, to point to a few credits of physical education as fulfilling the body part of holistic education, to involvement in campus ministries or spring break service trips as educating the spiritual part, and to the curriculum—especially to "objective," "value-free" sciences and social sciences—as targeting the intellect. By contrast, a truly integrative (Luther would say *incarnational*) education of the whole person in mind, body, and spirit should go beyond splitting learning outcomes into three buckets—the body bucket, the spirit bucket, the mind bucket—and then showing how different parts of the curriculum and/or different arenas on campus fill each. As these institutions tap their Lutheran roots, they are called to collaborate with one another and encounter whole students in ways that make this education truly integrative and holistic.

Practicing Wholeness across Whole Campuses

As noted above, late medieval Christendom elevated spirit and spiritual callings over the body and more mundane vocations. While that particular hierarchy may characterize some sub-cultures of North America, the dualistic temptations facing twenty-first-century educators are not the same as those of the sixteenth century. Since the Enlightenment, educated Westerners are much more likely to elevate mind over body or body over mind, while ignoring the spirit entirely.

Rationalist epistemologies, which privilege certitudes of the mind over body and spirit, can be glimpsed in professors who value the "pure" liberal arts and who lament an institution's expansion of preprofessional programs, which they see as encroaching on the "liberal free" model of liberal arts education. According to them, liberal arts education should encourage the free life of the mind and be less concerned with practical implications of knowledge and the credentialing of professionals. After all, these more "bodily" concerns are traditionally the domain of the "servile arts," in contrast with which the "liberal arts"—the free arts—originally got its name.

Against this position, Lutheran educator and researcher Mark Schwehn argues that educators at *Lutheran* institutions should not value the life of the mind over the training of body and soul. He makes his case based on Lutheran understandings of vocation, which, rightly understood, involve "both serious attention to matters of identity and self-knowledge *and* to matters of faithful action in the world, in other words to a seamless integration of the liberal and the professional, the theoretical and the practical."[6]

My own institution, Augustana College, has its share of lively debates between those valuing intellectual rigor and those also valuing practical and bodily/material opportunities, including the opportunity to play division III sports, which a third of Augstana students do. The debate recently manifested itself when the college added a new kinesiology major, housed in a new center for health and human performance, which also houses a new natatorium for our new water polo varsity teams. Promotional pamphlets currently found on tables in the new building defend the initiatives by recalling the institution's history and mission:

> Since the late 1880s, the Augustana College community has seen *physical* culture as necessary to the *intellectual* culture on campus. Good health is needed for good thinking, and attention to mind + spirit + body is the ideal balance for a great education in the liberal arts and sciences.

This "both/and" approach to bodily health and intellectual rigor has to be right. Still, balance is easier to name than to practice, especially

---

6 Mark Schwehn, "The Value of Evoking Vocation and the Vocation of Evoking Value," *Intersections* 38 (Fall 2013): 22.

in tuition-reliant schools facing demographic cliffs that feel pressure to market the college "experience."

Empiricist epistemologies, which privilege the sensory experiences of body over mind and spirit, may be a larger threat in a world where consumerism reigns and parents wonder about the "value added" by a college education in the first place. Many faculty across higher education complain that life of the mind is quickly getting eclipsed by the bodily needs and desires of college students, from getting a well-paying job to having a plethora of options in the campus dining hall. They ask whether the liberal arts are giving way to a consumeristic neoliberal arts.[7] Even in the curriculum, empirical observations of the physical world (the physical and social sciences) sometimes take priority over the knowing of the mind and especially of the spirit (humanities and the arts). Objective, fact-based knowledge trumps more subjective, value-laden knowledge.

Lutheran understandings of vocation again help deconstruct the hierarchies between rationalist and empiricist epistemologies, between the sciences and the humanities, between more "objective" ways of knowing and more "subjective" ways of knowing. Vocational discernment, knowing who one is and whom one is called to be, depends on ways of knowing that far surpass objective, technical, scientific reasoning. While technical proficiencies can be easily measured in terms of the accuracy and efficiency with which one brings about a desired end, questions of vocation invite—or demand!—deliberation about the ends themselves: What constitutes human flourishing? What are people for? What makes a life worth living? Such questions turn "subjective" rather quickly, but not in the sense that they are a matter of private opinion or idiosyncratic taste. Rather, they enable the subject to grow in *subjectivity*, which one philosopher describes as "an openness to be affected by (subject to, responsive to) deeply moral, religious, and aesthetic pulls,

7 Carolyn Hough and Adam Kaul, "Symbiosis or Entrepreneurialism? Ambivalent Anthropologies in the Age of the (Neo)Liberal Arts," in *Collaborations*, ed. Emma Heffernan, Fiona Murphy, and Jonathan Skinner (London: Routledge, 2020).

initiatives, invitations, pleas, calls, demands."[8] Growth in subjectivity also grows the virtues. The subjectively mature person comes to regard others as subjects as well; it encourages empathy and humility, and raises one's emotional intelligence.

It follows that a holistic education that resists dualisms and hierarchies must work between and below the distinctions between fact and value, objective and subjective truth. That the liberal arts are *liberal*—widely spanning the sciences, social sciences, arts, and humanities—helps in this regard. That the liberal arts are an *art*—a cultivated aptitude for making aesthetic, moral, and human judgments and for employing practical wisdom—is even more important. At best, holistic curricula issue in what the ancient Greeks called *paideia*—the "whole process by which ideals are shaped and cultivated in a culture and by which persons are formed for participating in a society."[9]

Luther College in Decorah, IA, calls its signature liberal arts curriculum *Paideia*, and so emphasizes this cultivation of judgment, character, and virtue. The *Paideia* curriculum is interdisciplinary, dealing with "important questions [that] draw on a range of perspectives for their answers." Moreover, it seeks to develop sensibilities and form character, rather than to focus only on objective knowledge. In program director Kathryn Reed's words, "the best answers draw not only on facts but on the wisdom of a well-developed sensibility." Finally, because holistic education also considers whole communities and ecosystems in which individuals are nestled, *Paideia* educates students "not just for a job, but for an active social, political, and inner life."[10]

Certainly, faculty and administrators at all NECU schools are working across the curriculum and campus in their own efforts to resist dualisms and educate holistically. Augustana College is currently bringing together scientific training with deep humanistic

---

8 Edward F. Mooney, *On Søren Kierkegaard: Dialogue, Polemics, Lost Intimacy, and Time* (Burlington, VT: Ashgate, 2007), 63.

9 Jennifer R. Ayres, *Inhabitance: Ecological Religious Education* (Waco, TX: Baylor University Press, 2019), 60.

10 Kathryn Reed, "Paideia." Luther College, https://www.luther.edu/catalog/curriculum/paideia/.

inquiry and practical colloquia and experiences in developing the contours of a new "integrative medicine and the humanities" immersive minor. It is also piloting a new living and learning program called ALIVE (Augustana Leaders in Vocational Exploration), where twelve sophomore fellows live together in a residence hall and participate in weekly conversations with the chaplain, career coaches, and faculty-in-residence. Finally, each of the varsity sports teams (now including water polo!) have at least one "faculty mentor" who helps student-athletes consider how their classroom learning and athletic training reinforce one another. Down the hall from the new natatorium and kinesiology classrooms is even a multifaith meditation and prayer room. Swimmers and kinesiology majors may one day use the space alongside Christians practicing centering prayer and Muslims meeting for Friday prayer, as the lines between mind, body, and spirit continue to blur.

Will the Center Hold? Ongoing Challenges and Responses

The call to holistic education issues out across the curriculum and campus. Educators are called to help students grow in mind, body, and spirit. They do so in the arts, humanities, social sciences, and sciences. Students develop holistically on the practice field or stage, during a wellness day, in the faculty-in-residence's apartment, and while discussing the chaplain's sermon.

But challenges remain. When the spaces and means of learning are multiplied in these ways, the temptation to categorize and compartmentalize almost inevitably reasserts itself. Augustana College now links virtually every campus activity, from internships and study abroad to Greek life and intramural sports, to one or more of its nine learning outcomes.[11] Other campuses slot programs into the seven dimensions of wellness, the seven intelligences, or various other

---

11 See the description of Augustana's nine learning outcomes (https://augustana. edu/academics/nine-learning-outcomes), where students are told that "Learning happens in the classroom, sure. But you also will learn on the athletics field, on stage, in a club, in your residence hall or working at a campus job."

metrics. We then unveil learning e-portfolios and extracurricular transcripts to track how various student experiences contribute to growth in mind, body, and spirit. All the tracking and categorizing is understandable, necessary, and often helpful, but it does often reinforce the assumption that the way to being well-rounded is to multiply involvements and check the many boxes on a list of graduation requirements.

This particular challenge may also arise from the Lutheran tradition that informs our work. Luther's sacramental understandings deconstructed hierarchies that pit mind, body, and spirit against one another, which leveled dichotomies in terms of *whose* work was valued, as we have seen. At the same time, it multiplied the many callings and responsibilities that each of us bears. This multiplication of callings easily leads to a compartmentalization and fragmentation of the self. In the words of Kathryn Kleinhans:

> Luther intended this recognition of our [many] existing responsibilities as vocation to be reassuring. Unfortunately, the multiplicity of roles is often experienced in modern times as overwhelming. Competing demands result in feelings of fragmentation and, on a practical level, in the compartmentalization of work, home, and community life for many of us [educators], just as our students often compartmentalize academics, co-curricular activities, student employment, and "fun."[12]

Perhaps the easiest "part" of our lives to compartmentalize and the hardest to integrate into holistic learning is the spiritual. Even though spiritual lives are increasingly visible on campus,[13] and even though today's college students want to talk about, explore, and be involved in spiritual and religious matters,[14] many educators still want to leave spiritual matters to personal choice, making them entirely private. For example, in introductory religion courses taught

---

12 Kathryn Kleinhans, "The Work of a Christian: Vocation in Lutheran Perspective," *Word & World* 25.4 (Fall 2005): 399–400.

13 Douglas Jacobsen and Rhonda Hustedt Jacobsen, *No Longer Invisible: Religion in University Education* (Oxford: Oxford University Press, 2012).

14 Barbara E. Walvoord, *Teaching and Learning in College Introductory Religion Courses* (Malden, MA: Blackwell, 2008), 11.

at some public, private, and religiously affiliated schools, there is a noticeable gap between what religion professors think is the primary goal of the course ("critical thinking") and what students think it is ("development of their own beliefs and values").[15]

My guess is that, compared with their counterparts at other schools, most NECU religion faculty are more practiced at combining objective knowledge and critical thinking with personal reflection and the formation of values.[16] Still, the tendency to compartmentalize and privatize spiritual matters affects NECU institutions too; I hear it every time student-led tour guides outside my office assure prospective students that the religion requirement is only one course and that chapel is entirely optional. Will we be able to educate whole students for wholeness without bringing spiritual growth into mission-centric programming, often by collaborating with programs aimed at mental and physical health? Three broad initiatives at three different NECU institutions are doing just that.

Midland University has recently commissioned campus ministries, student counseling, and the student affairs office to host a series of presentations and alternative learning days around mental, physical, and spiritual health. Called ImpactU, the weekly presentation series introduces topics ranging from mental health and domestic abuse to stress management and financial planning. With fall and spring breaks suspended during COVID-19, Midland's campus ministries have also helped organize "Warrior Wellness Days"—days during which all classes are cancelled and students take advantage of self-help resources, meditation sessions, Zumba, massage therapists, and even "cuddle time" with pets from a local animal shelter. Campus pastor Rev. Scott Johnson, the first full-time Lutheran chaplain to be called to Midland in the past fifteen years, sees the wellness days as following the Jewish and Christian commandment to honor the Sabbath. By hosting ImpactU under the student affairs umbrella (where campus ministries resides), he also finds that the ELCA's

---

15 Walvoord, *Teaching and Learning*, 13–55.
16 See the helpful reflections by John D. Barbour, "Professing Religion," *Intersections* 37 (Spring 2013): 22–26. See also the chapter by Martha E. Stortz in the present volume (57–71).

mission model of "accompaniment" can be faithfully lived out. Still, he adds, the spiritual side of these programs can sometimes get lost. "We [offer these programs] because we are a faith-based college," he says. "We should draw more deeply on Midland's Lutheran identity," he says, adding, "we don't have to reinvent the wheel."[17]

Grand View University reclaimed its Lutheran heritage as it attended to the interconnections of mind, body, and spirit. Grand View has roots in the Danish Grundtvigian tradition—a tradition incredibly important to a wide range of education opportunities that form students for citizenship and mutual service.[18] Historically, the ethos of Grand View was directly shaped by social practices such as folk dancing, gymnastics, and community singing. Each practice was meant to help form students to become fully human and form them not only for careers, but also and primarily "for social responsibility in their families, communities, nation, and world."[19] According to religion professor Mark Mattes, the challenge today is how to reconstitute such practices in a world where our overreliance on technology "enables people to live a disembodied life, free of hard physical labor, sport, or face to face social interaction with others."[20] Ongoing challenges notwithstanding, Grand View has reclaimed a focus on holistic formation through their annual summer NEXUS Institute, where high school students participate in group fellowship and work together in community service as a way of learning

17 Email and phone correspondence with Rev. Scott Johnson, Midland director of campus ministries, July 8 and August 3, 2021; email correspondence with Leaha Hammer, Midland director of student counseling, August 3, 2021.

18 President Obama said of "the great Danish pastor and philosopher Grundtvig," that, "among other causes, he championed the idea of the folk school—education that was not just made available to the elite but for the many; training that prepared a person for active citizenship that improves society. Over time, the folk school movement spread, including here to the United States." "Remarks by President Obama, Prime Minister of Iceland, and Prime Minister of Denmark in Exchange of Toasts," Obama White House Archives, May 13, 2016, https://tinyurl.com/yckmcdku.

19 Mark C. Mattes, "Reclaiming Grundtvig at Grand View College," *Intersections* 27 (Spring 2008): 29.

20 Mattes, "Reclaiming Grundtvig," 29. See the chapter by Deanna A. Thompson in the present volume (235–46) for a counterpoint to Mattes's worry about disembodiment via technology.

Lutheran theology, history, and traditions. Mattes told me that these spiritual/physical/intellectual practices are designed to help students find purpose in the wider community.[21]

Finally, Capital University's Center for Faith and Learning has put on a "Hinges Conference" since 2018, enabling the entire campus community to explore the intersection of spirituality and identity. Through TED-talk-styled presentations hosted on campus and livestreamed, student, faculty, and staff presenters narrate how their own or others' spirituality has positively or negatively intersected with other aspects of their identity, including race, sexuality, gender, and ability. Noteworthy aspects of the program include the fact that it brings spiritual identity beside identities that are more physically displayed (race, gender, ethnicity), a confluence often missing in other accounts of intersectionality and identity politics. Also, by inviting presenters to speak to their own spiritual commitments/practices or to those of others that have affected them positively or negatively, the sessions invite critiques of religion alongside the celebration of it. Critical thinking enters into these more interpersonal negotiations. Presenters over the past several years have included a gay preseminary student, as well as a female student who identified as "fat" and was raised in a Jain family that had specific religious ideals about bodily health. A young woman with cerebral palsy spoke about accommodations and belonging in her faith community; a student formerly addicted to opioids described how they found solace and hope in the church. I cannot imagine a better way to name the difficulty and importance of spiritual reflection and growth "in, with, and under" the development of body and mind.

Conclusion

Holistic education of whole persons depends on the willingness of NECU institutions to deconstruct hierarchies and explore synergies between the life of the mind, bodily health, and the spiritual lives

---

21 Phone conversation with Mark Mattes, August 20, 2021. See also Pam Christoffers and Josh Woods, "NEXUS Institute Program Evaluation" (unpublished report to the Lily Foundation/NetVUE Grant).

of students. They do so through interdisciplinary programs in the liberal arts and programmatic partnerships across campus. While institutions as a whole must answer their calling to educate whole persons for wholeness, individual educators hear and heed that call as well. They respond firstly by exercising their own practical wisdom and thus becoming whole people too. In other words, they enable students to simultaneously become whole and carry out a multitude of vocations when they exemplify this delicate balance or art themselves. With time and practice, each of us educators/humans—along with our students and graduates—can become an example of what it means to be a whole person created for wholeness, so that whole communities, in turn, may flourish.

For Further Study

Ayres, Jennifer R. *Inhabitance: Ecological Religious Education*. Waco, TX: Baylor University Press, 2019.

Jacobsen, Douglas and Rhonda Hustedt Jacobsen. *No Longer Invisible: Religion in University Education*. Oxford: Oxford University Press, 2012.

Schwehn, Mark. "The Value of Evoking Vocation and the Vocation of Evoking Value." *Intersections* 38 (Fall 2013): 17–25.

Thiemann, Ronald F. *The Humble Sublime: Secularity and the Politics of Belief*. London: I. B. Tauris, 2014.

Walvoord, Barbara E. *Teaching and Learning in College Introductory Religion Courses*. Malden, MA: Blackwell, 2008.

Part 2
Signature Strengths

6

Lutheran Values and Pedagogical Practices

Marit Trelstad, Pacific Lutheran University

> For you are powerful, not that you may make the weak weaker
> by oppression, but that you may make them powerful by rais-
> ing them up and defending them. You are wise, not in order to
> laugh at the foolish and thereby make them more foolish, but
> that you may undertake to teach them as you yourself would
> wish to be taught.
>
> —Martin Luther[1]

> We teach who we are.
>
> —Parker Palmer[2]

Martin Luther was a thinker who bristled at being boxed in. Instead
of merely accepting rules and traditions, he questioned the rationale
behind them and—perhaps more importantly—who or what those
traditions served. Luther dug deep into history, theology, and translation of sacred texts to understand the basis for the political and
church practices around him and found them lacking. He brought his
emerging questions and troubles straight to the top, writing in 1520
to Pope Leo X himself, to warn him of corruption that was leading

---

1 Martin Luther, "Two Kinds of Righteousness" in *Martin Luther's Basic Theological Writings*, 3rd ed., ed. Timothy F. Lull and William R. Russell (Minneapolis: Fortress, 2012), 123.

2 Parker J. Palmer, *The Courage to Teach: Exploring the Inner Landscape of a
Teacher's Life* (San Francisco: Jossey-Bass, 1997), 1.

the church astray. Like powerful contemporary revolutionaries such as Mahatma Gandhi and Martin Luther King, Jr., Luther was clear about the purpose and calling of his life. The schools, church, and authority figures surrounding him were, in his mind, negotiable and open to reform; they were not the ultimate point or authority of a life well lived.

Luther's reforms bear on who and how we educate today. Because his own studies were so radically enlightening, he sought to open education to all people at a time when the vast majority of people in Germany were illiterate. Though it began at the university, the Lutheran Reformation immediately committed to advancing literacy through public, accessible education at all levels. Education was not only for the elite.

Pertinent to the craft of teaching today, Luther's reforms addressed the *methods* of the classroom itself. To use the language of today, he was a fan of the "flipped classroom," where authority was decentralized. He was a charismatic lecturer but also met with his own students over beer at "Table Talk" sessions, where they discussed the meaning of Scripture and theology. He encouraged the art of asking good questions. Even though he was a rather impolite debater, he longed for deep debate on serious questions as a part of university life; his famous "Ninety-Five Theses" were a call to such debate. In the opening quotation in this chapter, one can see that he also encouraged a nonhierarchical, student-centered model of education in the classroom. He expected students to take their own responsibility in their education seriously so that they were prepared to engage in rigorous discussion. In short, Luther understood teaching and learning in a way that advanced particular ideals: shared authority, humility, justice, and compassion.

No matter what role we play at our college or university, most of us engage in teaching. The craft of teaching is profoundly linked to an instructor's deepest values and purposes. They are on display and integrated into the content, method, and interpersonal dynamics within each classroom or setting. Particular pedagogical practices and strategies embody the values of an individual teacher, the educational institution, society, the academy, culture, and more. In the second epigraph above, Parker Palmer asserts that "we teach who we are" and so highlights the way that personal shortcomings, quirks, and strengths uniquely shape each person's approach to teaching. It is therefore virtually impossible to simply share universal strategies for teaching success with one another. What one professor or staff member can carry off with ease, another will fumble. Teaching will be most effective when the methods come from one's own strengths and even, as will be discussed, from one's weaknesses. Additionally, as Brenda Llewellyn Ihssen notes, Lutheran higher education must be rooted in a "pedagogy of place" that connects to each of our NECU contents specifically.[3]

Still, Luther's own life and approach to teaching set the stage for pedagogical practices that inform Lutheran higher education today. These foundational instincts or values include the value of a good question, humility, compassion, shared power, multiple forms of knowledge, academic freedom, purposeful education, and a commitment to educational access. Lutheran higher education has inherited a particular approach from its tradition, one that makes it countercultural in an increasingly polarized society. Taken together, the various impulses each relate to what might be best described as *critical appreciation*, meaning the ability to hold something as deeply valuable while subjecting it to rigorous critical analysis. An idea, system, belief, or discipline can be simultaneously appreciated and critiqued, and this place of tension is a location of deep learning. This is ideally applied across all disciplines and contexts within the university or college, including religion, which—despite fears of some new students or even faculty members—does not want to make students more or differently religious, but rather invites learners into a deeply critical *and* appreciative consideration of religious traditions, including the tradition that helped shape the approach to learning being enacted.[4]

---

3 Brenda Llewellyn Ihssen, "From Olaf to Omar: Pedagogy of Place at a Lutheran University," *Dialog: A Journal of Theology* 54:1 (Spring 2015): 80–92.

4 Since its beginnings five hundred years ago, Lutheran higher education has been rooted in and has included the academic study of religion. Similar to Renaissance humanists, Luther devoted focused attention on detailed translation of texts; Lutheran scholars later pioneered contemporary biblical studies

The Lutheran educational tradition thus offers particular pedagogical emphases, "charisms," or gifts to our shared craft of teaching. Llewellyn Ihssen reports here that mission statements across our
ELCA colleges and universities hold these "emphases in common:
the ever-reforming education of free people must include critical
inquiry, it must aid in the development of the whole person and it
must, in turn, send whole people out to be care-givers for the world."[5]
These shared emphases are narrowed to pedagogical central practices, dispositions, and aims informing teaching and learning in our
network of ELCA colleges and universities.

This chapter will focus on (1) critical appreciation, a broad educational disposition that includes (2) the value of a good question,
as well as (3) attendant dispositions of humility, vulnerability, and
compassion, and, most important, (4) shared power as a primary goal
of life-giving teaching and learning. Many values related to teaching
within Lutheran higher education are particularly aligned with those
of critical pedagogy due to their shared attention to power, interests
served, questions, and the uplifting of all voices to shape and inform
the content and approach to teaching and learning. Therefore, insights
from critical pedagogy inform the discussion of practices and goals

---

that set the "data" of scriptural texts into social, historical, literary, economic,
political, and religious contexts in order to shed light on past and present possible interpretations. This contrasts with the approach of some religiously affiliated colleges and universities that may uphold Scripture or religious doctrine
as inerrant, ahistorical, and beyond question. NECU's shared vision document, *Rooted and Open: The Common Calling of the Network of ELCA Colleges
and Universities*, claims that our colleges and universities are called to equip
students with basic tools of "religious literacy" (2). See https://download.elca.
org/ELCA%20Resource%20Repository/Rooted_and_Open.pdf.

Some students and faculty see religion as a source for division and antiin-
tellectualism. The study of religion at our NECU schools challenges both parts
of this assumption. Through it, educators and learners seek to support a more
humane world and critical appreciation of a primary, global, individual, and
communal aspect of human experience. For the ways that Lutheran higher education offers a unique approach to the study of religion, see the chapter by Martha
E. Stortz in the present volume (57–71). The present chapter attends to broader
educational values and pedagogical methods shared among educators across the
liberal arts curriculum, including, but not limited to, the study of religion.

5 Llewellyn Ihssen, "From Olaf to Omar," 86.

of Lutheran higher education below, while Lutheran reflections on human nature provide a conversation partner regarding pedagogical dispositions. In Luther's large and small catechisms, documents designed to teach the key ideas of the Christian faith to both children and adults, Luther repeatedly poses the question, "What does this mean?" This chapter applies this question to ask: What do the values and principles of Lutheran higher education mean for how we teach in all contexts, regardless of the subject matter?

Critical Appreciation

In our contemporary culture, *critique* is often connected to the dismissal or negation of an idea. As mentioned earlier, the Lutheran tradition instead offers that one can deeply value one's own (or others') beliefs while simultaneously subjecting them to radical critique and examination. Critical thinking itself may result in an attitude of agreement or disagreement, but not necessarily either. Luther's own creative blend of scholarship and practice combined deep critical inquiry into religious beliefs, institutions, and texts while remaining committed to and valuing the tradition. In other words, when he leveled radical disagreement and critique, this did not indicate rejection, but rather his investment in renewal and reformation. Likewise, Lutheran higher education encourages critical thinking within all disciplines and subjects in terms of content and the ends they serve. Critique itself can be an element of holding something dear, even while calling it to accountability.

There is some deep congruence between this Lutheran disposition and the way feminist and womanist (Black, female) ethicists have defended the value of deep critique—and even anger—as a means to respond to and reform unjust structures. For example, ethicist Beverly Wildung Harrison, in "Anger in the Work of Love," claims that indifference is the opposite of love.[6] Anger indicates that passionate investment is still at play.

---

6 Beverly Wildung Harrison, "The Power of Anger in the Work of Love," in *Womanspirit Rising: A Feminist Reader in Religion*, ed. Carol Christ and Judith Plaskow (New York: Harper, 1989), 214–25.

This attitude of critical—and sometimes even angry—appreciation is rather countercultural. We live in a time when one must agree or be vilified and dismissed. To disagree and to stay in conversation, to value something enough to deeply critique it, these are unfamiliar. Sudents are challenged to conceive that Martin Luther could both love the church while harshly critiquing it. Another example can be seen in courses where students learn the critiques that womanist theologians level at historical Christian doctrines and their own church traditions. Some students automatically assume that these scholars equate all Christianity and its potential with racism. It requires a new mental muscle to hold value and dissent together. Critique can demonstrate investment rather than rejection. And critique can be used to instigate reform of something one loves and values. Lutheran higher education approaches all disciplines with the same approach of critical appreciation. This applies to economics, nursing and health care, art, the natural and social sciences, religion, philosophy, and more. In Lutheran higher education, one can hold a method, discipline, or set of beliefs as valuable *and* examine it critically, subjecting it to thorough analysis.

Central Practice: Good Questioning

Good questions are essential to teaching, learning, and self-reflection—for students, staff, administration, and faculty. No one is exempt from the growth, delight, and challenge of questioning. Critical thinking involves learning the style, format, and method for how knowledge is acquired through good questions that are shaped within a discipline or academic field. College educators are trained in these methods deeply during graduate studies and become experts at particular forms of questioning and research. In their teaching, they offer these methods of disciplinary inquiry, practices, and content to their students. Colleen Windham-Hughes of California Lutheran University suggests that "the cultivation of critical thinking" by learning to ask deep and broad questions certainly helps students now, but also "can be called upon later in life and career, even when discipline-specific knowledge has changed dramatically."[7] The same is true for professors, for whom a good question originally sparked and still sustains their own devotion to learning.

Across curricular and co-curricular areas in our institutions, NECU educators teach specific forms of inquiry, whether the natural and social sciences, the humanities, diversity and justice, the arts, professional studies, vocation, or communication. At the same time, we challenge students and each other with questions that sometimes cut to the core of identity. When the questions focus on a discipline, they may be felt neutrally. When critical questions engage a person's point of view, however, we enter a tender arena of learning. In our teaching, how do we respectfully and compassionately question our students' assumptions?

Conversely, are we open to receiving the form of questioning we teach? Sometimes the teacher and the very aims of education become the subject of critical inquiry. For example, students may level questions at the very content, scholarship, and disciplines that are a professor's intellectual home. Even more intimately, they may interrogate the professor's personal values and purposes. How do educators bring questions about our own disciplines and what is ideologically assumed as "good" into the process of learning? Do we allow for students to challenge our own deepest values and convictions?

Martin Luther leveled deep questions at the systems of education and power around him, asking whose interest they ultimately served. Likewise, critical pedagogy critiques both society and education, examining the "hidden curriculum" within pedagogies, course content, and institutions of learning—institutions that too often support the continuation of oppressive power and the reproduction of dominant social privilege. In the words of Henry Giroux, critical pedagogy claims that no teaching method or text is ideologically neutral, so it is important to uncover its explicit and implicit biases. Critical pedagogy seeks liberating and transformative education which is

---

7 Colleen Windham-Hughes, "Deep Roots, Big Questions, Bold Goals," *Intersections* 49 (Spring 2019): 28.

"simultaneously utopian but always distrustful of itself."[8] In a similar vein, feminist theologian Mary Daly accuses her own discipline of a "methodolatry," an idolatry of method, that stifles marginalized voices and maintains systems of power.[9] Invoking the spirit of Audre Lorde's famous quotation, students in our classroom may intuit that "the tools of the master will not dismantle the master's house"[10] and so resist or reject learning that is offered. While educators may, at times, respond defensively, many of us remember students or conversations that pushed and transformed their own approach to and assumptions about teaching. Indeed, the opportunity to learn and grow and be challenged is what makes teaching itself a life-giving process.

Even subjects and courses intended to address systemic injustice may be used by an institution in a disingenuous manner. For instance, Chandra Mohanty examined how gender studies and diversity—and the faculty and staff who teach them—can find themselves used as tools toward monetary gain and publicity for an institution while business proceeds as normal.[11] Additionally, courses or pedagogies that challenge dominant systems, values, and beliefs may inadvertently impose a new set of doctrine and policing of language, opinions, and ideas that do not actually build the student's ability to craft their own ideas or question freely.[12]

---

8 Henry Giroux, "Living Dangerously: Identity Politics and the New Cultural Racism," in *Between Borders: Pedagogy and the Politics of Cultural Studies*, ed. Henry Giroux and Peter McLaren (New York: Routledge, 1994), 52.

9 Mary Daly, *Beyond God the Father: Toward a Philosophy of Women's Liberation* (Boston: Beacon, 1985), 11.

10 Audre Lorde, *Sister Outsider: Essays and Speeches* (Berkeley: Ten Speed, 1984), 110.

11 Chandra Talpade Mohanty, "On Race and Voice: Challenges for Liberal Education in the 1990s," in *Between Borders: Pedagogy and the Politics of Cultural Studies*, ed. Henry Giroux and Peter McLaren (New York: Routledge, 1994), 145–66.

12 Even postmodern, postcolonial, and critical pedagogies have the potential to become as inflexible as the "traditional" ones they criticize. Elizabeth Ellsworth offers examples and analysis of how critical pedagogies can become oppressive rather than liberating for students in higher education. See Elizabeth Ellsworth, "Why Doesn't this Feel Empowering? Working through the Repressive Myths of Critical Pedagogy," *Harvard Educational Review* 59:9 (August 1989): 297–324.

Through antibias training, inclusive pedagogies, critical pedagogies, and engaging of the purposes of Lutheran higher education, our institutions can begin conversations concerning the values, ends, and beliefs we consciously and unconsciously support through our teaching. In their article, "Conciliatory and Queer: The Radical Love of Lutheran Higher Education," Kiki Kosnick (French) and Sharon Varallo (communication studies) of Augustana College (Rock Island, IL) write that teaching at their college "has changed us and what we think of ourselves, our students, our neighbors, and the possibilities for radical love. We are part of Augustana, so of course, our own transformations, when we have boldly claimed them (and have sometimes asked disruptive questions), have worked iteratively to change the College in (re)turn."[13] Varallo adds that "over the years I have been part of a culture that encouraged me to live in these very questions in a way that made my teaching better and my activism stronger, a culture that wasn't afraid to critique itself."[14]

Beyond this, it is good for our universities and colleges to be clear and transparent about their own values so they may be openly examined. Lutheran higher education is a value-laden form of education. *Rooted and Open* claims that we offer a holistic liberal arts education that encourages students to think about how their lives can contribute to human and ecological flourishing.[15] It is an education for purposeful living. Nonetheless, valuing good questions and academic freedom entails that we teach tools for critical thought rather than telling students what to value and believe.

As a result of their Lutheran foundation, classrooms in Lutheran colleges and universities are not a place to enforce particular doctrines, ideologies, beliefs, and values. In Lutheran higher education, learning cannot be equated with the adoption of others' values, even if those are central to the university or professor. Our universities and colleges are shaped by deep values, some of which are common across our NECU institutions and some unique to each institutional

---

13 Kiki Kosnick and Sharon Varallo, "Conciliatory and Queer: the Radical Love of Lutheran Higher Education," *Intersections* 50 (Fall 2019): 43.

14 Kosnick and Varallo, "Conciliatory and Queer," 45.

15 NECU, *Rooted and Open*.

context. Many of these values seem almost unquestionably good—such as sustainability, equity, inclusion, justice, and purposeful lives of care. Nonetheless, institutional values need to be distinguished from students' personal values. In the classroom and beyond, this heritage calls for creating space for students to question, challenge, and develop their own beliefs and values.

Dispositions: Humility, Vulnerability, and Compassion

In the 1970s there was a t-shirt that read: "Pobody's Nerfect." The Lutheran tradition upholds intellectual and personal humility as an important aspect of education.[16] This does not mean a diminishment of expertise or academic accomplishment. Here humility is given a different, more general sense; it means a simple acknowledgment that perfection is not possible and absolutely every person and institution is flawed. At its best, Lutheran higher education shapes teaching dispositions that allow educators to extend grace and compassion to themselves, one another, and their students.

In the words of L. DeAne Lagerquist of Saint Olaf College, Martin Luther believed that the world is "beautiful, broken and beloved."[17] He argued with humanist leaders like Erasmus who believed that reason and volition could lead us to overcome our "lower" desires. Quite the opposite, Luther argued that reason was especially susceptible to being bent to support horrible causes or justify awful actions. He also claimed that we not only are predisposed toward ill but, even worse, we love doing it.[18] Martin Luther King, Jr. followed his namesake by holding a strong doctrine of human fallibility. Indeed,

---

16 See the chapters by Caryn D. Riswold (173–87) and Martha E. Stortz (57–71) in the present volume for epistemological and dispositional humility as central marks of Lutheran higher education.

17 L. DeAne Lagerquist, "Convocation and Loving a World That's Beautiful and Broken," St. Olaf College, September 9, 2021, https://wp.stolaf.edu/lutherancenter/2021/09/convocation-and-loving-a-world-thats-beautiful-and-broken/.

18 See Martin Luther, "The Bondage of the Will," in *Martin Luther's Basic Theological Writings*, 3rd ed., ed. Timothy F. Lull and Williams R. Russell (Minneapolis: Fortress, 2012), 160–61.

he claimed that he would likely have taken all the power and privilege afforded to white people if the tables of racism were reversed. To be clear, neither of these men saw this to be an excuse to continue taking advantage of systemic racism or abusing the earth and one's neighbor. Acknowledging fallibility should not lead to resignation; it should engender compassion for others. This perspective tempers self-righteousness over and against others.

When it comes to classroom teaching and learning, the educational value of humility does not mean that students or faculty should be intentionally humbled—or humiliated. That is a power play and is certainly not constructive for learning. Not all people have even had the "opportunity" to be proud. There is a good reason that Pride Week encourages and celebrates pride in queer communities. Even Luther's unqualified idea of human sin and fallibility as fundamental can be challenged as an overgeneralized anthropology.[19] Humility in the sense I am supporting here ironically requires a great deal of bravery and self-confidence. One has to be able to stand with others as a flawed person and give up pretention of perfection.

In a polarized society (left and right, religious and secular, urban and rural), this type of humility is in short supply. Backed into ideological corners, generalization of the "other" and a fighting attitude lead to further calcification of positions. The wrong word, idea, or lack of knowledge quickly equates to being labeled a "stupid" and "bad" person. Being "good," "smart," and "acceptable" depends on knowing the correct things to say and do. When students believe their perspective or terms are the right ones, they may relish being in the right, correcting others in the classroom. There can even be a level of disgust and disdain for those other students not "in the know." Inevitably, however, the conversation turns and now one finds oneself in the wrong: using the wrong terms, the wrong ideas. Increasingly, in the classroom, students live in a precarious position of being fearful and self-righteous simultaneously. There is little to no safe space to

---

19 Marit Trelstad, "Lavish Love: A Covenantal Ontology," in *Cross Examinations: Readings on the Meaning of the Cross Today*, ed. Marit Trelstad (Minneapolis: Fortress, 2006), 109–24.

talk, learn, and make errors. In the opening epigraph, Luther writes, "You are wise, not in order to laugh at the foolish and thereby make them more foolish, but that you may undertake to teach them as you yourself would wish to be taught." Compassion for others and grace for our own errors are preconditions for trust and learning.

How do we provide space for risky learning? How might the classroom dynamic shift if we can help remove these judgments of good and bad and recognize that we are all flawed and in need of understanding? What do we need to do to cultivate an environment of curiosity and compassion rather than of judgment? While I do not have the answers to these questions, I can testify that sometimes effective teaching comes from moments when we publicly fail in the classroom, even if embarrassing failure is the stuff of professorial nightmares.

How can we invite students to be messy, real, and misunderstood when we fear that ourselves? How can we dispel the academic, professional, and social fear of being wrong? Within the past year, I participated in a small pedagogical workshop with professors from a wide variety of colleges and universities. We were asked to shared detailed descriptions of moments that we would call our "teaching at its best." Interestingly, the most common element across all of them was that these moments entailed being caught off guard by the unexpected. In moments of chaos and failure, we were pushed to be vulnerable with the students and they stepped up and made wonderful moments of learning. Somehow, our professorial failure and vulnerability in the classroom allowed students to take risks as well.

Compassion in the classroom is a twin sensibility that arrives with humility. Compassion can mark the attitudes and actions of educators in the classroom. This does not always come easily when a student is particularly challenging. I have come to believe that, unless I can find a place of generosity and compassion for each student, they should not trust me to educate them. Over the course of my own education, major turning points in learning have often occurred when generous and patient teachers have encountered my own ignorance with grace. From quite another angle, chemistry professor Cheryl L. Ney, formerly of Capital University, writes that empathy can be the basis of teaching in the sciences at NECU intuitions when one recognizes that science is done by fully contextualized human beings in relation to subjects of study that have their own inherent integrity. Scientific disciplines are shaped by technical, organizational, and cultural aspects and done by rational, emotional, culturally shaped people with specific values and intents.[20] Empathy and understanding of ourselves and others holistically is essential across the disciplines.

Another type of compassion in the classroom is embodied when we join our students in acknowledging the difficulties life holds. Caryn D. Riswold, professor of religion at Wartburg College, wrote an article in the ill-fated year of 2020 titled, "Called to a Pedagogy of the Cross."[21] She affirms the importance of acknowledging and sitting with suffering—together with our students—and how this can create spaces for an effective form of teaching. Riswold invokes Luther's idea that a "theologian of the cross" names our reality in all its suffering, pain, anxiety, and despair without sugar-coating or avoidance. Luther claimed that such moments of suffering, embarrassment, difficulty, failure, anxiety, and fear are where we encounter the holy. Over the course of decades of teaching, I can recall moments of shame, confusion, tears, ignorance, frustration, anger, and embarrassment in the classroom—both mine and the students'. When I have invited students into reflection on these times (e.g. "This class is becoming a hot mess! What can we do?"), this has almost always turned things around for the better. Students invest and lean in. They are kinder to one another and to me. Often trust begins to rebuild while fear and judgment subside. The classroom is a very human place. Martin Luther affirmed that grace often comes in the least likely places and times—times of sorrow, defeat, and anxiety rather than places of power and neat order. When we enter difficult

20 Cheryl L. Ney, "'Rooting Science in Empathy: Growing Towards a Sustainable Science Practice for the 21st Century' Or 'How a Feminist, Trained as a DNA Biochemist, Finds Freedom at an Institution Whose Heritage is German Lutheran,'" *Intersections* 7 (Summer 1999): 3–9.

21 Caryn D. Riswold, "Called to a Pedagogy of the Cross," *Vocation Matters* (blog), April 8, 2020, https://vocationmatters.org/2020/04/08/called-to-a-pedagogy-of-the-cross/.

times, we are not alone in that experience, and we are often surprised
to receive the very resources that we and our students need in order
to learn: wisdom, grace, and compassion.

Goal: Shared Power

Martin Luther's various forms of ecclesial, educational, and socie-
tal reforms each sought to empower the common person. Indeed,
as in many forms of Christianity, he held that power in relation to
others is found in love and vulnerability rather than domination.
While Luther appreciated the role of experts, officials, and authority figures, these people were not set apart as special or more holy,
but rather were simply those who held a particular job or function.
The "vernacular," everyday, and common were the realm of both the
sacred and the mundane.

As mentioned earlier, Lutheran reforms stressed literacy so individuals could read for themselves and not only rely on the interpretations of those in power. In church congregations, musical experts
and performers were replaced by congregational singing, involving
everyone (a tradition that has led to excellence in music and singing
at ELCA colleges and universities[22]). Even church authority structures took on a new "upside down" form of decision-making power.
An example of this is evident in the ELCA today. The Churchwide
Assembly, the primary decision-making body of the ELCA, is composed of roughly one thousand members of the church from every
region. The members vote on policies and statements after discussion
and communal spiritual discernment. Pastors serve their congregational members and bishops serve the pastors and congregations.

So, too, at best, learning and teaching is not unidirectional in
NECU classrooms and other arenas of learning at our institutions.
Professors bring valuable expertise, responsibility, and disciplinary
content to the craft of teaching. And yet, teaching and learning, critically questioning and responding to another's inquiry, ideally flow
in both directions.

---

22 See chapters by Marcia J. Bunge (13–29) and Anton E. Armstrong (127–41) in
   the present volume.

Elsewhere in this volume, authors emphasize the importance of equity and inclusion at the heart of Lutheran higher education.[23] Equity, access, and shared power are also primary pedagogical goals. Access in the classroom has to do with the forms of pedagogy we employ, as we lean toward inclusive and hospitable practices. In her article, "Radical Hospitality on Haunted Grounds: Anti-Racism in Lutheran Higher Education," Krista E. Hughes writes: "Hospitality is about receiving the other. Radical hospitality is about receiving the other in such a way that we open ourselves to being changed—and indeed being changed in ways we cannot predict or control. Opening ourselves to that which might disturb us is a practice that is at once active and receptive."[24] Hughes reflects on the NECU shared vision document *Rooted and Open* in light of this commitment to hospitality: "Rooted and Open articulates a common mission for the colleges and universities of the ELCA. Part of that mission, the document states, is to 'practice radical hospitality,' that is, to 'welcome all and learn from all' by valuing the unique gifts of each student who steps onto campus . . . 'hospitality makes deep learning possible'."[25]

In a wider, overall sense, to be open and rooted involves believing that all students merit inherent belonging. One brings one's whole self to one's education; belonging is not determined by worthiness or alignment with the university or college values. "All are welcome" is radical and complicated educational stance in an increasingly polarized society. It is one of the most challenging aspects of our work as teachers.

These understandings of authority, power, and access in the Lutheran tradition may be a generative springboard for considering shared power in the classroom. Many of us have learned that the "flipped classroom," or student-led education, is an effective form of teaching that fosters deep learning. It decenters the professor's authority and favors student agency and learning as the means of

23 See chapters by Courtney Wilder (109–26), Caryn D. Riswold (173–87), and Anthony Bateza (189–203) in the present volume.
24 Krista E. Hughes, "Radical Hospitality on Haunted Grounds: Anti-Racism in Lutheran Higher Education," *Intersections* 52 (Fall 2020): 15.
25 Hughes, "Radical Hospitality," 14.

education. Additionally, recent work in inclusive pedagogy invites us to develop teaching practices that engage and highlight the wisdom of a wide diversity of students and cultures. (Otherwise, many traditional pedagogical aims and methods are biased toward white, middle-to-high income students from families with generations of higher education.) Such critical pedagogy affirms that true authority is not granted by hierarchical status but is based in trust. When students trust the professor or institution, they grant them the authority to teach them. Indeed, the sensibilities of Lutheran higher education toward shared power resonate with many aspects of the field of critical pedagogy that includes feminist, postcolonial, and postmodern pedagogies.

First, feminist pedagogy encourages and presents a dialogue between multiple perspectives/voices to assess knowledge claims. It seeks voices from the margins, those who are denied full authority, especially—but not exclusively—women's voices. As a result of these commitments, it attends to issues of justice and empowerment as central. Another key component of feminist pedagogy is its recognition of the importance of the mind and body as integrated sites of learning. It offers a decentralization of the authority of the "expert" through a nonhierarchical, learner-centered, subject-centered classroom with a focus on community and shared responsibility.

Second, postcolonial pedagogy was founded in part by Paulo Freire, whose *Pedagogy of the Oppressed* frames education in terms of the interests of the oppressed and marginalized. Postcolonial teaching raises an analytical lens to the educational canon and content of the curriculum in order to examine who it ultimately privileges. Postcolonial approaches to learning and teaching challenge many traditional teaching models that are modes of indoctrination.

Third, postmodern pedagogy is based on an idea of power as an exchange rather than a possession. One has authority because it is given to them by the actions of others. In such a model, the authority of the teacher is understood in terms of the trust given to them by students rather than assumed or amassed by the teacher. In other words, true power is given rather than claimed. If students do not trust a professor, they will not learn from them. Postmodern pedagogy recognizes the situated, contextual nature of all knowledge as a part of larger cultural, economic, and religious systems. Since there is no single universal form of knowing, it embraces multiple voices, centers, and sources of knowledge; it calls for "multivocality."

Certainly, there is not a direct historical line from the Lutheran Reformation to feminist, postcolonial, and postmodern critical pedagogies. Still, as stated earlier, teaching and learning within Lutheran higher education ideally invites all voices to a shared table of learning, evaluates the interests and biases that are always at play, and does not hide in structures of unquestioned hierarchical power but rather teaches so that learning is a process of mutual learning where all are empowered.

Considering the insights of critical pedagogy and the heritage of Lutheran higher education, our students should question us when we seek to "transform" them.[26] Why should they trust an institution or educators who have this intent? And what is the effect by which we are gauging success? Shared power as a value of Lutheran higher education can take many forms and be informed by these branches of critical pedagogy that highlight multivocality, power analysis, trust, the perspectives and interest of the marginalized, and a strong suspicion of indoctrination. Asking students to replicate and reproduce our ideas, beliefs, and values is antithetical to Lutheran higher education. Shared power entails learning that is fundamentally reciprocal.

Conclusion

My own experiences as a religion professor suggest that, by gaining critical tools of historical, textual, and ideological analysis to examine one's own deepest beliefs, whether religious or secular, one is liberated from simple generalizations about religion—both positive and negative. Arguably, a wholly for-or-against mentality characterizes initial understandings of religion more so than other

---

26 See Marit Trelstad, "The Ethics of Effective Teaching: Challenges from the Religious Right and Critical Pedagogy," *Teaching Theology and Religion* 11.4 (2008): 191–202.

disciplines.[27] On closer analysis, however, any discipline can seduce students into entrenchment on one side of oppositional postures—of being for versus against something, of submitting to the teacher versus withdrawing from the course.

Against these cultural habits, Lutheran higher education offers tools and curricular space for students and educators to engage and hold their deepest commitments as valuable while simultaneously subjecting them to analysis and critique from multiple perspectives. These countercultural practices, dispositions, and aims are at the heart of Lutheran education. They are animated by reform and a commitment to social change, the pursuit of justice, humane citizenship, and service for the poor and vulnerable.

If the values of Lutheran higher education matter to us, we need to embody them in the classroom and other avenues of teaching and learning across our campuses. Based on the gifts of Lutheran higher education for teaching, I offer these final questions for your own pedagogical reflection: In what ways might your own classroom practices model the values of good questions, humility, compassion, and shared power? Is critical appreciation an aspect that is built into your discipline or teaching? In what ways might you allow students to push back against your own pedagogical sensibilities? What other pedagogical values may be particularly present in your college or university's present or past? Do these resonate or conflict with those present in this chapter or volume? And finally, which guiding values or commitments inform your own pedagogy, and how to do these relate to those within Lutheran higher education?

For Further Study

Chopp, Rebecca S. "Educational Process, Feminist Practice." *The Christian Century*. Feb. 1–8, 1995.

Ellsworth, Elizabeth. "Why Doesn't this Feel Empowering? Working through the Repressive Myths of Critical Pedagogy." *Harvard Educational Review* 59.9 (August 1989): 297–324.

---

27 For more on assumptions about (and the realities of) teaching religion within Lutheran higher education, see the chapter by Martha E. Stortz in the present volume (57–71).

Palmer, Parker J. *The Courage to Teach: Exploring the Inner Landscape of a Teacher's Life*. San Francisco: Jossey-Bass, 1997.

Riswold, Caryn D. "Called to a Pedagogy of the Cross." *Vocation Matters* (blog), April 8, 2020. https://vocationmatters.org/2020/04/08/called-to-a-pedagogy-of-the-cross/.

Trelstad, Marit. "The Ethics of Effective Teaching: Challenges from the Religious Right and Critical Pedagogy." *Teaching Theology and Religion* 11.4 (2008): 191–202.

7

Disability Accommodations and Institutional Mission

Courtney Wilder, Midland University

People with disabilities are present on college and university campuses throughout the United States and Canada. This does not mean they are recognized or that their needs are met. According to the National Center for College Students with Disabilities (NCCSD), "Many campus communities do not address disability as part of diversity and campus climate efforts. Even after addressing physical and structural barriers, the campus environment may be inhospitable for students, faculty, and staff with disabilities due to ableist attitudes about disability, as well as curricular, programmatic, and policy barriers."[1]

The US Department of Education estimates that students with disabilities make up about 11 percent of campus undergraduate populations, although this estimate may be low.[2] Mikyong Minsun Kim and Elisabeth Kutscher argue that, because colleges and universities that accept federal aid must comply with federal law regarding educational access, "almost all institutions of higher education are required to provide students with disabilities equal access to

---

1 Wendy S. Harbour and Daniel Greenberg, "Campus Climate and Students with Disabilities," NCCSD Research Brief 4. Volume 1, Issue 2, July 2017, https://files.eric.ed.gov/fulltext/ED577464.pdf.

2 Mikyong Minsun Kim and Elisabeth Kutscher, "College Students with Disabilities: Factors Influencing Growth in Academic Ability and Confidence," *Research in Higher Education* 62.3 (May 2020): 309.

all programs and services together with their classmates without disabilities. Institutions of higher education are therefore legally responsible for promoting the development and success of students both with and without disabilities."[3]

Beyond compliance with the law, what might drive (or fail to drive) disability accommodation? While Kim and Kutscher note that most institutions approach accommodations with the goal of legal compliance, it is also the case that disability accommodations are necessary to fulfill the missions of colleges and universities—in the case of the Network of ELCA Colleges and Universities (NECU), the shared mission to "equip graduates who are called and empowered to serve the neighbor so that all may flourish."[4] The fact that NECU schools are affiliated with the Evangelical Lutheran Church in America (ELCA) may suggest that they have an obvious motivation to ensure disability access. Yet, as we will see, Christian (including Lutheran) stances concerning disabled people have been mixed at best, and Christian colleges that directly bring their Christian worldview into the classroom (or into disability resource centers) risk reproducing theologically sanctioned misconceptions and stereotypes of disabled students.

In this chapter, I will show how Lutheran colleges and universities are well positioned to enact educational justice for disabled people. They are theologically grounded in a rich Christian tradition that informs their mission statements, long-term planning, and educational priorities. At the same time, because they distinguish the inclusive educational missions from the theological commitments that undergird them (that is, because their missions are *informed by* Christian priorities *without being synonymous* with them), they avoid some of the most dangerous Christian attitudes about people with disabilities. As both rooted and open, Lutheran institutions of higher education have a unique—or even paradoxical—combination of being deeply Lutheran while also being deeply critical of Lutheranism and

---

3 Kim and Kutscher, "College Students with Disabilities," 310.

4 NECU, *Rooted and Open: The Common Calling of the Network of ELCA Colleges and Universities*, 3. https://download.elca.org/ELCA%20Resource%20 Repository/Rooted_and_Open.pdf.

wholly open to calls for justice that emanate from elsewhere. NECU institutions can thereby both recognize disabled people as beloved children of God and frame disability rights as an ethical and humanistic issue of justice and inclusion.

The Ethics and Ethos of Inclusion

I mentioned above the charge by the National Center for College Students and Disabilities (NCCSD) that "many campus communities do not address disability as part of diversity and campus climate efforts." Disabled students are often not well served by colleges and universities, a failure that has as much to do with the overall campus climate as with particular policies. The NCCSD thereby suggests that removing barriers for students with disabilities and fostering a sense of belonging for all is the work of the campus as a whole:

> Even after addressing physical and structural barriers, the campus environment may be inhospitable for students, faculty, and staff with disabilities due to ableist attitudes about disability, as well as curricular, programmatic, and policy barriers. These barriers may be especially challenging for students with disabilities who identify as members of other marginalized groups, including students of color, LGBTQ students, and students who grew up in poverty. While there is often a tacit expectation that disability services offices will take sole charge for disability-related matters, a positive campus climate for people with disabilities needs to be an institutional responsibility involving multiple departments, offices, and individuals.[5]

Metrics the NCCSD used in determining the campus climate for disabled students included (but were not limited to) the students' perceived comfort in classrooms, in the student's department, and throughout campus. In each of these areas, nondisabled students rated their level of comfort more highly than disabled students. This matters for many reasons, including the fact that students who feel comfortable are more likely to be retained by their school and more likely to graduate.

---

5 Harbour and Greenberg, "Campus Climate," 4.

While the retention of students often is seen as a fiscal concern for institutions, it is also a pressing ethical issue. In an era of increasing cost of tuition, accumulating debt is a fact of life for many students; if the student does not complete the degree, that debt is not offset by access to jobs that require a bachelor's degree.[6] Students who do graduate from private nonprofit schools, such as those within NECU, had an average of $33,900 in student loan debt in 2021.[7] For disabled students, already facing potential employment discrimination and higher rates of poverty than their nondisabled peers, student debt in the face of lower graduation rates is an especially serious issue.[8] Federal data finds that "across all educational attainment groups, unemployment rates for persons with a disability were higher than those for persons without a disability."[9]

Disability accommodation is a developing aspect of higher education as students with disabilities are attending college in increasing numbers. One size does not fit all, and the stakes are high for students and institutions alike. Accommodation practices in higher education must go hand in hand with awareness of disability rights and affirmation of justice for disabled people. Finally, as the findings of the NCCSD show, such practices and ethics must go beyond compliance with the law in order also to shape the institutional ethos or climate of the whole campus.

---

6 For example, the estimated cost of tuition and room and board at a not-for-profit private four-year college or university in the US (a category that includes all ELCA colleges and universities) in 2018 was $47,662 annually. In 1985 that amount was $9,228; adjusted for inflation, the 1985 degree would now cost $21,478. See https://nces.ed.gov/fastfacts/display.asp?id=76. In 1985 the average household income was $23,620; in 2018 it was $63,179. See https://data.census.gov. In 1985 roughly speaking, one year at schools like those within NECU was 38.48 percent of an average family's income. Now that same year is 75.44 percent of an average family's income.

7 See https://www.credible.com/blog/statistics/average-student-loan-debt-statistics/

8 The National Council on Disability has found that "people with disabilities live in poverty at more than twice the rate of people without disabilities." See https://ncd.gov/newsroom/2017/disability-poverty-connection-2017-progress-report-release.

9 See https://www.bls.gov/news.release/pdf/disabl.pdf.

Regarding education as part of a person's vocation is one way in which colleges and universities within NECU shape their campus climate and institutional ethos. The long history of emphasizing vocation positions Lutheran schools to affirm and support students, staff, and faculty with disabilities. This is important not only to the individual education of disabled students but also to creating an environment where every member of the community participates in disability justice. Failure to support and nurture the vocations of disabled students is a violation of key tenets of Lutheran approaches to education. Moreover, even students who are not themselves disabled benefit immensely from being part of an environment where disability access is taken seriously. Accommodation affects all students' ethical formation; it shapes how they see themselves in relationship to their community and provides students with practical tools for inclusion.

Rooted and Open, the 2018 NECU foundational statement, has it that "Lutheran education is education for vocation. Students are called to do work that is both meaningful to them and helpful to the earth and its creatures."[10] The document continues to emphasize the way personal fulfillment is contingent upon the function and flourishing of whole communities: "Vocation-centered education equips students to understand how the world, human beings and communities function, as well as what they need to be personally fulfilled and healthy."[11] Many additional passages within *Rooted and Open* suggest that the flourishing of individuals depends on the functioning and flourishing of the communities in which they are inextricably nestled. Part of NECU's mission is to provide a teaching and learning context that illuminates for students what it might be like to live in a just and peaceful world. How students, staff, faculty, and administrators regard people with disabilities is both a test of the college's inclusivity and a practice that shapes the character of the community.

---

10 NECU, *Rooted and Open*, 5.
11 NECU, *Rooted and Open*, 5.

The Church's Ex/Inclusion of Disabled Persons

The Christian tradition has a mixed history on disability. Christians have certainly not consistently affirmed the humanity and value of disabled people. Two tropes within Christianity regarding disability continue to be common. One trope frames disability as a punishment from God, the other as a gift from God, wherein a disabled person's suffering is designed to serve as an inspiration or moral lesson for nondisabled people.

Nancy Eiesland calls the first of these characterizations the "sin-disability conflation."[12] This understanding of disability often comes with the express recommendation to the disabled person that they need to repent in order for God to "cure" them. This extremely harmful belief serves to justify the exclusion, abuse, and devaluation of disabled people on the grounds that they are obviously to blame for their disability.

The second trope is no less damaging; it instrumentalizes disabled people as occasions for pity or reminders to able-bodied people that things could be worse for them and they ought to count their blessings. In both of these scenarios, practicing Christians commonly touch and/or pray over disabled people without their consent, presuming to act on God's behalf. Such belief systems conveniently spare nondisabled people the work of examining their own behavior and the social contexts in which they live.

Church Practices and Scripture

Given these tropes and a host of theological justifications, disabled people are routinely excluded from not only the daily life of Christian churches, but even from the sacraments. One example from 2020 was reported in *The Washington Post*. Anthony LaCunga, a Catholic child who was then eight years old, was prevented from receiving his First Communion on the grounds that he could not affirm to his priest's satisfaction, verbally or physically, that he understood sin. Anthony is autistic, nonverbal, and has a diagnosis of apraxia, which

---

12 Nancy Eiesland, *The Disabled God: Toward a Liberatory Theology of Disability* (Nashville: Abingdon, 1994), 75.

limits his ability to respond with physical movement to instructions that he does understand. "My heart shattered," his mother said. "My first thought was, how do you take a child who was one of God's children and say that he is not good enough, basically, to be making the sacrament?"[13]

This is not an uncommon story, as Lutherans also know. Indeed, the ELCA's own history regarding disability is significantly if not equally problematic. As Ronald Duty recounts, one of the ELCA's predecessor bodies, the American Lutheran Church (ALC), specifically identified disabled people as unfit for ordained ministry. Duty examines policies for the admission of persons with disabilities into seminaries and for ordination. In June 1985, the ALC adopted the policy statement, "Seminary Admission and Certification Criteria in Relation to the Work ALC Pastors are Expected to Do." The statement listed not only the expected theological, academic, and ethical qualifications of pastors, but also their work performance expectations, including expectations for physical mobility and energy for the pastor's workload. Duty summarizes the implications for disabled persons called to ministry:

> In light of these [performance expectations], the statement issued guidelines for admission to seminary and certification for ordination that attempted to distinguish between those disabilities that were not a barrier to pastors serving congregations, on the one hand, and those physical conditions that were "potentially disqualifying," on the other hand. The latter conditions included progressive degenerative neurological and physical disorders (e.g., multiple sclerosis, ALS, juvenile onset diabetes, cystic fibrosis, some kidney diseases, non-correctable heart conditions, quadriplegia, and severe psychiatric disorders).[14]

---

13 Antonia Noori Farzan, "An Autistic Boy was Denied First Communion because He Can't Tell Right from Wrong, his Family Says" *The Washington Post*, February 28, 2020, https://www.washingtonpost.com/nation/2020/02/28/autistic-boy-denied-communion-church/.

14 Ronald W. Duty, "Actions Taken by the ELCA and its Predecessor Churches Regarding Persons with Disabilities and Disability Ministry," 2010 (unpublished manuscript provided by Ronald Duty), which cites Minutes of the Church Council, The American Lutheran Church, June 3–7, 1985, 96.

Happily, the policy sparked backlash and debate, but not before at least four months of being defended by bishop David W. Preus, at which time the controversy died down.[15] Although this particular policy was rescinded after significant negative public response, it represents too many church policies over the past several decades.

Christian Scripture itself is also mixed—sometimes reliably affirming (but sometimes failing to affirm) disabled people's identity as children of God and bearers of God's image who are worthy of respect. A positive example is John 9:1–3, which depicts Jesus correcting his disciples when they ask, "Rabbi, who sinned, this man or his parents, that he was born blind?" Jesus responds, "Neither this man nor his parents sinned; he was born blind so that God's works might be revealed in him." The pericope goes on to illustrate the man's faith and agency, and so serves as a positive lesson in the full humanity and faithfulness of disabled people.

A more problematic text is John 5:14, where after healing a man with a years-long illness, Jesus tells him, "See, you have been made well! Do not sin anymore, so that nothing worse happens to you." This essentially equates disability with sin and nondisability with righteousness or purity. The tension in these accounts illuminates some of the complex and contradictory accounts of disability within the Christian tradition. Many modern Christian communities struggle with these texts, both in interpretation and in preaching.

What is more, Christian congregations regularly sing hymns that adopt language from, for example, Isaiah 35:5–6, where God's rescue of God's people is prophesied in these terms:

> *Then the eyes of the blind shall be opened,*
> *and the ears of the deaf unstopped;*
> *then the lame shall leap like a deer,*
> *and the tongue of the speechless sing for joy.*

The envisioned rescue by God is depicted in images that specifically identify a range of disabilities as conditions that God will reverse. While in context these verses may have represented relief from

---

15 Duty, "Actions Taken by the ELCA" 96.

suffering, their repetition within hymns of praise by modern worshippers strikes a very different note. A blind or deaf or mobility-impaired or nonverbal member of the congregation should not have to serve, however obliquely, as a communal symbol, and may not need or want healing at all.

Lutheran Approaches to Disability

Clearly updated resources—not to mention better theology—are needed in Christian religious communities. There are some clear signs of improvement, including those within the ELCA. The 2019 ELCA *Social Statement on Faith, Sexism and Justice* is not specifically written to address issues of disability access, but it does helpfully suggest that every person is both disabled and abled—that each has gifts and dependencies that help sustain whole communities. The social statement declares: "We believe all people are created equally in the image of God. Every individual is dependent upon God, and all share in the God-given vocation to contribute their gifts to help all of creation flourish. Being in the image of the triune God means that we humans are relational, that we are interconnected. Just as we interact with God, we are social creatures relating with each other and all of creation."[16] This includes disabled people.

The ELCA directly addressed disability and inclusion in its 2010 "Message on People Living with Disabilities." The message affirms, "This church believes that God, as creator and sustainer, intends that society regard all people as of equal worth and make it possible for all—those without and those with disabilities—to participate freely and fully as members of society in all important aspects of common life."[17] It very clearly identifies the false ideal of an independent and perfectible human person as in opposition to Christian understanding of the self and the neighbor, and of human beings in relationship with God. There remains ample room for improvement. While the

---

16 ELCA, *Social Statement on Faith, Sexism and Justice: A Call to Action*, 2019, 15. https://download.elca.org/ELCA%20Resource%20Repository/Faith_Sexism_Justice_Social_Statement_Adopted.pdf.

17 ELCA, "A Message on People Living With Disabilities," 1. https://download.elca.org/ELCA%20Resource%20Repository/People_with_DisabilitiesSM.pdf.

social message provides many useful suggestions for congregations, seminaries, and broader social institutions—including schools—by its nature the document falls short of identifying specific benchmarks for the ELCA or its congregations or colleges and universities, and makes no specific financial commitment to the work of organizations, congregations, or educators seeking to work for disability justice.

Theologies of Disability

The well-established and flourishing field of disability theology is an important resource for Christians and Christian congregations. It is especially important for church-related higher education institutions—such as NECU institutions—who seek to reckon with the Christian tradition's sometimes problematic construal of disability and impairment. As we have seen above, and as Anthony Pinn argues, Christianity has both "buttressed oppressive activities" *and* been a tool for "oppressed communities [to] . . . critique and challenge this abuse."[18] Pinn is speaking specifically to the context of Black theology, but the same holds true for theology of disability. As both rooted and open, the twenty-seven NECU institutions are ideally situated to draw deeply on the best of Lutheran/Christian accounts of disability while unapologetically critiquing (and confessing) harmful theologies of the past.

Disability theology is also interdisciplinary, and so fits squarely within the educational priorities of Lutheran liberal arts colleges and universities. From its emergence in the 1990s through to our current context, theology of disability has been interdisciplinary, drawing from disability studies, biblical interpretation, and theology of liberation. Theology of disability frames disability rights as an issue of justice and calls religious institutions to recognize disabled people as beloved children of God. As such, disability theology is also *public* and *political* theology; it has developed in conversation with the

18 Anthony Pinn and Stacey M. Floyd-Thomas, "Introduction," in *Liberation Theologies in the United States: An Introduction*, ed. Stacey M. Floyd-Thomas and Anthony Pinn (New York University Press, 2010), 1.

disability rights movement more broadly and reflects the liberation-ist goals of the disability rights and other civil rights movements.

It is no coincidence that Nancy Eiesland, one of the first and most influential theologians of disability, was also trained as a sociolo-gist. While *inclusion* in religious institutions—whether churches, social agencies, camps, seminaries, or undergraduate institutions—continues to be an important goal of each community, disability theology cannot be disentangled from its origins as a *political liber-ation* movement. Friendliness is not enough, ramps are not enough, inclusive Sunday chapel or vocation retreats are not enough. Instead, church and church-related communities, including those within the ELCA and NECU, must reckon with their history of oppressing and demonizing disabled people and reject these practices. They need to dismantle theological and religious support for ableism (discrimina-tion against and stigmatization of disabled people) and instead use the tools of the Christian tradition to affirm the value of disabled people as children of God. This includes working actively to support the civil rights of people with disabilities, beginning within their own communities.

A theology of disability provides a clear theological grounding for an essential educational practice, namely, the offering of accessible education to students so that they can fully belong to communities that attend to the needs and gifts of all. Creating colleges and uni-versities that do not simply follow the letter of federal law in meeting the accommodation needs of disabled students, but that also enable each to flourish in the context of the whole, is necessary to live out the recognition of all people as created in the image of God.

Educational Justice in Practice

Lutheran colleges and universities are well positioned to live out this calling to full access and inclusion. Lutheran theological norms emphasize intellectual inquiry and education, religious and otherwise. Disability studies is an important partner in trans-lating this inquiry into action. While the educational practices established by the 1990 Americans with Disabilities Act (ADA)

and the 1975 Individuals with Disabilities Education Act (IDEA)
have shaped how colleges and universities provide access for disabled students, the students themselves are a powerful resource
for determining how access ought to work, and—theologically
speaking—what educational justice for disabled people looks like
in practice.

Inclusive Practices and Pedagogies

Key practices for a disability-informed teaching praxis include four
areas: First, *disabled thinkers* should be part of the canon of every
discipline, and identified as such in the process of teaching. Second,
as disciplinary practices allow, courses should include *analysis of disability rights issues* as integral to the course material. Third, in addition to providing accommodations to disabled students as required
by law, instructors should implement *universal design* into their
courses. Finally, as we will see below, intentional and strategic *institutional support for disabled students* is crucial for their well-being.

The disability rights movement has long used the mantra, "Nothing about us without us," and this includes integrating disability
perspectives into college courses. The best way to do this is to teach
disabled thinkers, which may be as straightforward as identifying
and discussing the disability experiences of writers and scholars who
are already on the syllabus. As with other marginalized groups, disabled people have been systematically excluded from access to education, including higher education; this does not mean that there are
no disabled scholars to draw from when considering who and what
to teach.

How does this work in practice? A course on bioethics, for
instance, should include work by disabled bioethicists in its assigned
readings. It should provide students with the opportunity to learn
the history of eugenics from a critical perspective, and the physical space and teaching techniques should be intentionally shaped by
inclusive practices. This may include offering remote access to students with chronic illnesses when needed, offering a wide range of
assessments for students, providing students the chance to choose
modes of learning and participation, and providing all students

access to lecture notes. Pedagogical strategies focused on universal design—which seeks to make education accessible for all students as a matter of course—play another key role here. Other areas of praxis cover all academic disciplines and students' access to key resources, including housing, academic support, tutoring, and a well-organized office for disability issues.

One example from an ELCA institution of thoughtful reflection on disability accommodation comes from Thiel College. The current interim director of Thiel's Disability Resource Center (DRC), Jodie Witherite, and the former director, Liza Schaef, spoke with me about best practices in student support for disabled students. Noteworthy is Schaef's centering of disabled students in decisions that would otherwise be made for or about them. Speaking to the college's renewed commitment to guide and support students, Schaef combines language of vocation (*vocare*) with self-advocacy (*ad + vocare*): "How do [disabled students] identify with their disability? What does it mean to them? How does it impact them?" She encourages disabled students to ask of themselves: "How do I advocate for myself here at Thiel? How do I advocate for myself in the real world? What does that mean, to be a student with this disability?" Schaef is committed to "let students be who they are and where they are in our [counseling] space."[19]

Institutional Mission
Thiel's Office of Disability Services Catalog Statement reads in part:

> The Office of Disability Services embraces the mission of Thiel College and works closely with faculty, staff and students to develop all aspects of the human character through education. This office works closely with faculty and staff in an advisory capacity and assists in the development of reasonable academic adjustments that allow individuals with disabilities to fully participate in all of the programs offered at Thiel College.[20]

19 Liza Schaef, phone conversation, August 23, 2021.
20 Thiel College, "Office of Disability Services Catalog Statement," https://www.thiel.edu/assets/documents/campus_life/office-of-disability-services-catalog-statement.pdf.

The second sentence resembles similar statements in catalogs of colleges and universities throughout the United States, and each school must determine what a "reasonable" accommodation includes. The first sentence, however, is relatively distinctive to church-related schools, especially those (like NECU institutions) that frequently link education to the development of the character of whole persons.

The Office of Disability Service's engagement with the overarching mission of Thiel College is important and noteworthy. It provides a means by which religious-affiliated institutions might navigate some of the difficult realities of the Christian tradition's response to disability. As we considered above, Christian institutions and Christian individuals have a mixed record on issues of disability. In her work with disabled students, Schaef has seen the same set of stereotypes that we explore above, and she, too, identifies their origin in religious teachings and Scripture:

> There's still a lot of stigma around disability. I think that is improving and the tolerance among the age group of the students we serve is getting better, but [there is still a] history of stigma [around mental health and physical disabilities] with regard to religion. It can be a disease-based model or a condemnation model, or that you've done something wrong to deserve this, or—if you survive this—then you get to a better place because you've endured all this. There can be very negative imaging . . . If that's what their doctrine or religion has brought them up with, there can be some barriers there that they need to overcome.[21]

In light of these negative stereotypes (or "imaging") that are named by disability theologians and confirmed by practitioners like Schaef, why is institutional mission so important? The answer involves the unique way that Lutheran colleges and universities (and NECU as a whole) have distinguished the central institutional missions and educational priorities from the theological tradition that undergirds them.

NECU institutions are "third path" colleges and universities, according to Darrell Jodock, and so can be distinguished from both

---

21 Schaef, phone conversation.

"secular" and "sectarian" schools. Secular schools do not claim a theological source below or behind their mission statements and strategic plans; they work directly from their college's mission in carrying out their daily work. More "sectarian" colleges (often called "Christian colleges" or "Bible colleges") do not distinguish Christian foundations from institutional mission; they thus often fail to incorporate into their mission those who are not Christian (and perhaps those whom some Christian traditions have particular stereotypes about, including disabled people). Lutheran colleges and universities have deep theological roots (unlike secular schools), which inform and shape their institutional missions in particular ways. At the same time (and unlike sectarian schools), the mission of the institution is not synonymous with its Christian foundation or church-relatedness, and so the school can be radically inclusive of—and deeply dependent on—the particular gifts and needs of all students, faculty, and staff, whether they are Lutheran, Muslim, or secular; able-bodied, disabled, or both; and so forth.[22]

When it comes to developing practices of inclusion, accommodation, and the deep belonging of disabled students, institutional mission—as informed by Lutheran principles but not synonymous with them—can be a more useful tool for enacting justice toward disabled students than direct religious conversation might provide. In Thiel's case, framing the rights of disabled students as part of a larger institutional conversation focused on serving the school's students both puts disability accommodation on par with other efforts to support and retain students and emphasizes that the school has made a commitment to the students it recruits to be part of the campus community.

Liza Schaef notes that, given the connections to institutional mission, the DRC staff person has recently become a full-time position.

---

22 See Darrell Jodock, "In A Diverse Society. Why Should Lutheran Colleges/ Universities Claim their Theological Roots?," *Intersections* 49 (Spring 2019): 10–12. See also Jason A. Mahn, "Roots and Shoots: Tending to Lutheran Higher Education," *Intersections* 49 (Spring 2019): 19–22; Martha E. Stortz, "Marked by Lutheran Higher Education," *Intersections* 49 (Spring 2019): 24–26; and Colleen Windham-Hughes, "Deep Roots, Big Questions, Bold Goals," *Intersections* 49 (Spring 2019): 27–30.

"With the last strategic plan," she says, "there was a really strong emphasis on trying to meet the needs of students academically and in every other way. Part of that vision within the strategic plan was to expand the role of the DRC on campus." Schaef also notes that access and inclusion are not the same as full support and a sense of belonging: "If we're going to actively recruit and enroll those students, we need to be able to support them at all levels . . . [The DRC office has had] constant growth and a constant recognition that you need to support students adequately, and in accordance with our mission."[23]

Thiel's mission is, of course, rooted in and sustained by the Lutheran intellectual tradition. It is not surprising, then, that disability support and religious leadership interface on campus. Jodie Witherite observed that the campus pastor at Thiel works closely with other support staff. "We do have a campus pastor . . . and he's great. Anything we really need, he's there for us."[24] This is certainly one important avenue for promoting the well-being and meeting the needs of disabled students, provided that campus clergy and other campus religious organizations are prepared to offer constructive responses to the needs of disabled students, and to welcome them as contributing members of the community. Liza Schaef also suggests that the mission of Thiel is shaped by its Lutheran church-relatedness, a connection she appreciates even as someone outside that tradition:

> For me, I choose to work at Thiel because I believe in their mission. So in my interactions with students and in the committees I serve on and in that capacity, I don't exclude religion from the conversation. Although I consider myself an atheist, I welcome conversations about religion. I've said a prayer with a student. If students come in the office and they want to talk about God, this is a welcoming space, and I'm comfortable with those conversations.[25]

At the same time, Schaef also appreciates the fact that the mission of Thiel is broader, more inclusive, and less *explicitly* Christian than the tradition that undergirds it. This, too, is an asset:

---

23 Schaef, phone conversation.
24 Jodie Witherite, phone conversation, August 23, 2022.
25 Schaef, phone conversation.

Is [religion] intentional to every conversation we have, directly? No! [What is direct and intentional] is helping [students] flesh out their experiences over four years, [of learning] what it means to be a college student, of really understanding your main purpose and vocation.[26]

Notice here how the emphasis on "purpose and vocation" uses an important Lutheran religious concept, available to any ELCA institution, to affirm the rights of disabled students, and their nondisabled peers, to reflect on their own personal and spiritual identities and their academic and career goals. At the same time, rooting disability inclusion and justice work in institutional mission rather than directly in the theological tradition that undergirds and shapes it avoids much of the complex and conflicting biblical and theological constructs of disabled bodies. As rooted and open, higher education institutions such as Thiel are able to leverage the most life-giving and liberatory elements from Lutheranism in their support and advocacy work with disabled students. They are also free to critique or nuance that tradition when it demonizes or instrumentalizes disability, and instead frame disability rights as an ethical and humanistic issue of justice and inclusion.

Conclusion

Institutions of higher education ought to prioritize equal access for disabled people. Lutheran colleges and universities have a strong theological foundation for providing this access: First, our long tradition of intellectual curiosity positions us to seek out a range of points of view, including those from disabled people, who have historically been underserved by educational systems. Second, we affirm our commitment to promoting justice and to the status of every human being as a child of God. By offering accessible classrooms and campuses, we promote the education of disabled people. By studying the work of disabled scholars and attending to the points of view of our disabled students, we more fully engage with the world as it is. By

---

26 Schaef, phone conversation.

engaging in theological reflection that affirms the value of disabled people, we bring these insights to our religious practices. Finally, by rooting all of these practices in institutional missions that are decidedly shaped by Lutheran traditions but not synonymous with them, we ensure that our particular support of disabled students will draw from the best of Lutheranism while also critiquing it, allowing it to be challenged and developed in conversation with the disability rights movement and other civil rights movements.

For Further Study

Brock, Brian. "Theologizing Inclusion: 1 Corinthians 12 and the Politics of the Body of Christ." *Journal of Religion, Disability & Health* 15.4 (2011): 351–76.

Brock, Brian and John Swinton. *Disability in the Christian Tradition*. Grand Rapids, MI: Eerdmans, 2012.

Carter, Eric W. *Including People with Disabilities in Faith Communities*. Baltimore: Brookes, 2007.

Eiesland, Nancy. *The Disabled God: Toward a Liberatory Theology of Disability*. Nashville: Abingdon, 1994.

Yong, Amos. *The Bible, Disability, and the Church*. Grand Rapids, MI: Eerdmans, 2011.

8

Music, Vocation, and Transformation

Anton E. Armstrong, St. Olaf College

From their founding and still today, institutions within the Network of ELCA Colleges and Universities (NECU) have given music a central place and function. Many NECU institutions are recognized nationally and internationally for their stellar music departments, choirs, and instrumental ensembles. Each offers opportunities for all students, whatever their majors or future goals, to engage in music. On NECU campuses, music is a major part of academic study and community events. Music departments offer courses about music and music lessons, support a wide range of concerts, and provide music for sporting events, worship services, and convocations. NECU institutions believe a high level of musical excellence should be offered to all students.

In Lutheran higher education, music is not understood as a peripheral endeavor or mere entertainment but rather as central to the aims of a rigorous liberal arts education and as a powerful vehicle for nurturing the whole person. Indeed, as the mission statement of Saint Olaf's music department recognizes, "Through music we affirm the college's mission to foster the development of the whole person in mind, body, and spirit" and seek to create "an educational experience that unites the artistic standards of a professional program with the intellectual rigors and academic breadth of the liberal arts in an environment of free, creative, and critical inquiry."[1]

---

1 Mission Statement, St. Olaf Music Department, https://catalog.stolaf.edu/academic-programs/music/.

In the same vein, the music department at Luther College connects music to the college's values of "excellence, community, scholarship, and service."[2] Such ideas are shared by many other, if not all, NECU institutions.

These institutions acknowledge that for listeners and performers alike, music can also be a powerful and transformative *voice*. Whether through choral or instrumental works, music connects people and creates community. Furthermore, the music explored on NECU campuses often calls for justice or renews the human spirit. In this sense, music often serves what could be called "prophetic and priestly roles." Whether in concerts or at special events, music has the capacity to serve as a clarion call for social and environmental justice, to delight the heart and mind, and to provide a healing voice of love and hope. In worship services on NECU campuses, communities of faith also sing for the glory of God on behalf of the neighbor. In these ways and more, music can spark social change, heal the spirit, and strengthen an individual's or an institution's own sense of calling and service to the world. In other words, music can be an influential element in shaping the *vocare* or vocation (from *vox*, or voice) of those pursuing Lutheran higher education.

One of my greatest mentors was the late church musician and professor of music emerita, Westminster Choir College, Dr. Helen Kemp. Her mantra, "Body, Mind, Spirit, Voice—it takes the *whole* person to sing and rejoice," has been core to my own personal sense of calling as a vocal music educator and conductor. Kemp admonished those she met to remember the following: "We are imprinting musical memories for the soul and a lifetime. For in this high-tech world, the music we sing with all people makes us responsible for what we put into their hearts, minds, and souls." Kemp often quoted the words of Tom Brokaw, "It is not enough to wire the world—if you short circuit the soul."[3]

---

2 Mission Statement, Luther College Music Department, https://www.luther.edu/music/department/mission-statement/.

3 Helen Kemp, workshop presentation at the National ACDA Conference, Chicago, March 1999.

The aim of this chapter is to introduce readers to some of the reasons that music is so widespread and significant in Lutheran higher education. The chapter first highlights the biblical and theological foundations for the significance of music in the Lutheran tradition and then focuses on the ways that students from all backgrounds, traditions, and academic disciplines are engaged in and empowered by music across NECU campuses today. The chapter also shows how music can be a transformative force for individuals, institutions, and communities, and how Lutheran higher education seeks to honor its rich musical heritage by including an ever-growing range of multicultural and global voices. Although music is often perceived as peripheral to academic study, the chapter affirms the centrality of music in Lutheran higher education and underscores its significance for nurturing body, mind, and spirit, providing a voice for justice, peace, and love, and cultivating the callings and courage of both individuals and institutions to serve their neighbors and the world.

Biblical and Theological Background

The multifaceted power of music is expressed in many passages of the Bible. In the Psalms alone, music is used to express lament and praise, sorrow and joy, losses and victories. Music can also be used as a vehicle for instruction. In Colossians 3:16, for example, we see one of the scriptures in which music is shown to be a method of biblical instruction: "Let the word of Christ dwell within you richly; teach and admonish one another in all wisdom; and with gratitude in your hearts sing psalms, hymns, and spiritual songs, to God" (NRSV).

Building on such passages and his own experience, Martin Luther wrote extensively about the power of music. He was not only a theologian and reformer but also a musician and composer. He played the lute and the German flute, and composed several hymns that continue to be sung today. He believed that music was a divine gift to all creation and an essential component of intellectual, emotional, moral, and spiritual life.

In 1538 Luther stated the power of music in these bold words:
"Next to the Word of God, music deserves the highest praise."[4] He
was "overwhelmed" by the "diversity and magnitude" of music's "virtue and benefits," and he described music as a divine gift that appears
in all creation, but reaches its highest manifestation in human beings:

> First then, looking at music itself, you will find that from the begin-
> ning of the world it has been instilled and implanted in all creatures,
> individually and collectively. For nothing is without sound or har-
> mony. Even the air, which of itself is invisible and imperceptible to
> all our senses, and which, since it lacks both voice and speech, is the
> least musical of all things, becomes sonorous, audible, and compre-
> hensible when it is set in motion . . . Music is still more wonderful in
> living things, especially birds . . . And yet, compared to the human
> voice, all this hardly deserves the name of music, so abundant and
> incomprehensible is here the munificence and wisdom of our most
> gracious Creator.[5]

The notion of music as a divine gift, next in importance only to theology, becomes an important foundation for the Lutheran tradition's
deep appreciation of music and its understanding of the essential
role that choral and instrumental music play in both worship services and education.

Luther instigated congregational song as a powerful musical
catechism for all ages and as a meaningful way of nurturing and
instructing believers. Congregational song—the people's song—
represented the depth and breadth of the church proclaiming God's
call for justice undergirded by God's mercy, grace, and love. The people's song, which has its origins in the German chorale, served as the
foundation for vocal/choral music in the Lutheran tradition. These
were songs that were meant to educate a largely illiterate population in biblical content and introduce them to theological thinking.
Some texts paraphrased elements of the Ordinary of the Mass into
the German vernacular and served as congregational responses to

---

4 Martin Luther, foreword to "Georg Rhau's *Symphoniae iucundae*" (1538), in
  Luther's Works, ed. Jaroslav Pelikan and Helmut Lehmann (St. Louis: Concordia Publishing House, 1955–86), 53:323.
5 Luther, "Georg Rhau's *Symphoniae iucundae*," 321–22.

Latin chant. Others were used to illuminate seasons of the church year, and others focused on theological teachings.

Luther also appreciated a range of chorale and instrumental music. He had the opportunity to meet musicians who served the nearby courts of Saxony and Bavaria, such as Ludwig Senfl and Johan Walter. He also deeply appreciated the music of the renowned Renaissance composer, Josquin des Prez (1440–1521), famously calling him "the master of the notes." Luther also advocated for the use of instruments in praise of God. Since the Reformation, the organ has had a very special place in the tradition of Lutheran church music, given its ability to effectively lead and enliven the singing of congregational song and liturgy. However, other instruments have also been used in worship services.

Luther, Melanchthon, and their followers are also recognized for their educational reforms and emphasis on rigorous training in the liberal arts, including music. Luther and Melanchthon strongly emphasized the benefits of music in the education and formation of young people, and they revolutionized ideas about incorporating music into schooling. They required teachers to have musical training, and they incorporated required music classes into the curriculum. Many scholars highlight Luther's understanding of the importance of music in education, quoting passages such as this one: "The young are to be continually exercised in [the art of music]; it makes good and skillful people of them. Those who are skilled in this art are possessed of good qualities and can be employed in anything."[6] Luther and Melanchthon based their curriculum on the medieval model of the seven liberal arts, wherein music was included. They created a community of students who joined together in song to nourish their faith as well as their knowledge of language and grammar. For Luther and Melanchthon, music enhanced learning and worked well when paired with grammar and rhetorical studies.

Given this emphasis on the power of music, many Lutherans from the Reformation to today are respected musicians and composers, and Lutheran educational institutions around the world are noted

---

6 Cited in John Derksen, "'Music is Next to Theology': Martin Luther and Music," *Touchstone* (2007): 50.

for their emphasis on music. Early Lutheran composers include Heinrich Schütz (1585–1672) and Dietrich Buxtehude (1637–1707). One of the most famous Lutheran musicians, who is well-known for both his choral and instrumental music, is Johann Sebastian Bach (1735–82). As for contemporary Lutheran composers and text writers, Marty Haugen (b. 1950) and Rev. Dr. Herbert Brokering (1926–2009) are known widely for their contributions to many modern-day Lutheran hymnals. Haugen's "All are Welcome" and Brokering's text of "Earth and All Stars" are just two of the beloved hymns by these composers.

Although Lutheranism began in Germany and first spread to Scandinavia, over the past one hundred years Lutheranism has been spreading rapidly in Africa, South America, and Asia. The fastest growing and largest Lutheran church in the world is currently in Ethiopia. Congregations and musicians in these areas and others are contributing much to the hymnbooks and rich heritage of Lutheran music. Furthermore, as Lutheranism spreads to other parts of the world, new music composed and performed in Lutheran schools and congregations incorporates diverse cultural and musical traditions and instruments.

Among Lutheran congregations around the world today, congregational song—the people's song—continues to be a living lesson in building community. Worshipping communities are one of the last vestiges where communal song occurs. Singing together is one of the best and easiest ways of bringing people together. It is also a powerful way of sharing faith and uniting communities in a priestly and prophetic way. Today, congregational singing in Lutheran communities across the globe offers healing and comfort as well as raises the needs and concerns of the neighbor and the world. As Lutherans today incorporate the music of the global church, they give themselves the opportunity to gain insight into how other Christians around the world find and express their relationship to God. Mark Sedio, cantor at Central Lutheran Church in Minneapolis, has written: "As any culture connects its experience of the holy to its music, a unique context for God's presence is created—we experience together the way God weaves a varied diverse tapestry of revelation among us."[7]

Hallmarks of Music in Lutheran Higher Education

Given this heritage, Lutheran-affiliated colleges and universities today continue to incorporate music into their curricula and a host of co-curricular activities, worship services, and special events. Many NECU colleges and universities were founded by German and Scandinavian Lutherans who incorporated music from the beginning. Although these institutions served primarily Lutherans early in their history, today they serve students from all faith backgrounds or none.

The Lutheran college choral tradition continues to be one of the hallmarks of Lutheran higher education. F. Melius Christiansen founded the St. Olaf Choir in 1912, and during the early decades of the twentieth century it became the exemplar for choral programs not only among Lutheran colleges but also college, school, church, and community choirs throughout the United States. The initial choral repertoire of the St. Olaf Choir and other Lutheran college choirs was founded on historic chorales and congregational songs of the Scandinavian-German Lutheran church tradition. F. Melius's chorale motets of the great hymns are still highly regarded works that deserve study and performance. Among these are his settings of "Beautiful Savior," "Lamb of God," "Praise to the Lord," "O Day Full of Grace," "Wake, Awake," "Built on A Rock," and "Lost in the Night."

A major distinction of the Lutheran college choral tradition is that, at its best, it sets out not to entertain, but to serve others. It seeks to transform the performer and, in turn, those who listen to the music. That is key to understanding the distinctive nature of the choral art in the Lutheran college choral tradition. Choirs and ensembles are often called upon to provide comfort, compassion, and healing through their music. At the same time, they often are

---

7 Mark Sedio, "Introduction," in *Leading the Church's Song*, ed. Robert Buckley Farlee and Eric Vollen (Minneapolis: Augsburg Fortress, 1998), 9.

the prophetic voice, leading cries for care of our neighbor and of our planet and demanding justice for all.

Increasingly, the Lutheran college choral tradition has been called to be a prophetic voice in sharing powerful messages of liberation and social justice through the music and texts of women, people of color, and others who have been so marginalized in our society. In recent programs of the St. Olaf Choir, for example, the repertoire has been more intentionally ecumenical and international, highlighting themes of social and racial justice, and has brought comfort and strength to those dealing with traumatic life issues, such as dementia, Alzheimer's disease, and world hunger. Some of the section headings of recent concert programs at St. Olaf have included: "Songs of Justice and Compassion," "We are Called to Compassion and Care of Our Neighbors," and "We Sing of Hope and Love."[8] In these ways and others, the St. Olaf Choir seeks to be a transforming force in society through choral performance, bringing understanding, mercy, justice, peace, and hope to a world that desperately cries out for the realization of these values.

The St. Olaf Choir is not alone in this refocusing of the choral literature their choirs are performing. We can see a similar direction in the concert programs of the many choral ensembles at various colleges of the ELCA, including their touring choirs.

A very good example of music that addresses events of recent history is Dr. René Clausen's *Memorial*, a work premiered in 2003 by the choirs and orchestra of Concordia College under the baton of the composer and based on subject material which reflects the horrific events of September 11, 2001. Though scored as one continuous movement, the composition follows a program that comprises four sections: September Morning, The Attack, Prayers and Petitions, and Healing, Cleansing, and Hope.

Most if not all NECU institutions have cultivated distinctive celebrations of Advent-Christmas, which are held on campuses and often publically broadcast locally, nationally, and even internationally. These worship/concert experiences attract and inspire diverse audiences for a host of reasons. They provide opportunities for musical

---

8 St. Olaf Choir concert tour programs, 2019 and 2020.

proclamations of healing and renewal in the promise of the birth of the Christ child. Powerful musical settings of social justice also permeate these Advent-Christmas commemorations—for example, the Canticle of Mary/The Magnificat. In addition, these Advent-Christmas programs often include voices of the global church as well the historical legacy of Lutheran church music.

Instrumental music also plays a vital role in the musical fabric of NECU institutions, whether in concerts, informal gatherings, or ceremonial and signature events. NECU institutions offer music lessons and sponsor a host of programs and opportunities for those who play a wide range of instruments. Campuses also support bands, orchestras, and a variety of instrumental ensembles, including jazz bands and string quartets.

In addition to offering a full array of concerts, most NECU institutions maintain a regular schedule of worship services, and here, too, musical instruments play an important role. The pipe organ is still the primary instrument invigorating and supporting the congregational song in a large majority of these gathered assemblies. However, many other instruments regularly participate in leading worship, including piano, strings, brass, winds, handbells, guitars, synthesizers, and various types of percussion. Instruments other than the organ have increasingly become the primary instrumental musical support in more recent liturgies based on folk, jazz, and other more contemporary popular musical genres.

At St. Olaf the two bands and two orchestras even lead separate chapel services each year, completely without choral collaboration other than the congregational singing of a hymn or liturgical music. These services are meaningful both for listeners and performers. As Dr. Timothy Mahr, professor of music and conductor of the St. Olaf Band, recently wrote these words about the experience of leading these worship services:

> I count the performances of the St. Olaf Band as part of a worship service in Boe Memorial Chapel to be among the most meaningful I've had over the past 27 years. There exists a rather unique power of expression within a worship performance that simply does not exist on a concert stage, or, for that matter, in front of an athletic crowd.

> We sense this special potential and become one with it. The musi-cal delivery itself seems to pick up on this purposefulness, deepen-ing the experience for the listener, the participant, no matter if it is within the concert hall, chapel, or gymnasium.[9]

Students, faculty, staff, and alumni, whether performers or listen-ers, recognize the value of instrumental music in Lutheran higher education and its power to address the whole person—mind, body, spirit—whether performed in a concert hall, a gymnasium, or a wor-ship service.

Professor emeritus and long-time conductor of the St. Olaf Orchestra, Steven Amundson, for example, has written eloquently about the spiritual depth of instrumental music:

> Music truly is the international language—words are not necessary for listeners to embark on a transcendent journey. For example, one of the most moving instrumental pieces I know is Edward Elgar's Adagio (subtitled Nimrod) from his *Enigma Variations*. This music expresses sincere, deep love beyond almost any other work I know. There is no text, but we do know Elgar wrote this in honor of one of his best friends. It's obvious Elgar had love in his heart when he composed this sublime music! This music is comforting, peaceful, loving and joyful all at the same time. And this is but one example among thousands that convey incredible beauty and depth enabling the listener to be moved, inspired, and spiritually alive—all con-veyed without a text to lead the way. Music is truly one of God's greatest gifts and it's so much better when shared with others.[10]

Dr. James Patrick Miller, Douglas Nimmo Endowed Professor of the Gustavus Wind Orchestra at Gustavus Adolphus College, has offered the following insights into the importance of instrumental music and ensembles to uplift and uphold values of justice, service, equity, inclusion, and academic excellence:

> Our music has no words, no text. Yet, it clearly reaches the human heart and spirit deeply. We are called upon to serve ceremonial functions that have, in many cases across academia, been replaced

---

9 Timothy Mahr, memo to Anton E. Armstrong, June 29, 2021.
10 Steven Amundson, memo to Anton E. Armstrong, June 28, 2021.

by recorded and amplified background music. I can comfortably say that within the Lutheran higher education model this call to serve is different and carries with it great meaning and spirituality. When the Lutheran college band is called to serve, the music becomes foreground; it not only complements the event but, more so, helps define it—even when the music is specifically intended to be prelude or postlude. Somehow the Lutheran college band has a sound that reaches the human spirit, turning service into artistry, ordinary into memorable.

The outreach and service components combined with the educational and artistic excellence we provide defines the institution of the Lutheran college band, and they are extraordinary examples of service, artistry, education, and inclusion within higher education and the greater community and world.[11]

Vision and Challenges for the Future

One major challenge in Lutheran higher education for the twenty-first century is creating communities of belonging where we cultivate a respect for tradition while being visionary, prophetic voices. This means understanding music as an active and fluid voice for social justice and the proclamation of the gospel of God's mercy, grace, and love for *all* of God's children. Music is relational and transforming, so our art must be in service to others. This in turn calls us to be humble and vulnerable in the sharing of our gifts.

Noted liturgical writer, the late Susan Palo Cherwien, wrote the hymn text entitled "Rise, O Church, like Christ Arisen." The fourth and final verse reads:

> *Service be our sure vocation;*
> *courage be our daily breath;*
> *mercy be our destination*
> *from this day and unto death.*
> *Alleluia, alleluia.*
> *Rise, O church, a living faith.*[12]

---

11 James Patrick Miller, memo to Anton E. Armstrong, June 30, 2021.

12 Susan Palo Cherwien, "Rise, O Church, like Christ Arisen," *Evangelical Lutheran Worship* (Minneapolis: Augsburg Fortress, 2006), #548.

Theologian and church musician Dr. Paul Westermeyer offers insights into Cherwien's text and provides a useful understanding of the central vocation of the church—a vocation shared by Lutheran colleges and universities. As he emphasizes, this vocation includes both service to those in need and attention to preventing suffering and injustice:

> The vocation of the church . . . is called to help others as the need arises in whatever way it can. This communal role that the whole church assumes includes not only binding up wounds after bad things have happened, however. It also includes trying to keep bad things from happening. Though it cannot solve all these problems any more than it can fix all the problems . . . the church's vocation is to work at these matters as best it can on the front end of prevention as well as on the back end of care.[13]

A clear example of service through the choral art was the benefit concert given by the St. Olaf Choir and the Luther College Nordic Choir in Austin, MN, on November 16, 1993. ELCA bishops in southeast Minnesota and Iowa reached out to Weston Noble and me, proposing a way that our touring choirs could bring much-needed aid to people of this region, who had suffered devastating damage and loss from summer floods. The event, the first time the two choirs had performed together in this format, raised $18,500 to provide relief funds for the residents of Iowa and southern Minnesota. As I said at the time: "We want to generate financial and prayer support for the victims. This is a message of love—to reach out and ease some of the pain."[14]

Many times, the resident and touring ensembles of NECU schools have collaborated with service agencies to serve the needs of people in the regions where they were performing. For many years, the St. Olaf Choir would partner with organizations such as Lutheran Social Services and Lutheran Volunteer Corps.

---

13 Paul Westermeyer, *Rise, O Church: Reflections on the Church, Its Music, and Empire* (Saint Louis: Morning Star Music, 2008), 18–19.

14 Joseph M. Shaw, *The St. Olaf Choir: A Narrative* (Northfield: St. Olaf College, 1997), 546.

Proceeds from our tour concerts would be shared to benefit the work of those agencies in cities throughout the country. In 2018 when the St. Olaf Choir was performing in Santa Barbara, we returned a portion of the concert income to several local social agencies working with victims of severe flooding and mudslides in that area.

While the curricula of our NECU music departments are heavily steeped in the music of the Western European canon, faculty members are actively working to create more equitable, inclusive, and culturally relevant learning environments for our students. The educational institutions of NECU are increasingly challenged to do more intentional work in the realm of access, diversity, inclusion, and equity. Currently, I increasingly observe this work in the repertoire selection of many of our NECU collegiate choral and instrumental ensembles. The repertoire and composers being studied in the private performance studios and classroom courses are gradually moving beyond the Western-Eurocentric music canon and including more voices of women, BIPOC, LGBTQ+, and other marginalized groups. This is important for all our students, perhaps especially for our BIPOC students, who now encounter composers and compositions that reflect their own cultural and racial identities.

There are other opportunities for music programs to serve others and participate in civic engagement work. Examples of work being done at St. Olaf College include a month-long Interim class, "Music and Social Justice," where students travel four times to the Shakopee Women's Prison to mutually share in making music with one another.

Another project started in the 2017 January Interim and continued until the pandemic hit in 2020. It involved our first-year sopranos and altos (SSAA) ensemble; Manitou Singers, conducted by my colleague Dr. Therees Hibbard; and members of Ruth's House, a women's transitional shelter and refuge located in Faribault, MN, which serves women and children in Rice County. Dr. Hibbard shared these thoughts: "During those four weeks each year, we brought our voices together in song to raise awareness, and to let music be common ground for us to share the messages of hope and strength and joy during our rehearsals."[15]

Finally, St. Olaf assistant professor of music, Tesfa Wondemagegnehu, spent the summer of 2021 traveling to forty cities in sixty days to speak to social activists in Black communities as part of his "To Repair Project." He is collecting their stories which will serve as the basis for his composition of the libretto for a new multimovement choral work. The piece illuminates the work of Black people and organizations who have been active in the struggle for racial civil rights.

The study and performance of music teaches patience, perseverance, and dedication. In our music-making, we also gain the opportunity to nurture empathy, compassion, and gratitude in our students. We are challenged in creating communities of belonging that not only nurture a respect for tradition, but also call us to be visionary, prophetic voices.

Conclusion

ELCA Bishop William O. Gafkjen says that Lutheran higher education "is a gift to be shared, not a fortress to be defended."[16] Our call is to become servant-leaders who create art to enrich and inspire others and ourselves for lives of purpose, service, and justice. We must use our art as a means of nurturing and nourishing whole people. We must break down the walls within and outside of us. Our music-making creates educational communities of belonging built on respect, trust, and love. We become, in turn, agents of *light* and *hope*.

For Further Study

Highben, Zebulon M. and Kristina M. Langlois, eds. *With a Voice of Singing*. Minneapolis: Kirk House, 2007.

---

15 Therees Tkach Hibbard, memo to Anton E. Armstrong, June 28, 2021.
16 Conversation between Rev. William O. Gafkjen, ELCA Bishop, Indiana-Kentucky Synod, and Dr. Jo Beld, Vice President for Mission, St. Olaf College, June 2021.

Leaver, Robin. *Luther's Liturgical Music: Principles and Implications*. Minneapolis: Fortress, 2017.

_____. *The Whole Church Sings: Congregational Singing in Luther's Wittenberg*. Grand Rapids, MI: Eerdmans, 2017.

Westermeyer, Paul. *The Heart of the Matter: Church Music as Praise, Prayer, Proclamation, Story, and Gift*. Chicago: GIA, 2001.

_____. *Let Justice Sing: Hymnody and Justice*. Collegeville, MN: The Liturgical Press, 1998.

_____. *Te Deum: The Church and Music*. Minneapolis: Fortress, 1998.

9

In the Garden of Science and Religion

Ann Milliken Pederson,
Augustana University (Sioux Falls, SD)

> Religious beliefs cannot remain what they were before the rise
> of modern science any more than ancient scientific beliefs can.
> It would be absurd to insist that ancient religious beliefs should
> remain unchanged when our whole view of the universe has
> changed radically.
>
> —Keith Ward[1]

When I first came to Augustana University (Sioux Falls, SD), I taught
a religion and science class with faculty from the chemistry department. As I was entering the Froiland Science Center, a student who
was in my first-year religion course looked rather puzzled and asked:
"What are you doing in this building?" While that question caught
me off guard, I realized the student was generally perplexed about
why a religion professor would care about science because, in his
view, they had nothing to do with each other. His religious faith and
his work in the lab were completely independent of each other.

What do science and religion have to do with each other? The
most common metaphor, perpetuated in our media and politics, is
that they are at war: science and religion locked into a fierce battle of
whose authority wins out in the public realm. Whether it's from the
famous Scopes Trial portrayed in the movie *Inherit the Wind*, or in

---

1 Keith Ward, *The Big Questions in Science and Religion* (West Conshohocken,
PA: Templeton, 2008), 4.

the current religious and political debates about whether the vaccine is a hoax, the idea of warring claims about ultimate truth and value has seeped into our collective consciousness. Given this widespread impression, some science faculty may come to our Lutheran colleges and universities and wonder if they will be able to teach evolution or genetics with disciplinary integrity and academic freedom.[2] They quickly find out that they can (and should!), just as many students quickly find out that what they grew up learning about religion and science are challenged in both their religion classes and biology labs.

Arguably better than the warfare model, but still rather limited, is the idea that the student encountering me in the science building implicitly expressed—that the discipline of science and the discipline of theology are entirely unrelated; each has autonomy within its own tightly guarded disciplinary boundaries, but have little or nothing to say to one another.[3] And so, just as the student was surprised to see me in the science building, newly hired scientists may be relieved to find out that they have full academic freedom to teach their disciplines, but then also surprised to find courses that bring their discipline into conversation with theology. At best, classes, curricula, and the institutional vocations within the Network of ELCA Colleges and Universities (NECU) push past both the warfare and independence models of science and religion.

What students and educators at NECU schools discover is what the opening quotation from Keith Ward, an Anglican priest and Oxford professor, tells us: that both scientific theories and religious beliefs change in relation to one another, as our understanding of the world in which we live also constantly changes. For Christians, the claim that God created the world is fundamental, but how to interpret and make sense of that claim is the marvelous challenge that we meet in our classes and in the labs. Four models reflect the ways that religion and science relate to each other: (1) the warfare model, (2) an independence model, (3) a model of dialogue, and finally, (4) a model of interdependence between scientists and Christian leaders

---

2 See also the chapter by Samuel Torvend (31–43) in the present volume.

3 Ian Barbour, *Religion and Science* (New York: Harper One, 1997), 3–30.

who work to tackle the tough problems our one world faces.[4] Many of the NECU schools exemplify this fourth model.

Reimagining Humanity

In the interdependence model, religion and science at best challenge and change one another around a central pressing concern: What does it mean to be human in a vast and interdependent world and cosmos?

Let's hit the refresh button on what we believe and have learned. What if we reimagine in new and powerful ways what it means to be a part of God's world?

To imagine what God is like is to imagine our own self-image reflected in the relationships we have with all of God's creatures. From science, I learn that 3–4 percent of my DNA is Neanderthal. I learn that I share much of the same genes with the fruit fly, the rat, and the dog. I learn that primates can use linguistic symbols to communicate and that dogs have taught humans to evolve along with them. What if the cow in the field has human genes? What about robots and artificial intelligence?

My family album is much richer than my human relatives; the album includes all of creation. According to Genesis, humans and other creatures are made from the same soil and breath of God. The more scientists discover about humans, the more they reveal how the rest of creation is necessary for human survival.

When I teach undergraduate students about the intersection of religion and science, I often use three books that challenge their ideas and images of what it means to be human. The three books work like a three-part invention, playing the themes of science, religion, and the role of God in the world. All raise the following questions: What does it mean to say that God created *all* of creation? If creation includes extraterrestrials and intelligent primates, then what does this say about what it means to be a human person?

---

4 Barbour, *Religion and Science*, 3–30. See also Ian Barbour, *When Science Meets Religion: Enemies, Strangers, or Partners?* (New York: Harper Collins, 2000), 7–38.

Would you Baptize an Extraterrestrial? is by two Jesuit priests and scientists, Guy Consolmagno and Paul Mueller. Contrary to the popular narrative that science and religion are at war with each other, these two Jesuits remind the reader that there is a deep, long tradition of the ways that science has been a conversation partner with Christianity. Imagine starting a class on religion and science with this very question: Would you baptize an extraterrestrial? The sheer shock of the question opens our minds to think about the relationship between religion and science in ways beyond its warlike image. What if? Would you? Why not? To be created in the image of God is to be open to the imagination of God. And this is a marvelous and challenging way to teach religion and science. Indeed, if God's grace is as wide and deep as Christians claim, then baptizing an extraterrestrial would be a confirmation of that grace.

The Sparrow, by Mary Doria Russell, catapults the reader into the strange world of Rakhat, a planet several light years away from Earth. Set in the early twenty-first century, a crew of explorers, headed by Emilio Sandoz, a Jesuit priest, sets out to discover the identity of the creators of music that they heard via Arecibo and the SETI Project. At one point on the new planet, Emilio cradles the young female Runa in his lap, a child of another species. Their tenderness stills the conversation between his compatriots. Russell challenges us to think about not only what it means to be human but also, and more importantly, what it means to be a creation of God.

Frans de Waal, a primatologist, in his latest book, *Mama's Last Hug*, sent me into tears as I read about the encounter between a scientist and his friend, a female chimpanzee (Mama) who was dying. In their last moments together, Mama recognizes the scientist who had cared for her and studied her. She reaches out to embrace him, to acknowledge his witness of her dying, and to create one tender moment between two different mammalian species. Frans de Waal claims that the differences between humans and other primates are not so much differences in kind as differences in degree. We are more alike our primate cousins than different.

After reading and discussing these books, students speak about how their imaginations open into a different kind of discussion between religion and science than the warlike caricature they had heard in popular culture. Their imaginations are fueled by listening and learning to look.

Learning to Look

Sometimes I take my students to our new outdoor classroom at Augustana University, built and designed under the tutelage of Dr. David O'Hara, director of sustainability and environmental studies. During one of our outdoor excursions, the students had just finished a chapter entitled "When We Look," from Elizabeth Johnson's book, *Ask the Beasts*. This chapter's title echoes the first words from chapter 1 of Darwin's *On the Origin of Species*: "When we look . . . ." Like a faithful Roman Catholic theologian would do, Johnson calls her readers to attend, to behold the creation, to look "upon the world in all its grandeur as [Darwin] did."[5] To listen and to behold is to gaze with an incarnational lens—with the insight that God dwells in all things. What can we learn when we ask the beasts? The plants of the earth?

When scientific and theological imaginations are in high gear, they generate such big, metaphysical questions rather quickly. What is our place in the cosmos, in the world? What is the meaning of life? What is true? How do I know what is true? Why does science matter to religion? Why does religion matter to science? How do they relate to each other?

Yet, in a Lutheran educational system that values reflection, personal appropriation, and vocational discernment, these big questions

---

5 Elizabeth Johnson, *Ask the Beasts: Darwin and the God of Love* (London: Bloomsbury Continuum, 2015), 44. Johnson quotes from the book of Job:

But ask the animals, and they will teach you;
    the birds of the air, and they will tell you;
ask the plants of the earth, and they will teach you;
    and the fish of the sea will declare to you.
Who among all these does not know
    that the hand of the Lord has done this?
In his hand is the life of every living thing
    and the breath of every human being. (Job 12:7–10 NRSV)

also stay rather concrete. For example, when students and I learn to listen to our questions, to the cultural idioms that surround science and religion, we turn quickly to the hopes and limits of modern medicine. Almost every student wants to ask, What does it mean to play God? A student once told me that she thought the charge against scientists for "playing God" was a paltry interpretation of both who God is and what scientists do. God's power is known through God's willingness to suffer with creation and to transform that suffering. God's power is shared. So she said, we *ought* to play God, as the creatures we are, by engaging with the neighbor in order to transform and share the neighbor's suffering, whether the pain of our canine companion or our human sibling.

When I teach Theology, Medicine, and Ethics to undergraduates, I am always amazed at the "eureka" moment when students discover that how they live their lives, whom they vote for, and what they believe actually makes a difference to them and others. Our intense discussions hone in on the opposites we create that polarize our worldview: pro-life or pro-choice, pro-mask or anti-mask, for organ donation or against organ donation. The list goes on.

However, when we construct the discussion so that there are at least three options, imaginations go wild. Life's puzzles and struggles become opportunities instead of threats. To imaginatively explore these options is not about finding some kind of generic middle ground. Rather, it is to declare that life is more complicated and amazing than we ever thought.

The complications are not easy to navigate, but they do seem more hopeful. We can touch the vulnerability of our lives, acknowledge our despair, and share it with others. Our imaginations are cut loose—graciously and widely.

Rootedness in God's Creation

Teaching theology and science interrupts both the warfare model and the independence model, which claims that science and religion have virtually nothing to do with each other. The Lutheran intellectual tradition overturns these assumptions by giving creation a central place for the self-revelation of God. Martin Luther and his fellow reformer Phillip Melanchthon believed that all of nature inheres in God's grace; both Scripture and nature reveal God. With such a generous theological background, Lutheran colleges and universities can pursue truth in deeply interdisciplinary ways—in particular, through the intersection of the natural sciences and Christian theology.

In other words, we learn about our place in the cosmos when we study the local practices of science alongside the study of religion. Where you are determines what you see. While Genesis 1 is cosmic in its emphasis, the location of Genesis 2–4 is more local. We attend to the cosmic scope of God's creative work as we listen to and learn from our local "garden."

In Genesis 2, God appears as the consummate farmer/gardener, who even walks in the evening breeze amongst the vegetation (see Gen 3:8). The centerpiece of the garden narrative is topsoil, the rich dirt from which God creates not only the animals but also Adam, the earth creature (Gen 2:7). Adam comes from *adamah* (Hebrew for *soil*). God's breath and the dirt on which God walks are the composite elements of humankind. But not just humankind. God also creates non-human animals from the same stuff (Gen 2:19). All of creation begins as dirt and returns to the dirt. In fact, God creates Adam, Eve, and all the animals as helpers to tend the garden and to cultivate the soil.

We remind ourselves again of the way that the story in Genesis 2 reflects the human being as one who is the cultivator of the land. This mirrors the way that God interacts with the world. We are co-creators and co-cultivators not only with God, but also with all the earth. The image of God is fully relational.

From Eden to the flood, the whole arc (no pun intended) of salvation unfolds: creation, destruction, new creation. Creation is a dirty business. God's hands get dirty. From Adam and Eve's disobedience to Noah's righteous obedience, those who would have listened to this account of Creation likely eked out a subsistence living from the soil.[6] They raised crops and tended to their flocks and herds of animals.[7]

---

6 Theodore Hiebert, *The Yahwist's Landscape: Nature and Religion in Early Israel* (Minneapolis: Fortress, 1996).

7 Hiebert, *The Yahwist's Landscape*, 51.

This rich land was irrigated just like the garden of Eden.[8] Eden and the world east of Eden stand side-by-side in the world of Palestinian agriculture. Whether the farmers waited for the rains in order to till the scruffy hillsides or used the rich springs to irrigate, the land is the center of this Genesis story. This agricultural "setting" is much more than a backdrop; it defines what being created in the image of God and being related to the rest of creation truly entails.

What God begins and continues in creation is what God accomplishes with redemption and new creation. Salvation includes all that God has created. This understanding of salvation as cosmic in scope and as congruous with God's original aim in creation was popularized in 1972, when Joseph Sittler, a renowned Lutheran theologian and pastor, reflected upon the talk he had given earlier at the World Council of Churches in 1961, long before theology took the environmental crisis seriously. Sittler's task was to reassess and reimagine the way that the natural world is part of what Christians believe about Jesus the Christ. His reflection and speech at the World Council of Churches marked the beginning of significant movements in Lutheran institutions of education, both undergraduate and graduate, that would now locate the relationship of humankind with nature as the center of the intersections of theological dialogue. Where we are rooted shapes who we are.

Of course, the convergence between salvation and creation—and the interdependence model of theology and science—did not begin with Sittler in the 1970s. The first chapter of Colossians from the Christian New Testament reflects the "incarnational" vision that, through Christ, God is pleased to dwell in all. God's home is with us:

> He is the image of the invisible God, the firstborn of all creation; for in him all things in heaven and on earth were created, things visible and invisible, whether thrones or dominions or rulers or powers—all things have been created through him and for him. He himself is before all things, and in him all things hold together . . . For in him all the fullness of God was pleased to dwell, and through him God was pleased to reconcile to himself all things, whether on earth or in heaven. (Colossians 1:15–21, NRSV)

---

8 Hiebert, *The Yahwist's Landscape*, 55.

The material cosmos is God's home sweet home. Humans, in turn, are called to learn about this shared home, and science is one of the best ways to learn about our place in the cosmos. Again, Scripture reinforces our imaginative task: to learn all we can about our world. I ask my students to read sections of the Wisdom of Solomon, one of the books of the Apocrypha—those biblical writings not in the Protestant Bible. They find in that text a vocational mandate to be lovers of wisdom, as well as lovers of creation:

> *May God grant me to speak with judgment,*
> *and to have thoughts worthy of what I have received. . . .*
> *For both we and our words are in [God's] hand,*
> *as are all understanding and skill in crafts.*
> *For it is [God] who gave me unerring knowledge of what exists,*
> *to know the structure of the world and the activity of the elements;*
> *the beginning and end and middle of times,*
> *the alternations of the solstices and the changes of the seasons,*
> *the cycles of the year and the constellations of the stars . . .* [9]

Redemption is cosmic and yet centers on the particular details of the land and those creatures who live there.

Indigenous communities have known this connection between health/healing (which translates as "salvation") and a land ethic for thousands of years. Many Native American scholars remind Christians that the choice of Israel by God to be the promised land and people finds its parallel in Indigenous traditions, which share stories of "Indigenous nations chosen by God to dwell here, in North America, over centuries of our spiritual development."[10] My own location at Augustana University is geographically situated on the ancestral lands of the Lakota, Dakota, and Nakota people, and in a state where reservations mark the fraught history of the Euro-American colonization of Indigenous people of North America.[11]

---

9 Wisdom of Solomon 7:15-19, NRSV, Apocrypha.
10 Elaine A. Robinson and Steven Charleston, *Coming Full Circle: Constructing Native Christian Theology* (Minneapolis: Fortress, 2015), 3.
11 In her chapter in the present volume (205–20), Krista E. Hughes explores this fraught history and calls for reparations and repair.

The account of creation in Genesis 2 repeats themes found in many Native American accounts of creation: the stories center on the land; the Creator is intimately involved with creation and shares the power of creativity with the creatures; the promises of the Creator's blessings apply to the whole of reality. For the Lakota tradition, the language of *mitakuye oyasin* reveals that all are kin, together in one created reality. One translation of *mitakuye oyasin* is as follows: "all the above me and below me and around me things."[12] No wonder that above, below, and around me resonates with the "in, with, and under" of Lutheran sacramental theology.[13] All are related.

Concrete Practices and Ongoing Challenges

At Augustana University, courses in science and religion have been taught since the 1980s. Augustana now has interdisciplinary programs in environmental studies and medical humanities and society, which permit students and faculty to work on the climate crisis and other wicked problems we face. Students demand this integration between theory and practice. Interdisciplinary teaching is one key toward telling the stories of how science and religion relate to each other.[14]

The title of my religion and science course is "God's Garden from Scientific and Theological Perspectives." During each section of the course, we examine creation from particular perspectives:

---

12 Clara Sue Kidwell, Homer Noley, and George E. Tinker, *A Native American Theology* (Maryknoll, NY: Orbis, 2001), 51.

13 The Formula of Concord (1577), Article X, in *The Book of Concord: The Confessions of the Evangelical Lutheran Church*, trans. Charles Arand, et al. (Minneapolis: Augsburg Fortress, 2000). See also Jason A. Mahn's chapter in the present volume (73–86).

14 A recent grant from the American Association for the Advancement of Science funded seminaries to create courses with scientific content for those who are preparing for ministry. Scientific literacy, along with religious literacy, is necessary for conversation to occur. Lutheran Theology Seminary at Gettysburg (now part of United Lutheran Seminary) partnered with Augustana University for this grant. Biologists, a neuropsychologist, and a physicist from Augustana created courses with biblical, historical, pastoral, and liturgical scholars at LTSG. The collaboration eventually led to a publication in *Zygon: Journal in Religion and Science* by faculty and students from both institutions.

from evolutionary science, from the perspective of plants and animals, from artificial intelligence, and finally, from the perspective of humans.

For each section of the course, students choose a practice that helps them understand the particular perspective we are studying. For example, when we read Michael Pollan's book, *The Botany of Desire*, some students choose to eat all of their meals with ingredients made in South Dakota or not to eat any red meat. They write journal reflections while they keep the practice, and then they write a thousand word essay answering the question: "How Then Shall We Live?" The response to the question must address the spiritual-religious, ethical, and scientific aspects of the theme and text.

Gustavus Adolphus College hosts two religion and science events each year: The Nobel Conference in the fall and a week-long academy for high school students in the summer that focuses on the theme of the Nobel.[15] A statement on the website summarizes the intent and perspective: "At the Academy, we believe that we need *both* faith and science to address the ethical issues of our time. The outstanding students accepted into the Gustavus Academy for Faith, Science, and Ethics explore the intersection of faith and science while diving into the ethical issues that define our decades."[16] In the summer of 2017, I was one of the teachers for the academy, and we focused on reproductive technologies. Finally, many NECU colleges and universities find the ELCA's social statements to provide a platform from which students can dive into the waters of science, religion, and technology.[17]

However, our practices also reveal our problems. To remain rooted, the ELCA and NECU must remain open. God's garden is more like a tangled prairie of flowering plants, herbs, weeds, and grasses than it is a sculptured British landscape. In order to sow the seeds for future generations, ELCA churches and organizations and NECU schools must work together to address many concerns. These include: the need for diverse religious and scientific voices and practices; the need for laying groundwork from diverse experiences

---

15 See https://gustavus.edu/events/nobelconference/about/.
16 See https://gustavus.edu/chaplain/academy/index.php.
17 See the ELCA social statements here: https://www.elca.org/socialstatements.

and backgrounds; the need to assess and trust the credibility and veracity of religious and scientific contributions to the public good; and, finally and most importantly, the need to act in concrete and hopeful ways in order to care for the crisis of our planet and all its inhabitants.

I write this chapter during a year in which the COVID-19 pandemic has swept around the world, in which the political climate of the United States is scarred from polemical and violent clashes, and in which many Americans no longer trust any institutions, religious or scientific. No wonder that our imaginations screech to a halt and switch to remote access when we face prolonged uncertainty. We face complex issues that demand decisions that cannot be addressed with a "no" or "yes." Founded on and fueled by the interdependence of religion and science, our imaginations must respond to the calling to know the created world with all the nuance, complexity, and beauty it demands.

Conclusion

I believe that one of the greatest strengths of Lutheran traditions is that they help us to be open to interruptions and disruptions. If, in the moment of interruption, we are awake to its possibilities, it can be an interruption of grace. Otherwise, the moment passes into a kind of sustained uncertainty, just another blip on the screen. What are imaginative practices that can change the way the image of God and images of God function? What if the image of God (*imago dei*) can be stretched to include all of creation? The differences between humans and nonhumans matter, but they are not nearly as distinct as humans have wanted to imagine. Would that matter for how we treat nonhuman animals? How do we see our future on this planet? How do we take care of each other and the environment? These questions cannot be answered with a simple "yes" or "no." They require imaginative and creative exploration, while paying attention to both what the Christian tradition and scriptures say and what we see and learn from the world around us through the sciences. May our scientific and religious imaginations be open to the surprises that await in the garden of God.

For Further Study

Barbour, Ian. *When Science Meets Religion: Enemies, Strangers, or Partners?* New York: HarperCollins, 2000.
Clayton, Philip. *Religion and Science: The Basics.* New York: Routledge, 2018.
Hefner, Philip. *The Human Factor: Evolution, Culture, and Religion.* Minneapolis: Fortress, 1993.
Johnson, Elizabeth. *Ask the Beasts: Darwin and the God of Love.* London: Bloomsbury Continuum, 2015.
Kidwell, Clara Sue, Homer Noley, and George E. Tinker. *A Native American Theology.* Maryknoll, NY: Orbis, 2001.
Ward, Keith. *The Big Questions in Science and Religion.* West Conshohocken, PA: Templeton, 2008.

10

Environmental Studies and Sustainability

James B. Martin-Schramm,
Luther College (Decorah, IA)

The challenges of the twenty-first century are manifold and grave. Socially, racism continues to be a scourge that denies and denigrates the gifts of far too many. Economically, the unrelenting expansion of wealth and income inequality is taking its toll on human health and civil order. Environmentally, accelerating rates of habitat destruction, pollution, and climate change imperil the ecological systems that sustain the diversity of life on Earth. Put simply, the present order is not sustainable.

Lutheran colleges and universities are addressing these complicated, interwoven, and "wicked" problems.[1] This threefold concern about social justice, economic welfare, and environmental well-being is addressed in various academic fields, but especially with robust curricular offerings and internship experiences in environmental studies, environmental science, and related disciplines. Outside the classroom, a growing number of Lutheran colleges and universities have offices, steering committees, or other organizational

---

1 Urban planner and designer Horst Rittel coined the term *wicked problem* in 1973 while discussing limitations of a linear systems approach to urban planning and design. See Horst W. Rittel and Melvin M. Webber, "Dilemmas in a General Theory of Planning," *Policy Sciences* 4 (1973): 155, 160–67. See also Willis Jenkins, *The Future of Ethics: Sustainability, Social Justice, and Religious Creativity* (Washington, DC: Georgetown University Press, 2013), 149–80.

commitments to promote sustainability on their campuses and in their surrounding communities.

This chapter explores how Lutheran colleges and universities are responding to the most pressing issues of our time through their environmental studies programs and sustainability efforts. These responses grow out of and are supported by institutional commitments to help educate a learned citizenry and to be good stewards of God's creation. Such commitments are also undergirded by robust theological work and environmental initiatives found across Lutheran churches and organizations worldwide. These and other responses reflect an understanding in Lutheran theology that addressing the world's "wicked" problems and contributing to the common good require interdisciplinary approaches, systems thinking, and collaborative action.[2]

Environmental Studies Programs at Lutheran Colleges and Universities

The academic field of environmental studies began to emerge in North America in the 1960s and quickly spread to Lutheran colleges and universities. The field developed in tandem with the scientific discipline of ecology and a growing understanding of the enormous impact human patterns of reproduction, production, and consumption are having on the planet.

From the outset, environmental studies programs have been somewhat countercultural since they have sought to be multidisciplinary

---

2 This threefold approach is related to a key insight in *Rooted and Open: The Common Calling of the Network of ELCA Colleges and Universities*: "Because the world is always larger and more mysterious than the lens through which it is known, intellectual humility nurtures genuine curiosity and an interdisciplinary search for truth" (4). See https://download.elca.org/ELCA%20 Resource%20Repository/Rooted_and_Open.pdf. For environmental work across Lutheranism worldwide, see the bibliography below, including the ELCA's Social Statement on *Caring for Creation*. In 2021 the ELCA also authorized the development of a forthcoming social message that will complement this statement and focus on the grave dangers posed by climate change. For ELCA social statements and messages, see https://www.elca.org/socialstatements.

in orientation and interdisciplinary with regard to student learning outcomes. The vast majority of environmental studies programs require foundational learning in life science and geoscience along with an understanding of how economics and politics shape the relationship of human beings with the planet. The connections between these subjects are explored further in courses in philosophy, literature, and other areas such as anthropology and religious studies. More recently, the environmental justice movement has lifted up a key insight in ecofeminist philosophy—namely, that the oppression of people and the destruction of the planet are both grounded in a logic of domination.

In general, environmental studies programs explore three key themes. First is the sheer *complexity* of the problems we face and how rooted they are in philosophical assumptions and socioeconomic systems. Solutions to the loss of biodiversity or the catastrophic impacts of climate change are not merely scientific or technological; they are social, political, and cultural. Second, the problems imperiling human civilization have an enormous *scale*. Spatially, climate change is a global problem, and the increase in anthropogenic greenhouse gas emissions extends temporally not only to the origins of the Industrial Revolution in the late 1700s but all the way back to the origins of agriculture over 10,000 years ago. Finally, another hallmark of environmental studies programs has typically been an explicit commitment to *activism* and social change. The directions of such activism are not always self-evident, however. For example, while many protest the construction of new oil pipelines or the expansion of hydraulic fracturing, there is no question that all citizens in industrialized countries are dependent upon fossil fuel energy systems and thus complicit in their existence.

This complexity, however, is driving considerable interest in environmental studies and environmental science. Students attending Lutheran colleges and universities in North America can major and/or minor in environmental studies or environmental science at almost every institution. Eighteen of the twenty-seven schools within the Network of ELCA Colleges and Universities (NECU) have environmental studies programs and fifteen have environmental science programs. Seven Lutheran colleges and universities provide both curricular options to their students.

In regard to environmental studies, several schools have tailored their programs to their unique locations. Augsburg University in Minneapolis offers a "focus on urban environmental justice and a rich array of resources in a diverse urban neighborhood near the Mississippi River."[3] This focus includes a remarkable opportunity for a small group of students to spend a whole semester canoeing the Mississippi River from the headwaters in Minnesota to the Gulf of Mexico. This interdisciplinary learning experience enables students to earn a full semester of college credits focused on environmental justice and social change in the Mississippi watershed.[4]

Four hours north, students at Concordia College in Moorhead, MN, have the opportunity to "study energy conservation and north woods ecology at the one-of-a-kind BioHaus, designed by a leading-edge German environmental firm."[5] In addition, they can "study a variety of issues related to prairie, forest and lakeshore habitat" at the Long Lake Field Station thirty-five miles from campus near Detroit Lakes, MN. Another example is found 1,300 miles east at Susquehanna University, where an 87 acre environmental field station and freshwater research institute are right on campus.[6]

Almost all NECU schools emphasize the importance of experiential learning through internships and study-away opportunities. Augustana College in Rock Island, IL, requires all environmental studies majors to "complete a field experience and/or internship with an agency or company involved directly with environmental management."[7] Gustavus Adolphus College offers an array of

---

3 "Environmental Studies," Augsburg University, https://www.augsburg.edu/environmental/.

4 "River Semester," Augsburg University, https://www.augsburg.edu/river/.

5 "Environmental and Sustainability Studies," Concordia College, https://www.concordiacollege.edu/academics/programs-of-study/environmental-and-sustainability-studies/.

6 "Environmental Studies," Susquehanna University, https://www.susqu.edu/academics/majors-and-minors/department-of-earth-and-environmental-sciences/environmental-studies.

7 "Environmental Studies," Augustana College, https://www.augustana.edu/academics/areas-of-study/environmental-studies.

sustainability-related study abroad programs in India, Sweden, and Malaysia.[8] Roanoke College has semester programs in the Yucatán Peninsula in Mexico and in Leipzig, Germany, that focus in large measure on environmental issues and related public policy.[9]

There are also some unique features that set some schools apart. Luther College builds in engagement with local city leaders in Decorah, IA, through a required course in their program's core curriculum titled, "Sustainability, Systems, and Solutions."[10] Muhlenberg College now offers a major in sustainability studies that combines "studies of ecological and environmental health with a calling for economic welfare and social justice."[11] At Pacific Lutheran University, the environmental studies program coordinates PLU's annual Earth Day Lecture, which has featured prominent scholars, noted activists, and political leaders.[12]

Sustainability Initiatives at Lutheran Colleges and Universities

The sustainability movement in society has grown in parallel with environmental studies in the academy. Faced with the prospects of nuclear war, rapid population growth, deepening poverty, and growing environmental degradation, members of the World Council of Churches (WCC) began in the 1970s to grapple with the complicated and interconnected problems related to social justice and environmental well-being. In fact, it was the WCC that elevated the concept of sustainability to a social norm when it challenged its members and the international community in 1974 to create a "just, participatory,

8 "Environmental Studies Program," Gustavus Adolphus College, https://gustavus.edu/env-studies/.
9 "Study Abroad," Roanoke College, https://www.roanoke.edu/inside/a-z_index/international_education/study_abroad.
10 "Environmental Studies," Luther College, https://www.luther.edu/catalog/curriculum/environmental-studies/.
11 "Sustainability Studies," Muhlenberg College, https://www.muhlenberg.edu/academics/sustainability/.
12 "Environmental Studies: Earth Day," Pacific Lutheran University, https://www.plu.edu/environmental-studies/earth-day/.

and sustainable society."[13] In 1987 the World Commission on Environment and Development defined sustainable development as "development that meets the needs of the present without compromising the ability of future generations to meet their own needs."[14] Today, many multinational companies, states, municipalities, and higher education institutions have ambitious sustainability goals and climate action plans.

Many Lutheran colleges and universities in North America have a strong commitment to environmental sustainability. They seek to live out this commitment in a host of ways—from offering courses on sustainability and refining waste reduction strategies to carrying out the major construction of LEED-certified buildings and wind turbines. Furthermore, many institutions are members of national organizations that champion sustainability in higher education. Nearly half are members of the Association for the Advancement of Sustainability in Higher Education (AASHE). Established in 2005, AASHE is comprised of over nine hundred members across forty-eight US states, one US Territory, nine Canadian provinces, and twenty countries. AASHE "defines sustainability in an inclusive way, encompassing human and ecological health, social justice, secure livelihoods and a better world for all generations."[15]

Seven NECU institutions have participated in AASHE's Sustainability Tracking, Assessment & Rating System (STARS), which is "a transparent, self-reporting framework for colleges and universities to measure their sustainability performance." STARS is a collaborative rather than a competitive framework. The goal is to share sustainability information and strategies among all member institutions. Based on the information and supporting evidence that is furnished, colleges and universities receive ratings (platinum, gold, silver, or

13 World Council of Churches, *Study Encounter 69*, IX.4 (1974): 2; as cited by Larry Rasmussen, "Doing our First Works Over," *Journal of Lutheran Ethics* 9.4 (2009), https://www.elca.org/JLE/Articles/385.
14 World Commission on Environment and Development, *Our Common Future* (New York: Oxford University Press, 1987), 26.
15 "Mission, Vision, and Commitments," Association for the Advancement of Sustainability in Higher Education, https://www.aashe.org/about-us/mission-vision-commitments/.

bronze) rather than rankings. These ratings are based on points earned in the following areas: academic (curriculum, research); campus and public engagement; operations (air and climate, buildings, energy, food and dining, grounds, purchasing, transportation, waste, water); planning and administration (including coordination, diversity, affordability, investment, finance, well-being, and work); and innovation and leadership.

Four NECU institutions have received a STARS gold rating: Luther College (IA), Muhlenberg College, Pacific Lutheran University, and Wartburg College. Three additional schools have received a STARS silver rating: Concordia College, Gettysburg College, and Susquehanna University. Most schools participating in the STARS program provide updated reports every two or three years.

About one-third of the Lutheran colleges and universities in North America are members of Second Nature. Since 1993, it has worked with over four thousand faculty and administrators at hundreds of colleges and universities to help make the principles of sustainability fundamental to every aspect of higher education.

At the heart of Second Nature's work is implementation of the American College & University Presidents' Climate Commitment (ACUPCC), which was initiated in 2006 by twelve college and university presidents "motivated by their conviction that higher education had the capacity and responsibility to lead on climate and sustainability action for the sake of their students and society."[16] One of the twelve founders of ACUPCC was Loren Anderson, President Emeritus of Pacific Lutheran University. Already by 2007, the presidents of five other Lutheran schools became charter members (Augsburg University, Gettysburg College, Gustavus Adolphus College, Luther College [IA], and Wagner College). Since then, California Lutheran University and Concordia College have both joined Second Nature.

Two core commitments of the ACUPCC are to make sustainability a part of every student's learning experience and to achieve carbon neutrality (net zero greenhouse gas emissions) at some point in the future. In 2010 Second Nature initiated their annual Climate Leadership Awards to recognize schools making great strides toward

16 "Our History," Second Nature, https://secondnature.org/our-history/.

these two commitments. Luther College (IA) was the recipient of a Climate Leadership Award in 2012 after it erected a 1.6 MW wind turbine on the western edge of campus.

In 2015 Second Nature expanded and rebranded the ACUPCC as the Presidents' Climate Leadership Commitments, which houses the Carbon Commitment (focused on reducing greenhouse gas emissions), a Resilience Commitment (focused on climate adaptation and building community capacity), and a Climate Commitment, which integrates both. Six Lutheran schools have made the Carbon Commitment (Augsburg University, Gettysburg College, Gustavus Adolphus College, Luther College, Pacific Lutheran University, and Wagner College), whereas California Lutheran University and Concordia have also taken on the Resilience Commitment and thus the all-inclusive Climate Commitment.

In 2020 the Bush Foundation recognized Concordia College's leadership on resilience planning and awarded a $207,000 grant over two years to enable the community in Moorhead, MN, to develop a community resilience action plan to become better prepared to face the impacts of climate change. The grant funding enabled the Moorhead Community Resilience Task Force, chaired by a Concordia faculty member, to develop a set of actionable goals and a plan for using collaboration among stakeholders to pursue the goals. Working groups are focusing on specific areas: infrastructure, ecosystem services, health and wellness, social equity, and economic health.[17]

Two additional examples of leadership in sustainability come from Gustavus Adolphus College and St. Olaf College. Gustavus was the first college or university in Minnesota to be designated a Fair Trade College/University by Fair Trade Campaigns, an organization consisting of fair trade groups from across the globe.[18] As a Fair Trade College, Gustavus strives to use responsibly sourced products and to make them available in its dining facilities, book store, and to offices and departments across campus. Gustavus also supports students,

17 "City of Moorhead Receives Bush Grant," Concordia College, https://www.concordiacollege.edu/news/details/city-of-moorhead-receives-bush-grant/.
18 "Fair Trade Colleges and Universities," Fair Trade Campaigns, https://fairtradecampaigns.org/campaign-type/universities/.

faculty, and staff as they work to create educational programs and increase awareness of fair trade.[19]

Less than fifty miles away, St. Olaf College recently achieved carbon neutrality with regard to electricity consumption on campus. St. Olaf currently leases forty acres of college-owned land to solar developers and subscribes to 40 percent of the solar project's output, which is the maximum allowable by state law. In addition to the solar project on college land, St. Olaf is subscribing to twenty-one other community solar gardens in nearby communities. The college's solar subscriptions, combined with the electricity generated by its wind turbine, have enabled St. Olaf to achieve 100 percent carbon-free electrical power.[20]

Relation to the Theological Roots and Aims of Lutheran Higher Education

To what extent are academic interests in environmental studies and civic commitments to sustainability related to the aims of Lutheran higher education? Are these subjects central or peripheral to major Lutheran theological claims? Does a Lutheran approach to higher education bring anything distinctive to these endeavors?[21] The following five characteristics help answer these questions.

The Life of the Mind and the Value of Interdisciplinarity

It is important to recall that the Reformation movement began with a heated debate at the university in Wittenberg. Perhaps this start in an academic setting is why Lutherans have always placed such a high priority on education. Lutheran colleges and universities see no

---

19 "Gustavus Adolphus College Becomes First Fair Trade College in Minnesota," Gustavus Adolphus College, https://news.blog.gustavus.edu/2015/12/16/gustavus-adolphus-college-becomes-first-fair-trade-college-in-minnesota/.

20 "St. Olaf Celebrates Carbon-Free Electrical Power," St. Olaf College, https://wp.stolaf.edu/news/st-olaf-celebrates-carbon-neutrality.

21 In what follows I draw on "Characteristics of Lutheran Higher Education," which was drafted by Karen Martin-Schramm, based on conversations with and articles by Darrell Jodock, David Preus, Wilfred Bunge, Kristin Swanson, and me. It is included in the Luther College Regents Handbook.

contradiction between faith and intellectual freedom, which means no questions are considered off-limits from vigorous debate and discussion. Lutheran higher education offers a third way between the polarities of sectarian fundamentalism versus purely secular education. The founders of Lutheran colleges recognized there was no specifically Christian math or science; they established colleges that would give young people interdisciplinary knowledge about all facets of life.

The Finite Bears the Infinite and the Goodness of Creation

Martin Luther explored the paradoxical claim that the "finite bears the infinite" in several of his writings. Can something without limits (God) inhabit something with limitations (humanity)? For Luther, this was most certainly true. He emphasized this connection in his reflections on the sacraments and on the incarnation. Throughout, he emphasized the hallowed nature of all bodies (not only human bodies) and the goodness of God's creation. This twofold affirmation for both people and the planet provides a strong theological basis for environmental studies and sustainability initiatives at Lutheran colleges and universities.

Paradox, Wisdom, and Systems Thinking

As noted above, a theological marker that defines Christianity in general and Lutheranism in particular is the notion of paradox. For example, God is both hidden and revealed, fully human and fully divine; the Christian is both free and a servant, both a saint and a sinner. Affirming such seemingly contradictory descriptions leads Lutherans to resist dualistic, either/or ways of thinking and easy answers to complicated problems. Lutherans acknowledge that truth often transcends our fallible reasoning. As a result, Lutheran colleges strive to be communities of moral and intellectual deliberation. Developing critical thinking skills is central to this work. Ideas are powerful and diverse perspectives need to be heard. One of the paradoxes is that truth and wisdom emerge from such deliberation in community. This intellectual approach is very consistent with a "systems approach" to problem-solving and sociopolitical analysis, which is common in environmental studies.

The Doctrine of the Two Kingdoms and Government Regulation

Martin Luther's doctrine of the "two kingdoms" refers to two ways God is at work in the world. On the one hand, God is at work through the church, which uses the Word of God to spread the gospel of love and mercy. On the other hand, God is at work in those governments that use the law to establish a modicum of peace with justice along with the preservation of ecological well-being. While some want to shrink the size of government, Lutherans have valued the divine benefits of a well-regulated society. While Lutherans distinguish between the sacred and the secular, they do not separate them because Lutherans believe God is at work in the world in both of these dimensions of human life. Since Lutherans believe God is at work in the secular world, they do not seek to transform it into the Kingdom of God; neither do Lutherans withdraw from the messiness of worldly affairs and the need for better regulations to develop and maintain a more sustainable world.

Vocation and the Common Good

While many understand vocation as a job or career, Lutherans understand vocation as a calling from God that encompasses all of life. The common vocation Christians share is the care and redemption of all that God has made. One lives out this vocation in varied occupations and the other roles people have as citizens, parents, spouses, and so forth. The goal of a Lutheran education is to help students discover this understanding of vocation so that they find a fulfilling career and a well-balanced, meaningful life. Increasingly, the concept of the common good is being viewed through the prism of sustainability, which is defined broadly as integrated action to address environmental, economic, and social challenges to ensure a more just, equitable, and ecologically healthy world.

Ongoing Challenges

Many Lutheran colleges and universities have clearly made impressive commitments to environmental studies in the classroom as well as sustainability work on campus and in their communities. Nevertheless, some challenges in both areas persist.

In environmental studies, one of the challenges (which is common to any interdisciplinary program) is whether a major in the field offers sufficient depth in any one of the various academic fields students are required to study. As noted above, students tend to take introductory courses in life science and earth science as well as other courses in political science, economics, and in the humanities that tend to be tailored to their program. One way that programs seek to address the depth issue is via tracks within the environmental studies major that typically reflect a focus in either environmental science, environmental law and policy, or environmental literature and culture.

Another challenge, which again is not unique to environmental studies, is whether there is a preferred canon of required texts for the major. Much of the history of environmental studies in North America has revolved around the American West, but the challenges explored by the field transcend this region and are relevant across the globe. While expansion of geographical relevance is important, it has produced a tension in some programs between focusing on local issues versus introducing students to a wide range of environmental concerns around the world. The most successful programs are those that help students see the connections between both.

In the area of environmental sustainability, many NECU and other educational institutions face three ongoing challenges. One major challenge has been to expand beyond what most assume is a sole or primary focus on *environmental* sustainability. As ongoing research and the testimony of individuals and marginalized groups have made abundantly clear, social justice and economic well-being are also important aspects of sustainability. As a result, and quite appropriately, AASHE member organizations and others have been exploring in earnest how efforts to promote diversity, equity, and inclusion on campus and in the classroom are consistent with institutional commitments to sustainability.[22]

---

22 In his chapter in the present volume (221–34), Vic Thasiah explores the perceived tension between commitments to social justice and commitments to sustainability/environmentalism.

With regard solely to *environmental* sustainability, however, another challenge involves achieving greenhouse gas emission reductions not only by investing in more energy-efficient technology and renewable energy systems but also to complement these technologies with efforts to increase resource conservation by promoting behavior changes among students, faculty, and staff. The same can be said for recycling infrastructure. It is one thing to invest in the equipment; it is another to educate the campus community to make use of it.

A third challenge arises when laudable and ambitious sustainability goals collide with limited financial resources. For example, Luther College (IA) is striving to achieve carbon neutrality by 2030.[23] The main obstacle is the college's continued reliance on natural gas to heat the campus. A recently completed Energy Master Plan has outlined ways the college can heat and cool the campus without the use of fossil fuels for the next fifty years, but all of these options require the expenditure of millions of dollars. Needless to say, there are many other demands for financial investment in student scholarship assistance, faculty and staff compensation, and deferred maintenance. Key to investments in sustainability-related initiatives like the one at Luther College will be the extent to which such investments are linked to the educational mission of the school as well its confidence in a long-term future.

Even as they face such challenges, almost all Lutheran colleges and universities continue to strengthen their commitment to environmental studies and sustainability both inside and outside the classroom. Through these efforts they are equipping students to help address the many "wicked," urgent, and interwoven social, economic, and environmental problems that communities are facing, locally and globally. As institutions informed by the aims of Lutheran higher education, they also have a responsibility to be more of a model for society rather than merely a mirror of it.

---

23 "Luther College Climate Action Plan," Luther College, 12–14 https://www. luther.edu/sustainability/assets/Luther_College_Climate_Action_Plan_ Final_and_Approved_01_26_21_.pdf.

For Further Study

ELCA. "Caring for Creation: Vision, Hope and Justice." 1993. https://www.elca.org/Faith/Faith-and-Society/Social-Statements/Caring-for-Creation.

Jones, J. R. "A Sustainable Campus: How ELCA Schools are Working Toward Climate Justice," *Living Lutheran*, August 31, 2020. https://www.livinglutheran.org/2020/08/a-sustainable-campus/.

Martin-Schramm, James B. "Bonhoeffer, the Church, and the Climate Question." In *Eco-Reformation: Grace and Hope for a Planet in Peril*, edited by Lisa E. Dahill and James B. Martin-Schramm, 110–24. Eugene, OR: Wipf & Stock, 2016.

Moe-Lobeda, Cynthia D. *Resisting Structural Evil: Love as Ecological-Economic Vocation*. Minneapolis: Fortress, 2013.

Orr, David. *Earth in Mind: On Education, Environment, and the Human Prospect*. Washington, DC: Island, 2004.

Rasmussen, Larry. *Earth Community, Earth Ethics*. Maryknoll, NY: Orbis, 1996.

_____. *Earth-Honoring Faith: Religious Ethics in a New Key*. Oxford: Oxford University Press, 2013.

Rhoads, David M. "A Theology of Creation: Foundations for an Eco-Reformation." In *Eco-Reformation: Grace and Hope for a Planet in Peril*, edited by Lisa E. Dahill and James B. Martin-Schramm, 1–20. Eugene, OR: Wipf & Stock, 2016.

Saler, Robert C. "Creativity in Earthkeeping: The Contribution of Joseph Sittler's *The Structure of Christian Ethics* to Ecological Theology." *Currents in Theology and Mission* 37 (April 2010): 126–35.

Simmons, Ernest L. "Liberal Arts for Sustainability: Lutheran Higher Education in the Anthropocene." In *Eco-Reformation: Grace and Hope for a Planet in Peril*, edited by Lisa E. Dahill and James B. Martin-Schramm, 197–216. Eugene, OR: Wipf & Stock Publishers, 2016.

_____. *Reformation & Resilience: Lutheran Higher Education for Planetary Citizenship*. Minneapolis: Lutheran University Press, 2017.

Part 3
Contemporary Callings

11

Diversity, Equity, and Inclusion in a White Supremacy Culture

Caryn D. Riswold, Wartburg College

In the aftermath of George Floyd's murder, there was renewed energy and attention directed toward racial injustice and work toward diversity, equity, and inclusion on college and university campuses around the country. I found myself wondering if there would be any lasting and structural changes as a result of this tragedy. Would anything new really emerge? Could lasting and structural changes really occur as a result of this latest generational awakening and potential sea change?

My colleague at Wartburg College, assistant athletic director and track coach Marcus Newsom, had another type of question. In his remarks at the opening chapel service of the 2020–21 academic year, he said: "If we are uncomfortable with what we have witnessed this summer, we need to ask ourselves why. If you are wishing this to go away, pass on, for the dust to settle, we need to ask ourselves why." He went on and repeatedly named "the sin of racism," noting that it is "a part of our core history." Ultimately, Newsom named the problem: "because we are uncomfortable to talk about it, speak about it in our public and private classrooms, we continue to repeat the mistakes of our past in this present."[1] For diverse college and university

---

1 "Weekday Chapel Service (August 26, 2020): Marcus Newsom," Wartburg College, https://livestream.com/wartburgknightvision/chapel20-21/videos/210290980.

campuses to truly transform toward equity and inclusion, we need to stop repeating the mistakes of the past. This chapter will name some of those mistakes.

I have some skepticism that lasting change will occur—a skepticism borne of two decades of working as a faculty member at three different predominantly white institutions (PWIs), two of which claim a Lutheran heritage and mission. As a white woman in academia, a Lutheran theologian teaching religion at church-related colleges and universities, I inhabit positions that have afforded me conditional privilege and protection. Privilege for white women academics has long been conditional on them upholding the basic structures of a white supremacist, capitalist patriarchy that has defined academia and the modern university. In addition, the value of teaching religion as part of a liberal arts education is as contested today as it is foundational for the whole enterprise. I was still a new teacher navigating these complicated positions when I watched jet planes slam into the World Trade Center's Twin Towers live on television. In the wake of 9/11, I heard students and neighbors decry entire nations, races, and religions. I committed then to always teach at the intersection of racial justice, religion, and gender equity.

More recently, I was a mid-career faculty member straining my way through a long pandemic winter break when a mob of white supremacists stormed the US Capitol, intent on disrupting a democratic process that had not favored their chosen leader in the end. These were insurrectionists wearing "Camp Auschwitz" t-shirts, and members of hate groups who proudly wore 6MWE ("six million wasn't enough") logos on their white and mostly male bodies. I recommitted then to the unfinished work of naming and deconstructing the evil structures that feed and breed this activity, that raise up terrorists in our own neighborhoods.

Images of the Capitol under siege brought to mind the query that Kevin M. Gannon, history professor at Grand View University, makes in his book *Radical Hope: A Teaching Manifesto*. In discussing the August 2017 "Unite the Right" rally in Charlottesville,

Virginia, and the fallout for some universities whose student leaders were identified as among the tiki-torch-bearing marchers, Gannon asks, "is it possible for a learner to both successfully move through the academic and intellectual spaces of a college or university and march in support of violent white nationalism?"[2] Stated more acutely, in the shadow of January 6, 2021: Is it possible that a student graduating from a Lutheran college or university could be part of a white supremacist insurrection at the US Capitol? And, as Gannon's follow-up question presses the point, "*should* it be?"

If that question can be answered with anything other than an immediate and resounding "NO!", we at NECU institutions need to hear Coach Newsom and "ask ourselves why." In this chapter I tackle two pressing and related issues: white supremacist culture as paradigmatic of entrenched structural power and the roots of the Lutheran tradition claimed by the twenty-seven institutions that are part of the Network of ELCA Colleges and Universities (NECU). Ultimately, I argue that the Lutheran tradition—through NECU—can support structural change for the project of higher education in the United States.

Yes, the Lutheran Church is 96 percent white. Yes, all NECU institutions are historically white. Yes, most remain predominantly and persistently so. Yet, there are theological resources in this Lutheran tradition to resist white supremacy: While white supremacy culture relies on an array of assumptions to maintain its legitimacy, including a perfectionist ethic, either/or thinking, and an alleged right to comfort, Lutheran theological concepts like the claims that humans are justified by grace, that we are all enmeshed in myriad paradoxes, and that to be a theologian is to be of the cross, provide intellectual resources for dismantling and delegitimizing white supremacy culture in our campus communities.

I will first discuss some of the characteristics of white supremacy culture as discussed by Tema Okun and the *Dismantling Racism*

---

2 Kevin M. Gannon, *Radical Hope: A Teaching Manifesto* (Morgantown: West Virginia University Press, 2020), 14.

Works project, noting how they intersect and reinforce one other. Then I will explore some key Lutheran theological roots that begin to provide an antidote to these toxins that continue to pervade our culture and our campus communities. Finally, I will note a few recent stories from NECU institutions where the disruptive work of transforming cultures is seeded and budding.

Challenge: White Supremacy Culture

White supremacy culture is defined by Tema Okun and the *Dismantling Racism Works* project as "the ways in which [the] ruling class elite or the power elite in the colonies of what was to become the United States used the pseudo-scientific concept of race to create whiteness and a hierarchy of racialized value in order to disconnect and divide."[3] In describing this as a "culture," Okun highlights that it is something "baked into the beliefs, values, norms, and standards of our groups, our communities, our towns, our states, our nation," and, I would add, into our colleges and universities.[4] This is consistent with Clifford Geertz's classic definition of culture as "a system of inherited conceptions expressed in symbolic forms by means of which men communicate, perpetuate, and develop their knowledge about and attitudes toward life."[5] Culture predates the individual, shapes and is shaped by each of us, and governs our lives. When we don't recognize that this is happening, culture is effectively doing its job.

Okun's description of some of the features of white supremacy culture are compelling because they are not overtly and obviously "about" race, gender, or any of the many aspects of human identity that serve to define and divide us. These features are about the preservation of power. In fact, some of the characteristics overtly reveal ways that "white supremacy culture is inextricably linked to all the

---

3 Tema Okun, "What Is White Supremacy Culture?," http://www.whitesupremacy culture.info/what-is-it.html.

4 Okun, "What Is White Supremacy Culture?"

5 Clifford Geertz, "Religion as Cultural System," in *Introducing Religion: Readings from Classic Theorists*, ed. Daniel L. Pals (New York: Oxford, 2009), 349.

other oppressions—capitalism, sexism, class and gender oppression, ableism, ageism, Christian hegemony—these and more are all interconnected and intersected and stirred together in a toxic brew."[6] Investigating these more subtle features illuminates the ordinary attitudes and practices that make our institutions resistant to structural change toward equity and inclusion at the intersections of race, class, gender, sexuality, and the many other facets of human identity. Recognizing and naming *intersectionality* is important. In their definition of that term, Patricia Hill Collins and Sirma Bilge note that:

> When it comes to social inequality, people's lives and the organization of power in a given society are better understood as being shaped not by a single axis of social division, be it race or gender or class, but by many axes that work together and influence each other.[7]

The nine specific characteristics of white supremacy culture named in Okun's work are thus interlinked. They are: fear, perfectionism, either/or and binary thinking, denial and defensiveness, the right to comfort and fear of conflict, individualism, quantity over quality, worship of the written word, and urgency.[8]

Three of these characteristics are particularly salient to campus culture at NECU institutions, and exploring them allows us to "understand the water in which we are all swimming so that we can collaboratively work together to build and sustain cultures that help us thrive as communities and individuals."[9] Social inequalities that persist on our campuses are the result of intersecting factors and features, reinforced by attitudes and practices that are more subtle than many think they are. Structural change must be rooted in an intersectional analysis of power.

---

6 Tema Okun, "White Supremacy Culture Characteristics," http://www.white supremacyculture.info/characteristics.html.

7 Patricia Hill Collins and Sirma Bilge, *Intersectionality* (Malden, MA: Polity, 2016), 2.

8 Okun, "Characteristics."

9 Okun, "Characteristics."

Perfectionism

Perfectionism shows up in "a tendency to identify what's wrong" along with "little ability to identify, name, define, and appreciate what's right."[10] This happens at the individual level as well as at the institutional level, when we know the problems but seem unable to implement solutions. In addition, "making a mistake is confused with being a mistake, doing wrong with being wrong." Here perfectionism is not to be confused with excellence, something for which many institutions and organizations strive, since "excellence requires making and learning from mistakes."[11] This should obviously be valued and championed. At predominantly white institutions, however, perfectionism leads to a paralysis when it comes to meaningfully engaging in antiracist work. The end result is to preserve the status quo of power structures.

If you can't make mistakes, you can't meaningfully address systemic inequalities. Antiracist work is complex, messy, and demanding of a vulnerability that perfectionist culture disallows. In some suggestions about antidotes to perfectionism, Okun notes the value of "a learning community or organization where the stated expectation is that everyone will make mistakes and those mistakes offer opportunities for learning."[12] Ideally, our campuses are already aiming to be these very learning communities. Yet, like any transformation of a culture, this work takes time, commitment, and earned trust.

Either/Or

Okun identifies another feature of white supremacy culture as either/or thinking. This shows up as "positioning or presenting options or issues as either/or—good/bad, right/wrong, with us/against us." Either/or thinking also includes "little or no sense of the possibilities of both/and," along with habitually "trying to simplify complex

10 Tema Okun, "One Right Way," http://www.whitesupremacyculture.info/one-right-way.html.
11 Okun, "One Right Way."
12 Okun, "One Right Way."

things."[13] Conflict and urgency arise from this, and power dynamics are exacerbated when a zero-sum game defines the landscape. Okun notes that this is closely linked with perfectionism, where muddled responses, partial measures, and incremental change are disallowed, mistrusted, or devalued.

One of the antidotes to either/or thinking insists that we "acknowledge the ways in which oppressions intersect and reinforce each other as well as the ways in which oppression can be operating at the interpersonal, institutional and cultural levels."[14] This statement points toward what Patricia Hill Collins calls the "matrix of domination" and "the more fundamental issue of the social relations of domination."[15] Such complexity practically insists that perfectionism be jettisoned and life and work relocated to a muddy middle ground. Having social relations and institutional structures in place that protect and guide the work toward equity and inclusion is our ongoing challenge.

Right to Comfort

A final feature of white supremacy culture that I will examine here is what Okun calls "the right to comfort" or, more precisely, an assumption that one has a right to be comfortable. This is "the belief that those with power have a right to emotional and psychological comfort" alongside "scapegoating those who cause discomfort."[16] When people and institutions operate as if they have a default right to feel comfortable, any discomfort is experienced as The Problem that they must handle before returning to the baseline state of comfort. On some college and university campuses, even calling attention to racism, sexual harassment, and gender inequities can be seen as the cause of the discomfort. This often effectively derails any meaningful discussion of equity and inclusion before it truly begins.

13 Tema Okun, "Either/Or & The Binary," http://www.whitesupremacyculture. info/eitheror--the-binary.html.

14 Okun, "Either/Or."

15 Patricia Hill Collins, *Black Feminist Thought: Knowledge, Consciousness, and the Politics of Empowerment* (New York: Routledge, 1991), 226.

16 Tema Okun, "Right to Comfort," https://www.whitesupremacyculture.info/ comfort--fear-of-conflict.html.

In 2021 various efforts to ban diversity, equity, and inclusion workshops and to curtail the teaching of Critical Race Theory emerged as
prime expressions of this right to comfort. After President Joe Biden
ended a Trump-era executive order that banned "divisive concepts
in federally funded diversity training," the Iowa House and Senate
proposed bills that "prohibit race and sex 'stereotyping' and 'divisive
concepts' in diversity training." This led the University of Iowa to
temporarily pause their diversity work as the matter unfolded in the
courts.[17] This is one example of efforts across the country to control
teaching about the origins and history of inequalities at every level
of education. Note that the discomfort here comes from diversity
training and the discussion of race and gender, not from the structural inequalities and dehumanizing attitudes embedded in white
supremacy and a heteronormative patriarchy. Thus diversity training and "divisive concepts" are effectively made the scapegoat.

These are just three features of white supremacy culture that begin
to point toward a more subtle and insidious set of problems that
a college or university campus committed to equity and inclusion
needs to confront. Seeing them is a first step, and finding resources
for resistance comes next.

Resources: Lutheran Theological Roots

When the majority of staff, faculty, and students on a NECU campus are not Lutheran, of what use are Lutheran theological roots?
Insofar as they shape institutional mission, culture, and strategy,
they help us understand the values that NECU institutions purport
to embody and enact. They can also be indicators of distinction in
a marketplace crowded with options. Here I suggest that a few basic
theological ideas that shape this tradition can be drawn upon as
resources for responding to and dismantling white supremacy culture and its intersecting inequities. Whether or not they are beliefs

---

17 Colleen Flaherty, "No More 'Divisive Concepts' in Iowa?" *Inside Higher
Ed,* March 18, 2021, https://www.insidehighered.com/news/2021/03/18/
trumps-diversity-training-ban-finds-new-life-iowa.

that individuals claim for themselves, institutions can function in such a way as to embody them. They share a theme of reimagining what it means to be human, a theological anthropology, that was at the core of much of the Protestant Reformation and Martin Luther's work in particular. I suggest today that they help us all reimagine these human institutions of Lutheran colleges and universities.

Always A Little Bit Wrong: Justification by Grace

First, the Lutheran theological root of justification by grace claims that human beings can let go of the pressure of having to do and say enough of the right things to merit salvation. From his study of the Christian New Testament, Martin Luther argued that human beings cannot do enough to merit the gift of grace that comes from God. All humans are inherently flawed and our institutions are as well. As the reformer said, "It is clear that the inner man cannot be justified, freed, or saved by any outer work or action at all."[18] Further, drawing on his own deep feelings of inadequacy, Luther names the distress inherent in this situation: "Being truly humbled and reduced to nothing in his own eyes, he finds in himself nothing whereby he may be justified and saved."[19] This has direct bearing on his understanding of the gospel and Christ's saving work.

An anthropology that boldly confesses human flaws and failings offers powerful resistance against tendencies that prop up the perfectionist ethic of white supremacy culture on our campuses. These tendencies are here exposed for what they are: delusions of human grandeur. Not only can humans and human institutions make mistakes, they must. They can't not get things a little bit wrong, and often they get things very wrong.

It's Complicated: Paradox

There is a crucial next point to be made, because colleges and universities can't afford to simply get it wrong. People's very lives and

---

18 Martin Luther, "The Freedom of a Christian (1520)," in *Luther's Works*, ed. Jaroslav Pelikan and Helmut Lehmann (St. Louis: Concordia Publishing House, 1955–1986), 31:347.

19 Luther, "Freedom," 348.

dignity are at stake. Facing the fact of human imperfection, a campus community can work through the many struggles inherent in the antiracist work of transforming its culture. A second Lutheran theological root I find relevant to this is paradox: a tendency to resist the binary. In Luther's thought, we see the claim that humans are saint *and* sinner, as well as the paradox of Christian freedom wherein a person is lord of all *and* servant of all at the same time.[20] There, too, we see the paradox of being embedded in sinful structures while being bound to hope and called to work for a more equitable community.

The paradox of being free and bound is central to the Lutheran theological tradition; when Luther argues that because Christians are freed from having to do and say and be the perfect things, they are liberated to attend to the needs of their neighbors. He draws on the New Testament writings of Paul, suggesting "that when each person has forgotten himself and emptied himself of God's gifts, he should conduct himself as if his neighbor's weakness, sin, and foolishness were his very own."[21] He also notes that a Christian should "be guided in all his works by this thought and contemplate this one thing alone, that he may serve and benefit others in all that he does, considering nothing except the need and advantage of his neighbor."[22] This statement captures an essential reorientation of human attention toward the need of the neighbor, needed particularly by persons and institutions with structural power.

At such a time as this, on predominantly white college and university campuses, attending to the needs of students of color is a life and death matter. If institutions can extricate themselves from the urgency and tyranny of perfectionism, allow themselves to admit mistakes while learning, and truly transform along the way, we can seek reconciliation and finally, truly, attend to the needs of all.

20 See Anthony Bateza's chapter in the present volume (189–203) for consideration of the Lutheran construct of sin as dialectical and confessional, alongside resources for hope when confronting racism.
21 Martin Luther, "Two Kinds of Righteousness (1519)," in *Luther's Works*, ed. Jaroslav Pelikan and Helmut Lehmann (St. Louis: Concordia Publishing House, 1955–86), 31:302.
22 Luther, "Freedom," 365.

Confessions and Failures: Theology of the Cross

This work is uncomfortable—and it should be. Letting go of the right to comfort is a final requirement where a third Lutheran theological root can help. Martin Luther's understanding of what it means to be a "theologian of the cross" requires seeing that human life is lived in the pain and the mess of this world. "The cross" for Luther is the moment of Jesus's tortured and painful death at the hands of the state. It is both *not* how one would expect "the son of God" to live and die, and it is *exactly* there that God is most fully experienced: in a shocking place of suffering and injustice. For Luther, it is also that God is there in the suffering precisely for the purpose of overcoming it. For Luther to argue that understanding this is prerequisite for being a theologian highlights that for him, the default human situation is pain, not comfort, and the essential truth about the divine is accompaniment in the midst of struggle. A central premise of Luther's theology of the cross is that "man must utterly despair of his own ability."[23] For him, this is specific to salvation and the (in)ability to earn grace.

This inability to earn grace inspires humility. Humans can't do it (whatever "it" is) themselves, and human institutions have not gotten it right. Theologians of glory, in Luther's words, are the ones who assume they know everything already and are able to get it right— even perfect. On the contrary, "God destroys the wisdom of the wise."[24] Knowing that we don't really know, seeing that we have not truly seen, listening to voices that we have not heard—these today are expressions of a theology of the cross.

Ultimately, this moment of humility and despair becomes a key to hope. For Luther, the triumph of life over death, of resurrection over crucifixion, is most deeply known via the complexity and the struggle that come to all of us eventually. NECU institutions are called to face and respond to the fact that struggle comes to some more than others, and that it comes to some *because of* others. Stated even more

---

23 Martin Luther, "Heidelberg Disputation (1518)," in *Luther's Works*, ed. Jaroslav Pelikan and Helmut Lehmann (St. Louis: Concordia Publishing House, 1955–86), 31:51.

24 Luther, "Heidelberg," 53.

sharply and discussed in the final section of this chapter, suffering has come to some because of their experiences on NECU campuses.

For NECU institutions, all will flourish only when we overcome the limitations of white supremacy culture and the intersecting inequities that it produces on our campuses. Reckoning with what we have gotten wrong and how our institutions have failed, we realize that we do not have a right to be comfortable until every student is seen and heard enough to flourish. The work begins in the places of struggle where it is painful and uncomfortable for some, and where it is dangerous for many. If we are not able to go to what Luther would describe as the foot of the cross, we will not be able to do the work necessary to transform a campus culture.

Snapshots of Cultures and Responses

Many of us have been reminded anew since the summer of 2020 of the ways that our campus communities have failed to serve and benefit all of our students. The voices of young alumni of color reverberated across social media and into presidents' offices with humbling evidence of this point. Empowered by their NECU campus experiences and education, these young people actually articulated some of our failures back to us, while calling our campuses deeper into the work toward equity and inclusion. In Lutheran theological terms, they manifest hope at the foot of the cross.

Two campuses illustrate the challenges and resources I have described in this chapter. Nick Hayes, a 2008 graduate of Texas Lutheran University, found TLU's initial response to the uprising following the murder of George Floyd insufficient. Hayes "wanted TLU's leadership team to be more direct in the fight for racial justice. 'I sent an email to [President Debbie Cottrell] voicing my concerns and, to my surprise, she agreed and was passionate about wanting to make it right.'"[25] In addition to the president's own initiatives of learning and listening, and at the suggestion of other alumni, Hayes

---

25 "Student-Led Podcast Addresses Experiences of Black Students & Alumni," Texas Lutheran University, https://www.tlu.edu/news/student-led-podcast-addresses-experiences-of-black-students-alumni.

decided to "start a podcast to amplify Black voices in the TLU community and connect people from all over." Four student hosts and Black Student Union advisor Chris Bollinger ultimately came up with the idea for *Learning Boldly*.[26] The podcast now has ten episodes available, featuring conversations with current students, alumni, and community leaders, like the Seguin Chief of Police, and President Cottrell herself.

Similarly, several young alumni of Wartburg College used social media to share video accounts of their past experiences on campus after finding the institution's initial response to the murder of George Floyd inadequate. Though graduates from as many as ten years ago, their memories of dehumanizing moments on a predominantly white campus emerged as newly relevant. In his public response to them, President Darrel D. Colson stated that "as a College, we must acknowledge our history of racist acts. As an individual, I confess that I, and others on this campus, while enjoying white privilege, have been complicit, and have betrayed our missional values, falling short in our vocation to serve a college of the Church."[27] In addition to this humble statement, he responded directly to the experiences shared by the young alumni as he sought to lead the institution through the work to come: "Trust also comes with transparency, so let me respond explicitly to something we've all learned in recent days. Wartburg College did not do enough for the students of color who've shared their stories of racist victimization."[28] The message further discussed investigation processes and several new initiatives set up for the coming academic year. What is most striking and noteworthy is the tone of honesty and vulnerability. For many and good reasons, presidents and institutions are not quick to admit failure, and a willingness to do so here highlights a first step in resisting perfectionism and an assumed right to remain comfortable. Many initiatives at Wartburg grew from that response. These included a presidential task force on diversity, equity, and inclusion comprised

---

26 "Student-Led Podcast."

27 Scott Suhr, "Wartburg President Addresses Allegations," KWAY Radio, June 18, 2021, http://kwayradio.com/wartburg-president-addresses-allegations/.

28 Suhr, "Wartburg President."

primarily of college alumni of color, as well as multiple professional development opportunities for staff and faculty, and co-curricular efforts championed by coaches like Marcus Newsom, who led a community prayer vigil in Waverly during the summer and spoke at a student-led rally in the fall.[29]

In her own responses to student and alumni voices, TLU's President Cottrell launched a podcast series "All Are Welcome" to expand conversations about past and present issues of racial justice. In addition, she acknowledged that "top-level initiatives must occur for institutional change to truly happen and plans to hire a vice president for diversity, equity, and inclusion who will provide leadership for work related to racial justice and equity."[30] This came to pass with the hiring of Dr. David Ortiz in 2021.[31] This move toward senior-level leadership around equity and inclusion has seen a number of NECU campuses include cabinet-level positions for the first time, including Augustana College in Rock Island, IL, when Dr. Monica Smith was named its inaugural Vice President for Diversity, Equity, and Inclusion in 2018.[32] New people in new positions alone will not change culture, as Smith herself put it in a 2019 essay when she described her position as that of "a disrupter of patterns, processes, and systems that are barriers to change."[33] This is the kind of work that ultimately matters in these and all NECU communities, as this is the work that transforms culture.

29 "Creating an Antiracist Campus," Wartburg College, https://www.wartburg.edu/creating-an-antiracist-campus/#1591969624752-22d20316-e733.
30 "Podcast Series Encourages Community Conversations About Racial Justice," Texas Lutheran University, https://www.tlu.edu/news/podcast-series-encourages-community-conversations-about-racial-justice.
31 "TLU Announces New Vice President for Diversity, Equity, and Inclusion," Texas Lutheran University, https://www.tlu.edu/news/tlu-announces-new-vice-president-for-diversity-equity-and-inclusion.
32 "Dr. Monica Smith Named Inaugural Vice President of Diversity, Equity, and Inclusion," Augustana College, https://www.augustana.edu/about-us/news/dr-monica-smith-named-inaugural-vice-president-diversity-equity-and-inclusion.
33 Monica Smith, "Making Diversity Matter: Inclusion is Key," Intersections 50 (Fall 2019): 6.

Conclusion

In these brief episodes and recent initiatives, we see a few ways that meaningful responses became possible when mistakes were admitted, when leaders became vulnerable, when complicated conversations truly began, and when patterns and processes were disrupted. When leaders and institutions are able to admit mistakes and become vulnerable enough to do hard work, perfectionism can be dented. When the voices of young alumni who were both harmed by and empowered from their experiences on our campuses were fully heard, the paradox of that reality could begin to start to have meaningful impact. And, when institutions are humbled and disrupted, they can be compelled and even freed to speak truth and work on lasting structural change.

White supremacy culture may be a part of our history, along with racism and many intersecting inequities, but NECU institutions have an intellectual and theological legacy that provides resources for the work of disrupting it. The question remains: Will we learn from this heritage and transform our campuses toward equity and inclusion? If we do not, we need to ask ourselves why.

For Further Study

Kendi, Ibram X. *How to Be An Anti-Racist*. New York: One World, 2019.

Riswold, Caryn D. "Called to a Pedagogy of the Cross." *Vocation Matters*. Blogsite of the Network of Vocation in Undergraduate Education (NECU). https://vocationmatters.org/2020/04/08/called-to-a-pedagogy-of-the-cross/.

_____. "On Women's Freedom" *The Cresset*. LXXXII.3 (Lent 2019): 44–46. http://thecresset.org/2019/Lent/Riswold_L19.html.

Smith, Monica. "Making Diversity Matter: Inclusion is Key." *Intersections* 50 (Fall 2019): 6–11.

12

The Tragedy of Racism

Anthony Bateza, St. Olaf College

On April 11, 2021, Daunte Wright was shot and killed by officer Kimberly Potter in the Minneapolis suburb of Brooklyn Center. The following day, St. Olaf's president sent a short email entitled, "The pain and tragedy of the murder of Daunte Wright." Recognizing the gravity of the moment, the email encouraged community members to support one another. It denounced "all acts of racism and systemic oppression," acknowledged the "fear and pain" of many in the Black community, and called Wright's murder a "tragic incident" that is a part of "the continuous violence against communities of color."[1]

The language of tragedy is invoked but unexplained. This is likely because of the email's brevity. Given the immediacy of the reaction, there was little time to know what precisely had happened that prior spring day. But the language of tragedy struck me as fitting.

We see tragedy in print and on stage with stories where soaring ambitions never take flight or suddenly come crashing down. In everyday moments we speak of tragedy when confronted by extreme suffering and loss, lives taken by a natural disaster or a sudden illness. Tragedy upends our expectations, our sense of how things ought to go, leaving a painful road ahead for those left to move along as best they can.

In this chapter, I suggest that Lutheran colleges and universities need to draw on the language and meaning of tragedy to better

---

1 President David Anderson and the President's Leadership Team, email message, April 12, 2021.

understand and address racism. The Lutheran theological tradition provides valuable resources—ways of seeing, thinking, feeling, and acting. Through its understanding of sin's complexity and a tragic sensibility, the Lutheran tradition is well positioned to understand racism's presence. By commending a measured hope and practices of love, embodied in both individual lives and shared institutions, the Lutheran tradition positions NECU institutions to respond to racism in the present. Throughout this chapter, I connect these theological insights to experiences of campus life and culture at St. Olaf and Wagner Colleges, two Lutheran institutions wrestling with the reality of racism.[2]

A Lutheran Account of the Sin and Tragedy of Racism

For millennia, Christians have spoken of sin. In the sixteenth century, a young friar and college professor, Martin Luther, pushed against commonly held views of sin and God's judgment. Presented with an angry and punishing God whose expectations seemed unachievable, Luther experienced deep anxiety and despair. Time spent reflecting on biblical texts, Christian theology, and his own life experience led Luther in a different direction. He focused less than before on individual acts and divine scorekeeping, instead describing sin as broken relationship with God that spills over into damaged ways of seeing, desiring, and living with God, neighbor, and self. As human beings, we teeter between prideful overconfidence and hopeless despair. We frequently love the wrong things or—what can be even harder to recognize—we love the right things in the wrong way. These are lamentable features of the human condition, a constant and inescapable tendency to serve ourselves and stare at our own navels, as he liked

---

2 I am indebted to two colleagues at Wagner College for making time to share their experiences and perspectives with me: Ruta Shah-Gordon, the vice president of Internationalization, Intercultural Affairs, and Campus Life, and Jazzmine Clark-Glover, the vice president of Workplace Culture and Inclusion. I have done my best to represent their words and sentiments honestly and faithfully.

to put it.[3] Sin is not merely an individual flaw, it is also a systemic reality, a shared condition of human communities and institutions. There is the need for accusation to call out sin, but also confession to address things done and left undone individually and communally.[4]

There are vigorous debates about the meaning of racism. Is racism only present in overt and acute acts of malice toward people of color, for example, or is it a more diffuse and chronic condition? Should we focus on individual wrongdoing or systemic issues? Recently there have been fierce attacks on Critical Race Theory and other academic disciplines, with claims that all of this attention on racism is too pessimistic and ideological, and that it condemns all people and betrays the goodness of the nation and the progress that has been made.[5]

Institutions steeped in the Lutheran tradition should be in a better position to see what is wrong with these debates and attacks. While there is room for conversation and valuable disagreement, the idea that human beings are mired in broken systems we did not create and yet still perpetuate should come as a no surprise to a tradition accustomed to the language of sin. Guilt is never reducible to intentions. Almost thirty years ago, the ELCA Social Statement "Freed in Christ: Race, Ethnicity, and Culture" took a clear position on these issues:

---

3 Luther employed the phrase "*incurvatus in se*" to describe this curved-in nature of the sinful self. See, for example, his *Lectures on Romans*, in *Luther's Works*, ed. Jaroslav Pelikan and Helmut Lehmann (St. Louis: Concordia Publishing House, 1955–86), vol. 25.

4 For a summary of Luther's views on sin, see L'ubomír Batka, "Martin Luther's Teaching on Sin," in *The Oxford Handbook of Martin Luther's Theology*, ed. Robert Kolb, Irene Dingel, and L'ubomír Batka (Oxford: Oxford University Press, 2014).

5 As of March 2022, at least sixteen US states have passed laws banning discussions of Critical Race Theory in classroom spaces, with many written broadly enough to forbid issues tied to the historical realities and ongoing legacies of racism in general. Other legislation is pending in over a dozen states, with explicit bans proposed for educational institutions and within state agencies, in addition to numerous policy proposals and punitive budgetary moves that have been advanced by local and county governments.

When we speak of racism as though it were a matter of personal attitudes only, we underestimate it. We have only begun to realize the complexity of the sin, which spreads like an infection through the entire social system. Racism infects and affects everyone, with an impact that varies according to race, ethnicity, or culture, and other factors such as gender or economic situation.[6]

The battle against sin is perpetual. Or as Luther phrased it, every day human sinfulness must be confronted and put to death. The same is true for racism. Finding ourselves not only subject to, but complicit and conspiring with these forces that cause such suffering and sustain oppression can overwhelm our emotional and volitional resources, our ability to feel and respond.[7] But it is precisely these affective and intellectual resources that are needed and are shaped by tragedy.[8]

Actually *seeing* the suffering of Black and brown peoples requires many to be reshaped. Seeing this suffering as *tragic* requires more training still. The challenges here cannot be easily pushed aside. Some in our communities believe there is no suffering to speak of, that racism and its effects are either nonexistent or grossly exaggerated.

---

6 ELCA, "Freed in Christ: Race, Ethnicity, and Culture" (1993), https://www. elca.org/Faith/Faith-and-Society/Social-Statements/Race-Ethnicity-and-Culture, 4.

7 I presuppose that this complicated relationship with racism is experienced differently based on one's own racial or ethnic identity, in conjunction with other identities and social realities. I leave unaddressed important debates about the extent to which differently socially marked peoples experience and participate in racism or, simply put, whether or not people of color can be simultaneously the victims and perpetrators of racism.

8 Philosopher Martha Nussbaum argues that tragedies make clear the importance of the "sensuous imagination," the affects or feelings that move us and require us to eschew the over-rationalization of human life. She suggests that the "catharsis" that comes from tragic literature should be understood not as a release but instead as a clarification, a moment where obstacles are removed and vision restored. Tragedy "contributes to human self-understanding" as it explores emotions like fear and pity, and "the way it carries out this exploratory task is by moving us to respond with these very emotions. For these emotional responses are themselves pieces of recognition or acknowledgment of the worldly conditions upon our aspirations to goodness." See *The Fragility of Goodness: Luck and Ethics in Greek Tragedy and Philosophy* (Cambridge: Cambridge University Press, 1986), 390.

The perspective here shifts quickly to white people, making them the victims of a burdened legacy or overzealous and misguided activists today.[9] For others, while the suffering of people of color is real, its cause is attributed to some internal flaw in individuals or whole communities. Whatever tragedies befall Black and brown people are caused by their poor choices and cultural deficiencies, or so the thinking goes.[10]

It can sometimes be difficult to speak to the pain and suffering of racism on Lutheran college and university campuses. Speaking up and speaking out against injustice ought to be a signature strength of those who stand in Luther's wake, and doing so in ways that move hearts and minds to perceive and respond to suffering should be second nature.[11] Lutheran campuses must address the sin of racism and the tragic suffering it creates.

The two colleges I focus on in this chapter, St. Olaf and Wagner, are located in very different geographical locations and institutional contexts. At St. Olaf, domestic students of color comprise approximately 20 percent of the student body, while at Wagner that number has been closer to 35 percent in recent years.[12] While both schools have experienced increased demographic diversity, this has

---

9 Elizabeth Spelman observes that the national dialogue about slavery and its legacy often functions this way, making racism an American tragedy where the emphasis falls on the regrettable failings of the founding fathers and their white descendants who never embodied the ideals of freedom and equality for all. Their unrealized potential is lamented instead of the realities of violence and legacies of suffering borne by Black and brown bodies. See Spelman, *Fruits of Sorrow: Framing our Attention to Suffering* (Boston: Beacon, 1998), 34–58.

10 Eduardo Bonilla-Silva labels this a form of "cultural racism" prevalent in so-called colorblind America. For more see his *Racism without Racists: Color-Blind Racism and the Persistence of Racial Inequality in America*, 5th ed. (Lanham MD: Rowan & Littlefield, 2018).

11 Attending to other traditions that have also made the recognition of suffering central is also commendable. See, for example, James Cone's *The Cross and the Lynching Tree* (Maryknoll NY: Orbis, 2011).

12 For St. Olaf's recent data, see https://wp.stolaf.edu/ir-e/st-olaf-students-raceethnicity-profile/. Wagner's student data is available at https://wagner.edu/about/facts/reports/. Institutions of higher learning have been encouraged to isolate data on *domestic* students of color to provide greater transparency and to avoid potentially misleading representations of their student body by leaning on the international student population in an effort to project greater diversity.

often not come with a similar growth in inclusivity. It is one thing to admit more students of color, another to address structures and power and to critically assess campus culture and longstanding habits, so that Black and brown people feel seen and are truly valued.[13] At St. Olaf, this challenge has been made clearer as the campus has responded to larger national demands for Black equality and social justice.

In September of 2020, at the start of a new academic year and in the middle of the COVID-19 pandemic, a group of St. Olaf students, the Oles Against Inequality, organized an event to respond to the shooting of Jacob Blake in Kenosha, WI. The event, called "7 feet for 7 shots," began with speeches at the football field followed by a socially distanced march across campus. The event was embraced by college administrators, and this official embrace sparked fierce controversy. Student organizers, Bruce King, then the college's vice president for Equity and Inclusion, and President Anderson, all offered their reflections as a part of the official program. Then unofficial speakers from the Black student association, the Cultural Union for Black Expression (CUBE), stepped up to the microphone.

Senior Joshua Wyatt challenged the coopting of events against racial injustice as weak, public relations-driven exercises that avoid hard questions and harder institutional changes. Wyatt also questioned the privileging of cis-heterosexual Black male experiences and the silencing of Queer, female, trans-, and nonbinary voices. Brianne Smith, a sophomore, spoke about the lack of attention to and inclusion of Black women in conversations about *which* Black lives matter and the construction of systems of power and leadership on St. Olaf's campus. With powerful and raw testimony, Smith spoke about her sense of abandonment and betrayal, which was tied in part to a promise that St. Olaf is a welcoming campus and a place where Black students can thrive.[14]

---

13 For more on campus culture and inclusion, but related to disability, see Courtney Wilder's chapter in the present volume (109–26).

14 Both Joshua Wyatt and Brianne Smith granted me permission to use their names and to share their experiences for this chapter.

While I have focused on St. Olaf here, given my own location and experiences, a similar pattern has been observed at Wagner College. In 2008, for example, their Black Student Union organized a sit-in in response to a racist event on campus. The students articulated demands for change on campus while also doing the important work of simply articulating their experiences and making the demand to be seen and heard. This student work challenged members of the college to question how effectively they respond to racism, how they might move from merely showing sympathy to enacting solidarity.

The testimony of these students peeled back layers of suffering and tragedy. They gave voice to their pain and suffering, showing just how frequently the colleges' efforts to address racism are undone by inaction and ignorance. The very place that extended promises and created optimism for the next chapter of these students' lives far too often left these students wounded and disillusioned.

From Passive Spectators to Hopeful Agents

In the theater we sit, transfixed as a tragedy unfolds before us. Charging the stage to warn King Oedipus or Prince Hamlet would not be well received by the actors or the audience. But too often we are just as immobilized in the face of tragedies in real life, especially when it comes to the tragedy of racism. Cornel West, the philosopher and social critic, makes suffering and tragedy a central component of his analysis of racism and other injustices in the United States. As he sees it, the tragic features of life have invited different responses. For some a tragic sensibility leads to a loss of agency and hope as the forces at work seem too large and beyond human control. Another tendency has been to deny that tragedy is even possible in the modern world; ironic detachment emerges as one acknowledges the indifference of the world and sees that justice is a fiction.

Rejecting these options, West looks to the Black experience for guidance. Black peoples have refused to ignore or paper over suffering and pain, raising "the problem of evil in its concrete forms in America." What is more: "Black folk historically have reminded people of the prevailing state of denial."[15] The Black Christian and prophetic tradition, West argues, "puts a premium on change, transformation, conversion and future possibility, [where] the temptation of despair is not eliminated, but attenuated."[16] This stance toward tragedy is captured in the idea of a "strenuous hope" or a "strenuous mood," which ultimately supports and motivates "the worthwhileness of our struggle to endure."[17] Doe-eyed optimism and stoic withdrawal are two sides of the same problem, namely, avoiding responding to the problems before us. The work that needs doing is hard, and yet the desire and expectation for change remains real.

There is no formula for how to effect change and sustain the kind of action that West commends. But there are examples from individuals and communities that have done this work successfully. West draws from an eclectic cast of church leaders, political activists, authors, musicians, and artists to highlight the features of a strenuous hope.[18] These various figures see the future differently, as a source of ethical significance that motivates their agency in the present. There is a need, a drive, to create a better tomorrow even though the struggles of the day and the possibility of failure are real and unavoidable. Living in a strenuous hope can lead to suffering and loss, but the greater tragedy would be to succumb to a vision of life ruled by "brute chance" and "diabolic irrationality."[19]

In a very different but analogous way, Martin Luther wrestled with Christian responses to suffering, describing an ongoing battle

15 Cornel West, "On Black-Brown Relations," in *The Cornel West Reader* (New York: Basic Civitas Books, 1999), 504.

16 Cornel West, "Black Strivings in a Twilight Civilization," *Cornel West Reader*, 113.

17 Cornel West, "Pragmatism and the Sense of the Tragic," in *Cornel West Reader*, 181. Here West makes connections between the American philosophical tradition of pragmatism and the work of Josiah Royce to flesh out his account of tragedy.

18 Joseph R. Winters also uses Black literary and artistic figures to speak about a "melancholic hope" that stands in contrast with optimistic triumphalism and resignation as it "cultivates a difficult attunement to the ruins and remains" of our lives. See his *Hope Draped in Black: Race, Melancholy, and the Agony of Progress* (Durham, NC: Duke University Press, 2016), 248.

19 West, "Pragmatism," 181.

with diabolic forces and the ever-present temptation toward fatalistic resignation. Despite these dangers, Luther insisted that God's activity in the world and on behalf of goodness and life would always have the final word, even when we can only see this in hope.

Lutheran colleges and universities must draw from the Lutheran heritage in ways that subvert simple narratives and resist valorizing the past.[20] At St. Olaf and Wagner, this has looked different. St. Olaf places a premium on Lutheran identity, claiming in its mission statement that the community is "nourished by the Lutheran tradition." It continues to debate what is and is not nourishing, both in response to the changing demographics of the campus and in painful recognition of the ways that what appears to be a warm Norwegian embrace to some is experienced as a suffocating blanket of whiteness to many.

Wagner, in contrast, has shifted its focus from cultural Lutheranism, even as the cultural whiteness of its Staten Island location, staff, and board composition all continue to pose challenges. Wagner has looked to its history as a Lutheran pro-seminary, a preparatory program for those pursuing a call to ministry, to emphasize a longstanding commitment to social justice and civic engagement. Joel Martin, who became Wagner's nineteenth president in 2019, called upon the words of his predecessor in response to racism in our own time, writing:

> In 1938, President Clarence Stoughton, the first lay leader of Wagner College, decried anti-Semitism in Nazi Germany and challenged the US to root out its own racism. Eighty years later, bearing witness to the recent horrific murders of George Floyd in Minnesota, Ahmaud Arbery in Georgia, Breonna Taylor in Kentucky, and Sean Reed in Indiana, I echo his cry.[21]

---

20 For a helpful suggestion of how to do this recovery and interrogation of the past, see Shannon Sullivan, "Whiteness as Family: Race, Class, and Responsibility," in *Difficulties of Ethical Life*, ed. Shannon Sullivan and Dennis J. Schmidt (New York: Fordham University Press, 2008), 162–78.

21 "A message from President Joel W. Martin," June 1, 2020, https://wagner.edu/newsroom/message-president-joel-w-martin/. I am thankful to Dr. Shah-Gordon for this reference.

Because so many tragedies are caused by forces larger than any one of us, one way to make tragedies less common is to remake these systems and resist these forces. The Lutheran tradition has long emphasized the importance of "good order," a commitment to freedom paired with duty and the human need for guidance and organization. At times our work on campus can become overly bureaucratic and managerial, especially for faculty and staff, leading all parties involved to feel that we are merely piling meetings on top of meetings in ways that distract from or avoid the real work of combatting racism. There is, undoubtedly, something right in this sentiment. But at the same time, this attitude can breed cynicism; it underestimates the value of establishing policies and mechanisms to effect systemic and institutional change.

This work has been slow at St. Olaf and Wagner. Building structures has gone hand-in-hand with efforts to increase representation and facilitate conversations on campus. Both colleges have moved toward making antiracism and diversity trainings mandatory for all students, faculty, and staff. In some areas, such as tenure-track searches for faculty members, the changes have been easier to implement. In other areas, such as the process of tenure and promotion or the composition and oversight of boards of trustees, change has been slower and more difficult. For example, at Wagner, the election of Donald Trump in 2016 presented a unique challenge given the fact that the college had conferred an honorary degree on Mr. Trump in 2004. The tension and conflict this generated were productive insofar as the Wagner Board of Trustees had to discuss the rationale behind honorary degrees, and to construct policies that ultimately led them to revoke the degree in January of 2021 after the Capitol riots.

Love in the Face of Tragedy

As we aspire and work for the good, one of the insights of Martin Luther and the Lutheran tradition has been that good works often go wrong. In Lutheran thought there is a constant return to the "both-and" of human existence. People are simultaneously sinners and saints, faced with commands and promises, struggling to make progress and seeing ourselves regress.[22] The picture of the stereotypical racist, the malicious white supremacist wearing KKK robes or wielding a tiki torch, is a comforting distraction from the true evils committed by common people in mundane ways.

The philosopher John Kekes writes about a tragic view of life that speaks more honestly to evil and the human condition. Our evil and human suffering come as we pursue some goods and are undone by unintended outcomes and unexamined habits, with wrongdoing commonly caused when "part of ourselves colludes in sabotaging the efforts of the other part." As Kekes further observes, "What makes situations tragic is that the agents who cause great evil to themselves and others through their characteristic but unchosen actions and the agents who endeavor to live good lives are one and the same."[23]

On Lutheran campuses, recognizing the messy and painful mixture of virtue and vice remains a challenge. In reflecting on events at St. Olaf and in conversing with colleagues at Wagner, I notice several patterns of alleged virtues and good deeds going wrong.

Embracing the language of *grace* and *gift* is common in the Lutheran tradition, inspired as it is by a commitment to God's goodness and the way that God brings people into a loving relationship with God and neighbor. At the same time, the language of gift also places burdens on people, especially people of color. Black students, faculty, and staff can be reminded in ways both subtle and not so subtle that they should be grateful for the opportunities provided in a place of higher learning. Pointing out microaggressions or calling for concrete changes can leave one looking *ungrateful* in a place where gratitude is prized.[24]

Stewardship of limited financial resources is laudable, as places like St. Olaf and Wagner work with budgets that are largely

---

22 For more on the simultaneity of sinners and saints and Luther's hamartiology (understanding of sin) as it relates to a white supremacy culture, see Caryn D. Riswold's chapter in the present volume (173–87).

23 John Kekes, *Facing Evil* (Princeton, NJ: Princeton University Press, 1990), 37, 43.

24 Mrs. Clarke-Glover relayed this sentiment to me in our conversation together about Wagner, and I have gleaned a similar sentiment from colleagues at St. Olaf.

tuition-driven. There is genuine concern about the affordability of a college education and the rising realities of student indebtedness. But our ability to connect stewardship efforts with questions about justice both on and off campus is often underdeveloped. At its worst, the need to manage an institution's financial resources is played off of efforts to improve the campus experience for people of color. Their needs are seen as superfluous or gratuitous, things that it would be nice to have if more money were available, but which must be sacrificed in the present for the good of the budget. Add to this the confluence of economic and racialized obstacles, and one can see how financial decisions that seem minor to those in power and possessing adequate financial resources can have a major impact on the experiences of Black and brown students, faculty, and staff.

Given the focus on teaching at relatively small liberal arts colleges like St. Olaf and Wagner, being *student-focused* and cultivating *effective teaching* are shared values. After all, the Lutheran movement began in a college town, where the priest and friar Martin Luther was employed as a professor. But Black and brown faculty at Lutheran institutions today have spoken powerfully about the weight that they have to bear, and how these goals place a large amount of power in the hands of predominantly white student bodies and administrators. Given the recent departure of several Black women faculty members, St. Olaf has been forced to address these issues.

In an email to the campus community, Dr. Michelle Gibbs recounted her experience of being "in constant fear" of her white students because of their power over her evaluations and tenure process. Students' negative reactions were clearly driven by their racist and sexist prejudices, expectations for how white students should be treated and what kind of behavior is expected from Black women. What was equally disheartening was the unexpected lack of support encountered from faculty colleagues and ostensible allies in the administration, leading Dr. Gibbs to conclude that her "differences as a Black female educator were a hindrance at St. Olaf College, not a gift."[25]

---

25 Michelle Cowin Gibbs, email message to St. Olaf faculty, June 13, 2020.

Beyond not offering love for the gifts given by people of color on our campus, campus cultures often demand that *they* (people of color) show signs of love and affection for our institutions. This occurs in subtle and insidious ways. Reporting on admission data or new hires around the college or university can reduce people of color to numbers, tick marks on a wall that show how the institution is building a diverse community. When the numerical becomes personal, the particular stories of people of color can also become mere public relations window dressing, where warm stories of success and welcome are expected as people effusively share their love for this institution. This is no simple matter, and this love might even be genuine and heartfelt. But at historically and persistently white institutions, those in power are too often unaware of the damage these displays effect. Invitations to celebrate your school flow from a desire to confirm the goodness of white people and to publicly mark their forward progress, instead of seeking out the messy realities and complicated experiences of their Black and brown community members.

One of Martin Luther's insights about human relationships, with one another and with God, was our pernicious desire to control these relationships for our own, often myopic benefits. The relationship with God becomes one of crass exchange, and our neighbors are reduced to mere means serving our own ends. This is tragic, in our lives generally and particularly as our misguided paths to love collaborate with our racialized and racist ways. The other kind of love that Luther identified was God's unconditional love for creatures, a love that creates goodness and value, often in ways that oppose and subvert ordinary expectations. Strength looks like weakness, while weakness is seen as strength. Self-sufficiency is idolatrous, while vulnerability is venerated.[26]

Luther also insisted that love, when exercised rightly, can be understood as both freedom and bondage, a liberty to provide help and comfort to neighbors. Neighbors are not simply people who live in my immediate vicinity, but truly any and all who have need.

---

26 See especially Martin Luther, "Heidelberg Disputation (1518)," in *Martin Luther's Basic Theological Writings*, 2nd ed., ed. Timothy F. Lull (Fortress, 2005), 57 (theses 19 and 20).

Traditionally, this has inspired a strong focus on social welfare institutions that provide food, housing, and health care to others.[27] Making a social ill like racism a central focus of our work, seeing the harms it causes as requiring loving, embodied action, remains a challenge. For Lutheran colleges and universities to respond to the tragedy of racism in ways that address our challenges in a Lutheran voice, a return to this fundamental commitment of neighbor love is required. This would be love that seeks neither what it already views as beloved nor what is in the best material or political interest of the institution. A different mode of relationship is required, one that is sacrificial and does not presume to know what the other needs, but instead humbles itself.[28]

Conclusion

To say, as St. Olaf's President Anderson did, that the death of a young Black man is a "tragic incident" is an important beginning. Recognizing this loss is difficult in a world marred by racism and white supremacy, a world where white lives and deaths consistently matter more than Black ones. Before the recognition of tragedy can bear the fruit of hope, however, more must be done. I have suggested here that there are resources within the Lutheran theological tradition for doing more. Claiming a long tradition of reflection on sin better enables one to address racism's presence and persistence. Sin moves in the complex interaction of individual faults and systemic realities, personal and communal failings, things done and left undone. Facing sin requires introspection and honesty without navel-gazing and defensiveness. Unlike some philosophical and literary accounts of tragedy, where the forces that bear down upon the pitied subject are beyond their control, the view of tragedy and racism offered here has highlighted the interplay between our activity and passivity. When it comes to racism, we, as human beings in

---

27 Lutheran Social Services in America, for example, is comprised of over 300 member organizations, making it one of the largest service providers in the nation.

28 For a reconstruction of service and service-learning along these lines, see Mindy Makant's chapter in the present volume (45–55).

general and in our roles on college campuses, are both the victims and perpetrators of tragedy.

Following Luther's guidance and example, we can interrogate our loves, question the reasons behind our commitments and the real impact they have on people in general and people of color in particular. At our institutions of higher learning, this will entail some weighty losses, such as giving up power and wealth, or giving up a purified narrative about ourselves that serves our public image. These losses are real, and the outcome of our efforts are not assured, but love in service of neighbor is an ongoing project and not a mere means to an end. The tragedy of racism will continue in our communities, but hope struggles on as the work continues.

For Further Study

Ahmed, Sara. *On Being Included: Racism and Diversity in Institutional Life*. Durham, NC: Duke University Press, 2012.

Bonilla-Silva, Eduardo. *Racism without Racists: Color-Blind Racism and the Persistence of Racial Inequality in America*. 5th ed. Lanham, MD: Rowan & Littlefield, 2018.

Kay, Matthew R. *Not Light but Fire: How to Lead Meaningful Race Conversations in the Classroom*. Portsmouth, NH: Stenhouse, 2018.

Oluo, Ijeoma. *So You Want to Talk About Race*. New York: Seal, 2018.

Stjerna, Kirsi. *Lutheran Theology: A Grammar of Faith*. London: T&T Clark, 2021.

West, Cornel. *The Cornel West Reader*. New York: Basic Civitas, 1999.

West, Traci. *Solidarity and Defiant Spirituality: Africana Lessons on Religion, Racism, and Ending Gender Violence*. New York: NYU Press, 2019.

13

Lutheran Institutions on Unceded Indigenous and Former Slaveholding Lands

Krista E. Hughes, Newberry College

Take a deep breath. This chapter begins with a bracing confession. Every institution in the Network of ELCA Colleges and Universities (NECU) makes its home on unceded Indigenous lands, and all were founded within a national political economy that was reliant on the bodies, minds, and ingenuity of enslaved peoples. Yes, treaties and agreements were signed. Yes, only a handful of NECU institutions sit on former slaveholding lands. A fuller appraisal of history, however, leads us to acknowledge the staggering power at play in the European settlement of North America.[1] If we who work at these NECU institutions are honest with ourselves, then we acknowledge that we work, teach, mentor, and coach on haunted grounds.[2] This means that the education NECU institutions offer their students is rooted not only in a life-giving theological tradition and histories of educational uplift but also in a death-dealing history of settler colonialism

---

1 Consider, for example, the Homestead Act, the Morrill Act, and the Pacific Railroad Act, all passed in 1862 during Abraham Lincoln's presidency, which transferred millions of acres of Indigenous lands to states and private corporations for development, breaking multiple treaties with Indigenous nations in the process. For a fuller history of broken treaties, see Roxanne Dunbar-Ortiz, *An Indigenous People's History of the United States* (Boston: Beacon, 2014).

2 Krista E. Hughes, "Radical Hospitality on Haunted Grounds: Anti-Racism in Lutheran Higher Education," *Intersections* 52 (Fall 2020): 12–16.

and enslavement. As NECU institutions make positive steps toward justice on their campuses, it is vital to acknowledge, alongside generative forces, the historical violence that has made their institutional lives possible.

This chapter considers the intersection of land, history, and peoples and looks to Lutheran theology and practice as fruitful tools for more attentively engaging the local histories and living legacies of NECU institutions. At the same time, this piece acknowledges that Lutheran immigration patterns in North America and the strong cultural identities that emerged from that transcontinental movement have often occluded the cultural and material destruction that resulted from European settlement. The impact on the Indigenous peoples of Turtle Island (an Ojibwe name for North America) and the enslaved peoples from Africa took different forms, but the consumptive-destructive impulses of white European colonialism wrought fatal consequences for both Indigenous and African peoples.

In this chapter, I call on NECU institutions to consider a fuller, more honest history than often is told of the lands that are now NECU campuses. I ask how particular campus histories shape who and what institutions are today. While this chapter deliberately seeks to provoke some discomfort, it ultimately is a chapter of hope, offered in the conviction that, in the words of James Baldwin, "nothing can be changed until it is faced."[3] This chapter invites readers to consider the challenges and promises of confronting the local-regional histories of their campuses and also to look to resources within Lutheran theology and practice to support institutional courage in facing those histories. The Lutheran practice of confession and repentance is one model for how NECU institutions might face themselves as predominantly white institutions (hereafter, PWIs), and as inheritors of the fruits of white settler colonialism. A consistent practice of facing themselves opens the possibility for what Christians call

---

3 James Baldwin, interview featured in the film *I Am Not Your Negro*, directed by Raoul Peck (2016). This is akin to Martin Luther's demand "to call a thing what it is" as a key movement of confession and repentance. See Luther, "Heidelberg Disputation (1518)," in *Luther's Works*, ed. Jaroslav Pelikan and Helmut Lehmann (St. Louis: Concordia Publishing House, 1955–1986), 31.

repentance, which involves not simply expressing contrition for harms done but also a change of disposition and a commitment to act differently moving forward. This chapter also offers glimpses of how a few NECU campuses are imperfectly but with deep conviction and commitment answering their missional call to confess their history as PWIs situated on unceded Indigenous and former slave-holding lands. Their efforts suggest some strategies that other NECU institutions might consider as all work toward a more just society.

White Identity, Memory, and History

Facing History and Ourselves is an organization that equips K-12 teachers with history lessons and activities. Their organizational name is striking. It suggests that simply facing history, as if it were an object removed from who people are today, is insufficient. Rather, to face history meaningfully, people must also face themselves. NECU institutions are historically, structurally, predominantly white, even in contemporary contexts where the student, staff, and/ or faculty populations may be significantly non-white. It is important for NECU institutions to understand themselves as "institutions of whiteness" regardless of demographic composition or recent diversity efforts so that they can more clearly identify and interrogate white ways of thinking, functioning, sustaining structures, and perpetuating norms that work against their own missional commitments to reparative justice.[4] Black theologian and higher education administrator Willie James Jennings narrates how institutions of Western education continue to function according to what he calls a colonial "plantation logic," where the guiding image of the truly educated person is "a white self-sufficient man, his self-sufficiency

---

4 See Joseph Barndt, *Understanding and Dismantling Racism: The Twenty-First Century Challenge to White America* (Minneapolis: Fortress, 2007), chapters 5 and 7; and Tema Okun's contemporary "Characteristics of White Supremacy Culture," https://www.whitesupremacyculture.info/uploads/4/3/5/7/43579015/okun_-_white_sup_culture_2020.pdf. See the chapter by Caryn D. Riswold in the present volume (173–87) for extensive use of Tema Okun's work in diagnosing and responding to white supremacy culture in higher education.

defined by possession, control, and mastery."[5] In turn, Jennings claims, the ideal educational institution becomes this image writ large. Many NECU institutions are able to boast histories that resist this image. For example, Gustavus Adolphus College admitted white, non-Indigenous women at its founding in 1862, a full century before some of the "Ivies"—an echo of Martin Luther's commitment to the education of both boys and girls. Jennings's analysis nonetheless serves as a critical call for NECU institutions to attend diligently to their missions for vocation.

The first challenge of facing their histories is the contested nature of history itself. Professional historians are aware that history is continually being "revised" as more is learned, acknowledged, and understood. In addition, history looks different through different eyes. Because of these contestations, history, like memory, is vulnerable to being distorted beyond factual recognition, leading to such assertions as "slavery was not so bad for most slaves" and "the Civil War was not about slavery but about states' rights."[6] Such contested narratives, which circulate widely in US society, can impact NECU institutions in the form of constituencies who are not interested in or, worse, may feel threatened by a reconsideration of institutional histories that take honest account of injustices perpetrated by the institution. In 2009 my institution, Newberry College, replaced its mascot "the Indians" with "the Wolves." The college lost some key donors over the change, and even to this day, certain donors financially support the college while publicly protesting the mascot change. But it was a vital reparative step.

Subsequent challenges relate to the nature of whiteness itself. For white people like myself, "confessing our history" requires a critical racial gaze so that we might both acknowledge the ways whiteness has operated historically as well as the ways white persons and institutions today perpetuate the oldest of patterns, intentionally or not. This is to

---

5 Willie James Jennings, *After Whiteness: An Education in Belonging* (Grand Rapids: Eerdmans, 2020), 6.

6 For an examination of how these distortions occur, see "Blandford Cemetery" in Clint Smith's *How the Word Is Passed: A Reckoning with the History of Slavery across America* (New York: Little Brown, 2021).

say, it is crucial that NECU institutions learn about the specific Indigenous and/or slaveholding histories of the lands on which they sit.[7] Simply learning for the sake of interest is insufficient, however. Honest and searching inquiry ultimately provides an indispensable foundation for tracing how that history informs the ways institutions still function today. Charles W. Mills cautions about "the mystification of the past"—namely, an "airbrushed white narrative of discovery, settlement, and building of a shining city on a hill" that completely denies "the extent of Native American and black victimization"—because the mystification of the past "underwrites the mystification of the present." He offers the example of the "erasure of Jim Crow" that allows white persons to assume income inequality between Blacks and whites is due to Black people's laziness, not the utter lack of a level playing field.[8]

Beyond giving an honest and searching account of institutional history lies a yet more challenging challenge: accepting *responsibility* for what white people and white institutions have inherited, whether they would have welcomed that inheritance or not. This can be difficult for those who consider themselves "good white people." Whiteness studies scholar Shannon Sullivan analyzes the ways that "good white people"—that is, those white people actually engaged in racial justice work—remain in certain respects Martin Luther King's "white moderates" of today.[9] She explains that many white people who engage in social justice work often project racism onto "bad white people," both those who today are overtly racist in their attitudes and behaviors and those who lived long ago. Both these tendencies can and do operate at the institutional level. The first case manifests as a conviction that a college campus just needs

---

7 Campuses in former slaveholding states have the most obvious work to do. Campuses located further north might decide to trace whether and how their original founding may have benefited from the broader slavery economy, given, for example, the fact that enslaved persons picked cotton in the South to provide raw materials for Northern textile mills.

8 Charles W. Mills, "White Ignorance," in *Race and Epistemologies of Ignorance*, ed. Shannon Sullivan and Nancy Tuana (Albany: SUNY Press, 2007), 31.

9 Shannon Sullivan, *Good White People: The Problem with Middle Class Anti-Racism* (Albany: SUNY Press, 2014); Martin Luther King, Jr., "Letter from a Birmingham Jail" (April 3, 1963), in *Why We Can't Wait* (New York: Signet, 2000).

more good intentions rather than policy change, as if to say, "Sure, there is much work to do to improve our campus climate, but mostly we just need to be kinder and more aware." In the second case, one might hear, "Well, we know better now. We just need to move on and finally leave that sordid past behind us." Both approaches convey a desire to distance oneself, personally and institutionally, from those who have so clearly perpetuated white supremacist values. Contemporary white people distancing themselves, as individuals or institutions, from white people of the past, however, means failing to sufficiently notice or acknowledge the ways that history lives on. From where might NECU institutions draw courage to do such uncomfortable work?

Confessing and Repenting White Histories

The Lutheran practice of confession and repentance offers a tool to support NECU PWIs as they seek courage and conviction to draw closer to the problematic parts of their heritage. Offering up the practice of confession and repentance may seem rather obvious in the context of racial justice efforts. But a closer look at how the Lutheran tradition understands and engages this common Christian practice can support fresh institutional practices that challenge prevailing sociocultural tendencies and help campuses engage their missional imperative to grapple with the fullness of their institutional legacies.

Martin Luther posited that humans without exception are "curved in on themselves" (*incurvatus in se*), that is, self-concerned at the expense of life-giving relationship to either God or neighbor or the wider world. In contemporary terms, this might manifest in various postures, from pride or grandiosity/narcissism to even depression. Intriguingly, this self-oriented posture, however it manifests, involves not simply static navel-gazing but a dynamic movement of drawing into one's orbit anything that might shore up one's ego or standing in the world. With this image, Luther illustrates that the existential mistake of the *incurvatus* is relying on the self and one's own capacities for salvation rather than relying on God's grace. I believe—and Luther would agree—that the ethical mistake of the *incurvatus* is using other people and creatures as objects and means to one's own ends.

In the context of racial justice and the historical reckoning it requires, considering the *incurvatus* image as descriptive of not just an individual but a group is useful. Specifically, the *incurvatus* profoundly captures the movement of white settler colonialism and its practices of displacing and killing Indigenous peoples and enslaving African peoples. Narcissistically self-concerned, white settlers to North America engaged other peoples only on European terms (at best) and as disposable objects (at worst). Employing a collective understanding of the *incurvatus* can also support NECU institutions as they consider patterns of collective self-involvement or self-preservation that may be habitual but not necessarily missional.

The move from the personal to the collective can be both theologically and psychologically uncomfortable, even threatening, for some, but there are strong traditions of corporate confession in Lutheran and other Christian churches. Along with other Christian theologians, Luther appreciates that individuals are born into a broken world, in which perfect action is impossible.[10] People do harm to others knowingly and unknowingly, not only directly but by participating in unjust systems, again knowingly and unknowingly. That is to say, sin operates relationally and often collectively. The primacy of the individual within Western philosophical and theological thinking, combined with the vast complexity of such systems, can make thinking collectively a challenge. But it is necessary, especially for persons and institutions formed primarily by white Western values that prize individualism without considering its shadow side.

Resonating with Sullivan's insight about white people's tendency to distance themselves from other "lesser" white people, Black Buddhist teacher Ruth King observes that white people "tend to experience the world through individual identity" rather than group

---

10 See Anthony Bateza's chapter in the present volume (189–203) for an extended account of sin and tragic/constrained action.

identity, "as well-meaning, hardworking individuals unaware of themselves as a racial group."[11] This allows the distancing that Sullivan describes and also problematically occludes participation in collective and structural forms of racial privilege and racial supremacy. If this is true on the individual level, it is equally important at the institutional level for predominantly and persistently white NECU institutions. NECU schools must ask themselves, "In what ways did our institutional ancestors function as excessively self-concerned? Whom did they harm? As predominantly white institutions today, how do we continue to function as self-concerned? Do we prioritize loyalty over truth-telling, hubris over humility, expedience over mission?"

These are just a few questions to ask as part of moving into an institutional practice of collective confession and repentance. Nourished by the Lutheran tradition, NECU institutions have a missional calling to such work. It is possible for institutions to learn from this liturgical discipline and to engage in their own forms of it, even when institutions are comprised of people who claim a wide range of wisdom traditions and worldviews. Specifically, "confessing history and ourselves" requires institutions to confess their affiliation with institutional founders who created campuses on unceded Indigenous land and, for some, funded their new ventures on the backs of enslaved persons. Instead of attempting to distance themselves from these uncomfortable realities, they must confess that they are the direct beneficiaries of displacement, enslavement, and genocide. Such work will be neither comfortable nor easy. It will require deep and steady courage. Seeing their histories more clearly will reveal threads that remain woven in institutional culture. Thus with confession comes repentance, for deeds done and those ongoing.

Institution confession of racist histories has two levels. The first is to confess ignorance, both chosen and unchosen, about the history of displacement and destruction that has made institutional lives possible. At my own institution, Newberry College in South Carolina, this means grappling with the fact that its founder John Bachman

---

11 Ruth King, *Mindful of Race: Transforming Racism from the Inside Out* (Boulder: Sounds True, 2018), 46.

wrote sophisticated theological defenses of slavery and explanations of the inferiority of people of African descent. It also means examining the even earlier history of German and Scots-Irish settlers violently displacing the Cherokee peoples from their ancestral land. Each campus will have its own journey.

The second component of institutional confession asks more of NECU campuses than just investigating and learning untold histories. It is none other than confessing institutional responsibility as descendants and beneficiaries of the white colonizers and enslavers that made institutional lives possible, even if current campus constituencies believe they would have made different choices. Harder still, to do this with real integrity involves also holding open the possibility not only that they perhaps would *not* have acted differently, but also that they may perpetuate patterns today that continue to do harm.

Healer and therapist Susan Raffo powerfully describes how thousands of well-meaning white Christian women in the mid-nineteenth century answered the federal Indian Service's call to work in boarding schools for Native Americans, becoming "the primary force for the intimate work of forced assimilation; the violent remaking of home, children, and bodies that was the next wave after military occupation." Yet, Raffo astutely observes, these women understood their call to be to "give and serve and care and love," leading Raffo to challenge her readers to ask themselves how they too might perpetuate "giving, serving, and caring" on their own terms also.[12]

Although Raffo is speaking to contemporary healing practitioners, her article models and advocates for a process of collective self-inquiry that NECU institutions would do well to engage. Raffo demonstrates that callings, past and present, may feel deeply faithful while harboring deep harm. In their efforts to be positive vehicles for

---

12 Susan Raffo, "The Lineages Healers have to Contend with . . . Working with Ancestors of Purpose" (blog), www.susanraffo.com/blog/the-lineages-healers-have-to-contend-with-working-with-ancestors-of-purpose. To be clear, I am not commending Raffo's "ancestral inquiry" under the assumption that Lutheran institutions were involved in the residential school system for Indigenous children. This is part of the historical inquiry that each campus needs to engage.

education and enlightenment, what have NECU institutions failed to see in both the histories they narrate and the patterns that persist today? The practice of confession is a sort of vessel that can hold such inquiry, which, when done well, requires the courage of vulnerability and transparency. To confess is to participate in the process of "uncurling" from one's own ways of seeing, knowing, and doing. It may even prompt NECU schools to reassess their institutional identities by returning them afresh to vital questions of mission.

Confession alone will require much of NECU institutions, but confession works in tandem with repentance, a commitment not only to cease harmful behaviors but also to actively do otherwise. Put simply, confession without repentance is empty, while repentance without confession risks perpetuating harm. Repentance is where the work of relational repair really begins to happen. Within the Lutheran tradition, there is a natural flow from repentance to reparative justice, that is, justice that seeks to mend the social fabric and foster communal relations generative for all involved. This is an outflow and reflection of God's grace which functions to free the faithful precisely so that they can turn toward their neighbor. Below are profiles of several NECU institutions doing reparative work, for example, proactively fostering educational access for Native American and Black students. Bold consideration of repatriation for Indigenous peoples and reparations for descendants of enslaved persons should also be on the table. The challenge of imagining what forms these might take should motivate conversation, not foreclose it.

It is worth noting that in the Lutheran tradition, confession and repentance are a regular practice and thus a continual, iterative process. Likewise, the institutional work should also be iterative. For those of us doing this work on NECU campuses, we investigate, we learn more, we go deeper. We confess, we repent. Repeat. It is also important to note that this practice is not about self-flagellation or inducing guilt or shame. Rather, confession is about self-honesty at the personal and institutional levels. It is about asking how we are falling short of our calling, whether to God or to the mission of our institutions. It is ultimately about turning again and again to the neighbor and pursuing the work of repair. With this theological wellspring, it is no surprise that many NECU institutions are engaged in reparative justice, which focuses on healing the social fabric through reconciliation, never forgetting the past but always working toward common flourishing.

NECU Institutions Facing History and Themselves

NECU institutions have much reckoning to do with the histories of violence that have made their institutional lives possible. While much remains to be done, many schools are working hard to live into a missional commitment to face those histories as a broader expression of the Lutheran commitment to reparative justice. At the time of this writing, Augsburg University, Augustana College (Rock Island, IL), Augustana University (Sioux Falls, SD), Concordia College, Gustavus Adolphus College, and Luther College at the University of Regina (SK, Canada) all have noteworthy initiatives underway that wrestle with where their histories intersect with the legacy of settler colonialism.[13] Two are profiled below. Colleges in the southeastern United States are likewise striving to make the slaveholding legacy of their campuses a central part of their institutional storytelling, and Roanoke College's work is also profiled below.

Luther College at the University of Regina in Regina, Saskatchewan lives out a bold commitment to justice for First Nations, as indicated by the "Indigenous Initiatives" link appearing among major institutional priorities on their home page. Luther College has institutionally pledged to the "94 Calls to Action" of Canada's Truth and Reconciliation Commission on residential schools. One central initiative, *Project of Heart*, is an eight-week experience that uses an artistic approach to teach participants about

---

13 Augsburg University and Augustana College have received "Reframing the Institutional Saga" grants from the Network for Vocation in Undergraduate Education (NetVUE). The grants enable the institutions to reframe and re-narrate institutional histories and renew institutional vocations with an eye toward previously excluded groups and marginalized perspectives. For a description of these projects, see https://www.cic.edu/p/NetVUE/Documents/2021-NetVUE-Reframing-Institutional-Saga-Summaries.pdf.

the history of the residential school system forced upon Indigenous children in Canada. The program not only teaches about this violent legacy but also commemorates the thousands of children who died in the schools, seeks to understand the intergenerational trauma that continues to impact Indigenous peoples in Canada, and calls all Canadians to work for justice and build right relationships. Over two hundred students, staff, faculty, and community members have participated in the program. Luther College also provides financial support and mentoring for the University of Regina's *Canadian Roots Exchange* (CRE) cohort. CRE is a national organization that trains Indigenous and non-Indigenous young people, ages 18–29, to form Reconciliation Teams that work to teach about the living legacy of colonialism and to envision a more just and inclusive Canada.

Augustana University (Sioux Falls, SD), located on the ancestral territory of the Oceti Sakowin (Seven Council Fires), also has a long history of learning about and celebrating Indigenous peoples while working toward expanding educational access to Native American students. Augustana's commitment to advancing appreciation for Native American studies spans the university, with programs sponsored by the Center for Western Studies; Augustana Campus Ministry; and AU's Center for Diversity, Equity, and Inclusion, among others. Local churches also partner with the university to sponsor educational and artistic programs. Expanding educational access is an institutional commitment in alignment with the university's Vision 2030 strategic plan. Building on past programs that have paired Augustana students with local Native American youth in order to offer a window into postsecondary education, the university's commitment to diversify its student body includes a specific focus on access for Native American students. Established by faculty and alumni, the Prairie Sage Scholarship Endowment currently supports one full-time Native American student studying anthropology. The long-range goal is to provide scholarship support for multiple Native American and First Nations students studying "academic storytelling disciplines," from journalism, literature, and history to law, art, philosophy, and religion.

Institutions in the southeastern United States are called to face histories not only of Indigenous displacement and genocide but also of enslavement. As a member of the Universities Studying Slavery consortium, Roanoke College is leading the way among NECU institutions in the Southeast. In summer 2020, Roanoke established a *Center for Studying Structures of Race*, whose explicit aim is to link contemporary questions of race to the legacy of slavery. A venue for teaching, research, and community engagement, the center is housed in renovated slave quarters and thus sits physically inside the history of the area. Although the college itself did not own enslaved persons, it is proactively working to have an honest and ongoing conversation about the college's physical and financial heritage from slavery, according to center director Dr. Jesse Bucher. Like many buildings on southern campuses, Roanoke's oldest, most prominent building was built by enslaved persons, and in spring 2021, the college held a ceremony to unveil permanent commemorative plaques honoring the lives of those skilled yet enslaved laborers.

There is no way to undo the destructive harms of settler colonialism and the institution of slavery. NECU institutions must always be open to listening and learning, aware that some of the steps they take may be faltering.[14] Land acknowledgments are important, but they can be vacuous, and institutions should be in conversation with local Indigenous communities about how they would like to be acknowledged. Likewise, calls to "decolonize" course syllabi risk treating the concept of decolonization as a metaphor instead of what it really means: to repatriate lands to Indigenous peoples and, equally vital, to "rematriate," by returning materials and artifacts to their original owners and by restoring cultures, knowledges, and ways of life.[15] A

---

14 Inspired by poet and professor, Phil Bryant, many at Gustavus Adolphus College speak about "missteps" and "faltering steps" in their diversity, equity, and inclusion efforts. See his essay, "Dancing with Diversity: Our Strides, Missteps, and Hopes" in *Rooted in Heritage, Open to the World: Reflections on the Distinctive Character of Gustavus Adolphus College*, 2nd ed., ed. Marcia J. Bunge (Minneapolis: Lutheran University Press, 2018), 101–5.

15 Eve Tuck and Wayne K. Yang "Decolonization Is Not a Metaphor." *Decolonization: Indigeneity, Education & Society* 1:1 (2012):1–40. The authors note that while repatriation, the return of land, is the ideal, it is both equally important

truly decolonized curriculum leads to action for justice. Similarly, as
Roanoke has shown, unearthing the ongoing legacy of slavery is only
the beginning. Will NECU institutions in the southeastern US challenge themselves to consider what reparations might look like? With
a significant proportion of Black students on NECU campuses—
over 30 percent of Newberry's student body, for example—there is
potential for creative solutions and significant impact.

From the institutional initiatives profiled above and at other
NECU institutions, there seem to be several key strategies for doing
this vital but challenging work. Here I name five.

First, NECU schools should begin with the institutional mission
as rooted in the Lutheran tradition. Although the missions of NECU
member schools vary in the details, they share a common calling
as outlined in *Rooted and Open*: NECU institutions are "called and
empowered to love the neighbor so that all may flourish." This means
engaging in a process of repair as much as the fresh pursuit of the
common good.

Second, because the Lutheran liberal arts heritage celebrates freedom of inquiry, such inquiry, if truly free, can encourage genuine
curiosity about specific institutional histories and how they might
inform institutional patterns and habits that persist today.[16] What
institutions discover may haunt them, but staying curious can infuse
their inquiry with energy.

Third, the Lutheran tradition proclaims the imperfection of
humans. This should not serve as an excuse for inaction or indifference. Rather, it can liberate institutions to keep moving forward—
even when knowledge is dim and steps are imperfect. Knowing that
neither humans nor their creations are expected to be perfect, institutions can stay courageous—even when paths of discovery lead to
uncomfortable or haunting truths.

---

and within closer reach to "rematriate" the other elements of Indigenous culture that colonialism stole or destroyed.
16 For more on the intersection between intellectual curiosity and self-critical
institutional postures, see Samuel Torvend's chapter in the present volume
(31–43).

Fourth, and by the same logic, the Lutheran tradition proclaims the limitations of humans. The full task of reparative justice is monumental, even at a single institution. Rather than an excuse for inaction, this reality can motivate institutions to start in just one or two places and focus.

Finally, the Lutheran tradition challenges and empowers imperfect, limited humans to channel holy love and mercy into the world. This takes myriad forms. It may be as quiet and subtle as gathering a small group to take a deep dive into local history. Or it may be bolder. What might rematriation or reparations look like on a particular NECU campus, and what courage is required to even consider the question, much less try to start to answer it?

Conclusion

At the time of this writing, Canada is facing a renewed reckoning with the violence that European settlers perpetrated against First Nations peoples through a system of residential schools that kidnapped, incarcerated, and attempted to assimilate Indigenous children into European culture. Recently, mass graves for these children have been discovered in Canada, and more are expected to be found throughout North America. The United States is not far behind in reckoning with its own legacy of residential schools. Secretary of the Interior Deb Haaland (of the Pueblo of Laguna peoples and the first Native American to serve as a cabinet secretary) has launched a comprehensive review of residential schools in the United States. Yet resistance to this work persists. Critical Race Theory (CRT), a sub-discipline of the legal field, has been turned into a political flashpoint. The accusation is that CRT is being taught in K-12 classrooms, causing white students to experience shame over their cultural heritage. In response to this misinformation about CRT, public school boards across several states have banned the teaching of anything related to race in the classroom with hefty fines for violations.

What leads some communities to face with courage the fullness of history—including violence perpetrated by their ancestors—while others seem unwilling to face the same atrocities or to acknowledge that the past lives on? As Lutheran institutions, NECU schools have a missional calling to model how to face the violent histories that are woven into their institutional histories, not as a means of shaming and silencing, but as a means of better understanding their present circumstances and of more richly imagining a future in which "all may flourish." The Lutheran practice of confession and repentance situates itself firmly within the larger context of God's grace: the appreciation that the faithful can neither earn God's love and mercy nor do anything to stop their ceaseless flow. Likewise, an institutional practice of facing itself in history and repenting situates itself firmly within a broader context of hope and possibility—and amidst community. If, as Martin Luther King, Jr. says, "the arc of the universe bends toward justice," we who work at NECU institutions need not fear facing history and ourselves. We do so courageously and step forth both humbly and boldly along that arc.

For Further Study

Dunbar-Ortiz, Roxanne. *An Indigenous People's History of the United States*. Boston: Beacon, 2014.

Mahn, Jason A. "The Cheap Grace of White Privilege and the Costly Grace of Repentant Antiracism." *Currents in Theology & Mission* 47:3 (July 2020): 8–14.

Okun, Tema. "Characteristics of White Supremacy Culture." https://www.whitesupremacyculture.info.

Smith, Clint. *How the Word Is Passed: A Reckoning with the History of Slavery across America*. New York: Little, Brown and Company. 2021.

Tuck, Eve and Wayne K. Yang. "Decolonization Is Not a Metaphor." *Decolonization: Indigeneity, Education & Society* 1:1 (2012): 1–40.

University's Studying Slavery Consortium. https://slavery.virginia.edu/universities-studying-slavery/.

Upstander Project. www.upstanderproject.org.

14

Race, Climate, and Decolonizing Liberal Arts Education

Vic Thasiah, California Lutheran University

> The logic that led to slavery and segregation in the Americas, colonization and apartheid in Africa, and the rule of white supremacy throughout the world is the same one that leads to the exploitation of animals and the ravaging of nature. It is a mechanistic and instrumental logic that defines everything and everybody in terms of their contribution to the development and defense of white world supremacy. . . . The fight for justice cannot be segregated but must be integrated with the fight for life in all its forms.
>
> —James H. Cone[1]

Facing existential threats in the United States is nothing new.[2] The bare existence of Black and Indigenous peoples in this country has been under threat for over four hundred years. As the climate changes, though, more and more people in this country are facing existential threats that were relatively unknown before.[3] Increasing average temperatures, rising sea levels, extreme weather, ecosystem

---

1 James H. Cone, *Risks of Faith: The Emergence of a Black Theology of Liberation, 1968–1998* (Boston: Beacon, 1999), 138.

2 Mary Anaïsse Heglar, "Climate Change Isn't the First Existential Threat," *Zora*, February 18, 2019, https://zora.medium.com/sorry-yall-but-climate-change-ain-t-the-first-existential-threat-b3c999267aa0.

3 See Nylah Burton, "Meet the Young Activists of Color Who are Leading the Charge Against Climate Disaster," *Vox*, October 11, 2019, https://www.vox.com/identities/2019/10/11/20904791/young-climate-activists-of-color.

degradation, biodiversity loss, and mass extinction directly related to climate change endanger public health, water supply, food security, decent livelihoods, economic opportunities, and international relations. Like the above threats to Black and Indigenous peoples, these environmental and humanitarian crises, caused by similar colonial and capitalist dynamics, disproportionately and unjustly affect Indigenous communities, communities of color, and low-income communities.[4] Simply put, climate disruption is one of the largest looming factors in our country's present and future, as college-age youth are well aware.[5]

Meanwhile, the Association of American Colleges and Universities (AAC&U) published the guide, *What Liberal Education Looks Like*, to "clearly describe the learning all students need for success in an uncertain future and for addressing the compelling issues we face as a democracy and as a global community."[6] However, this program for liberal arts education, while grounded, in principle, in equity and inclusion, does not seem to engage anything regarding ecology in general or climate disruption in particular. This makes sense, perhaps, given the traditional orientation of a liberal arts education to the three spheres: life, work, and democracy. Given the many above ways that the climate is significantly and progressively destabilizing these three spheres though—not to mention the very basis of all three, the planet itself—liberal arts educators must better orient higher education by adding a fourth sphere—that of ecology, or human–Earth relations. Even on its own terms of equity and inclusion, climate disruption should be of major concern to the AAC&U.

A key UN study observes a "*vicious cycle*, whereby *initial* inequality causes the disadvantaged groups to suffer *disproportionately*

---

4 M. Ballew et al., "Which Racial/Ethnic Groups Care Most about Climate Change?" Yale Program on Climate Change Communication, 2020, https://climatecommunication.yale.edu/publications/race-and-climate-change/.

5 See, for example, "Climate Change Ranks Highest as Vital Issue of Our Time: Generation Z Survey," Amnesty International, December 10, 2019, https://www.amnesty.org/en/latest/news/2019/12/climate-change-ranks-highest-as-vital-issue-of-our-time/. Over 10,000 youth from twenty-two countries in this survey ranked climate change as the most important issue of our time.

6 AAC&U, *What Liberal Education Looks Like*, May, 2020, https://secure.aacu.org/imis/ItemDetail?iProductCode=E-WHATLELL.

from the adverse effects of climate change, resulting in greater *subsequent* inequality."[7] The study identifies three main channels (both within country and across countries) "through which the inequality-aggravating effect of climate change materializes," namely: (1) "increase in the *exposure* of the disadvantaged groups to the adverse effects of climate change"; (2) "increase in their *susceptibility* to damage caused by climate change"; and (3) "decrease in their *ability to cope and recover* from the damage suffered."[8]

Activist and academic climate justice efforts confronting environmental destabilization and social inequality are the places to start in developing a liberal arts education along the above lines. In their introduction to the *Routledge Handbook of Climate Justice*, Tahseen Jafry, Michael Mikulewicz, and Karin Helwig summarize the concerns of these climate justice efforts well:

> Historically, industrialized countries have developed by implementing an economic model which has disproportionately exploited the Earth's resources and exacerbated socio-economic inequality across scales. Meanwhile, evidence indicates that the less-industrialized countries feel more severely the detrimental effects of this development model and the impacts of climate change that it has produced . . . The faces of this climate injustice have often been those who are in the frontline of climate-related impacts—the poorest and most marginalized in both the Global North and the Global South, who frequently lack access to the economic, social and political structures necessary to ensure that their views are recognized, their interests represented and their needs addressed.[9]

In what follows, I urge Lutheran colleges and universities to begin here and now, and make climate justice—that is, active "responsibility for the impacts of greenhouse gas emissions on the poorest and

---

7 S. Nazrul Islam and John Winkel, "Climate Change and Social Inequality," DESA Working Paper No. 152 (October 2017), UN Department of Economic and Social Affairs, https://www.un.org/esa/desa/papers/2017/wp152_2017.pdf. See also Tahseen Jafry, Michael Mikulewicz, and Karin Helwig, "Introduction: Justice in the Era of Climate Change," in *Routledge Handbook of Climate Justice*, ed. Tahseen Jafry (New York: Routledge, 2019).

8 Islam and Winkel, "Climate Change and Social Inequality," 1.

9 Jafry, Mikulewicz, and Helwig, "Introduction," 2.

most vulnerable people in society by critically addressing inequality and promoting transformative approaches to address the root causes of climate change"—central alongside vocational preparation for life, work, and democracy. They must educate students also for climate justice, for the sake of all species and the planet itself.[10] Lutheran educational communities understand themselves as places that "equip graduates who are called and empowered to serve their neighbors so that all may flourish."[11] Climate disruption is among the most serious threats to all of us, both human and nonhuman, and our flourishing.

One challenge is that, as Lutheran higher education undergoes reform based on BIPOC (Black, Indigenous, and People of Color) activism on campus and beyond for racial and Indigenous justice, disconnects and competitive perceptions tend to put climate change on the backburner. For example, there is a frequent misperception that any increase in institutional attention and resources dedicated to minimizing climate change entails a corresponding decrease in attention and resources dedicated to maximizing racial and Indigenous equity. As Lutheran colleges and universities respond to such activism and reconceive their liberal arts education, a return to the guiding principles of the Network of ELCA Colleges and Universities (NECU) set out in *Rooted and Open* can help them resist and reframe such disconnects and competitive perceptions. Thus they will better prepare students to serve, as *Rooted and Open* puts it, both "natural and human communities."[12] For as BIPOC activists

---

10 Mandy Meikle, Jake Wilson, and Tahseen Jafry, "Climate Justice: Between Mammon and Mother Earth," *International Journal of Climate Change Strategies and Management* 8:4 (2016): 497.

11 NECU, *Rooted and Open: The Common Calling of the Network of ELCA Colleges and Universities*, 3. https://download.elca.org/ELCA%20Resource%20 Repository/Rooted_and_Open.pdf.

12 NECU, *Rooted and Open*, 7. See also Cynthia Moe-Lobeda, "Climate Justice, Environmental Racism, and a Lutheran Moral Vision," *Intersections* 36 (Fall 2012): 22–27; Ernest Simmons, "*Semper Reformanda*: Lutheran Higher Education in the Anthropocene," in *The Vocation of Lutheran Higher Education*, ed. Jason A. Mahn (Minneapolis: Lutheran University Press, 2016), 191–200; and *Eco-Reformation: Grace and Hope for a Planet in Peril*, ed. Lisa E. Dahill and James B. Martin-Schramm (Eugene, OR: Cascade, 2016).

themselves have taught, there is no racial or Indigenous justice without climate justice.

BIPOC Climate Justice Leadership

After the killing of George Floyd, protests inspired by Black Lives Matter in Minneapolis and across the United States, combined with reporting on the disproportionate impacts of COVID-19 on BIPOC communities, forced many environmental and climate activists, especially those not necessarily identifying as environmental or climate *justice* activists, to reconsider the relation between racial justice and equity work on the one hand, and climate action and environmental stewardship on the other.[13] Two important interventions, representing long-held clarity on this relation among environmental and climate *justice* activists, made at the time were by Elizabeth Yeampierre, co-chair of the Climate Justice Alliance, and Hop Hopkins, the Sierra Club's Director of Organizational Transformation.[14] They each show how racial dehumanization and social inequality, on the one hand, and environmental degradation and climate disruption, on the other, historically coincide, develop side by side and will remain inextricably and inescapably intertwined. Both Yeampierre and Hopkins therefore recommend that they be engaged together. As Hopkins puts it, "You can't have climate change without sacrifice zones, and you can't have sacrifice zones without disposable people, and you can't have disposable people without racism."[15]

---

13 Environmental and climate activists questioned themselves, for example, about connections between histories of redlining, pollution levels, heat islands, and public health (e.g., preexisting respiratory conditions).

14 See the interview of Elizabeth Yeampierre in Beth Gardiner, "Unequal Impact: The Deep Links Between Racism and Climate Change," *Yale Environment 360*, June 9, 2020, https://e360.yale.edu/features/unequal-impact-the-deep-links-between-inequality-and-climate-change. (The Climate Justice Alliance is a coalition of over seventy organizations focused on addressing racial and economic inequities together with climate change). See also Hop Hopkins, "Racism Is Killing the Planet," *Sierra Club Magazine*, June 8, 2020, https://www.sierraclub.org/sierra/racism-killing-planet.

15 Hopkins, "Racism Is Killing the Planet."

The major factors causing climate disruption and directly related inequalities, according to these climate justice activists, are rooted in the colonial oppression of Black and Indigenous communities and the capitalist plundering and destruction of the environment. Regarding their historical connections and continuities, Yeampierre maintains,

> Climate change is the result of a legacy of extraction, of colonialism, of slavery . . . The idea of killing black people or indigenous people, all of that has a long, long history that is centered on capitalism and the extraction of our land and our labor in this country . . . .
>
> With the arrival of slavery comes a repurposing of the land, chopping down of trees, disrupting water systems and other ecological systems that comes with supporting the effort to build a capitalist society and to provide resources for the privileged, using the bodies of black people to facilitate that. The same thing in terms of the disruption and the stealing of indigenous land. There was a taking of land, not just for expansion, but to search for gold, to take down mountains and extract fossil fuels out of mountains.[16]

Such connections and continuities are instances of what activist-writer Charles Eisenstein calls "morphic resonance." He observes, "The demonization and dehumanization of the enemy is little different from the desacralization of nature upon which ecocide depends. To render nature into an *other* undeserving of reverence and respect, an object to dominate, control, and subjugate, is of a kind with the dehumanization and exploitation of human beings."[17] Hopkins views the connections and continuities in these terms:

> The pollution-spewing global mega-corporations that created Cancer Alley are just the latest evolution of the extractive white-settler mindset that cleared the forests and plowed the prairies. And just as the settlers had to believe and tell stories to dehumanize the people they killed, plundered, and terrorized, today's systems of extraction can only work by dehumanizing people. Back then we had the Doctrine of Discovery, and today it's the doctrine of neoliberalism that

---

16 Gardiner, "Unequal Impact."
17 Charles Eisenstein, *Climate: A New Story* (Berkeley, CA: North Atlantic, 2018), 20.

say it's OK to value some lives more than others, that it's OK for some people to have clean air while others struggle to breathe.[18]

Bundling the global pandemic, the protests surrounding George Floyd's murder, and the myriad and complex environmental and social issues this country faces, Yeampierre concludes with this:

> The communities that are most impacted by Covid, or by pollution, it's not surprising that they're the ones that are going to be most impacted by extreme weather events. And it's not surprising that they're the ones that are targeted for racial violence. It's all the same communities, all over the United States. And you can't treat one part of the problem without the other, because it's so systemic.[19]

So what should we do? Hopkins calls for the dismantling of white supremacy, and Yeampierre calls for a just transition, "a process that moves us away from a fossil fuel economy to local livable economies, to regenerative economies."[20] Hopkins explains,

> If our society valued all people's lives equally, there wouldn't be any sacrifice zones to put the pollution in. If every place was sacred, there wouldn't be a Cancer Alley. We would find other ways to advance science and create shared wealth without poisoning anyone. We would find a way to share equally both the benefits and the burdens of prosperity. If we valued everyone's lives equally, if we placed the public health and well-being of the many above the profits of a few, there wouldn't be a climate crisis. There would be nowhere to put a coal plant, because no one would accept the risks of living near such a monster if they had the power to choose.[21]

As Lutheran colleges and universities "equip graduates who are called and empowered to serve their neighbors so that all may flourish," Hopkins's dismantling of white supremacy and Yeampierre's implementation of a just transition suggest key conditions for such flourishing. The latter goal, based on Climate Justice Alliance's

---

18 Hopkins, "Racism Is Killing the Planet."
19 Gardiner, "Unequal Impact."
20 Gardiner, "Unequal Impact."
21 Hopkins, "Racism Is Killing the Planet."

mission, has to do with "approaching production and consumption cycles holistically and waste free. The transition itself must be just and equitable; redressing past harms and creating new relationships of power for the future through reparations."[22] This kind of climate justice is environmentally, culturally, scientifically, and politically challenging. And yet it should be of central intellectual and practical concern, alongside vocational preparation for life, work, and democracy, to a liberal arts education.

Decolonizing Liberal Arts Education

The above climate justice work informs the task of decolonizing liberal arts education. Both strive to hold race, class, gender, and the Earth together, and to acknowledge Indigenous and slaveholding lands and legacies. Such acknowledgment includes both recognition and reparation.[23] Decolonizing liberal arts education specifically involves revising campus mission statements accordingly, implementing statement values across campus, and setting up effective oversight to see such implementation through.

The current President of California Lutheran University (CLU), Lori E. Varlotta, recently charged CLU's dean of the College of Arts and Sciences, Jessica L. Lavariega Monforti, to lead a general education task force. Varlotta remarked that "many students and their families are struggling to discern what type of postsecondary education best prepares twenty-first-century learners for the personal and professional changes, challenges, and opportunities that mark today's world."[24] In response, Lutheran theologian and former CLU professor of religion Lisa Dahill started organizing professors already working on several environmental and sustainability fronts.

---

22 See Climate Justice Alliance's principles for a just transition: https://climatejusticealliance.org/wp-content/uploads/2018/06/CJA_JustTransition_Principles_final_hi-rez.pdf.

23 See the chapter by Krista E. Hughes in this volume for more (205–20), including how "decolonizing" must entail the concrete work of reparations, repatriations, and "rematriations."

24 Email from the CLU Office of the President to the CLU faculty on June 29, 2021.

With faculty from the departments of religion, English, sociology, and earth and environmental sciences, Dahill called the CLU faculty to develop a liberal arts education modeled on CLU graduate school Pacific Lutheran Theological Seminary's teaching and learning at the nexus of race, class, gender, and Earth that "advances students' adequate understanding and skills/capacities for leadership toward local and global sustainability, resilience, innovation, environmental justice, and human/interspecies survival befitting the urgent crisis we and the larger planetary community are facing."[25]

Like the BIPOC activists above, Dahill insists that climate justice is a key concern around which to develop CLU's liberal arts education. She writes,

> The global exploitation of carbon resources driving this accelerating climate chaos is the result of historical and ongoing racist and colonial exploitation of people of color and their environments, in which those who have contributed least to climate change are most vulnerable to its effects, while those (largely white North Americans and Europeans) who have contributed most to climate chaos are least vulnerable, with the effect that climate upheavals both mirror and undergird all other forms of white supremacy.[26]

While driven by global existential threats to humans and other-than-human life, Dahill's call to action is place-based. She reminds CLU of being on "the unceded ancestral homelands of the Chumash peoples, the original stewards of the land [who] understand the interconnectedness of all things and maintain harmony with nature." CLU's liberal arts education should thus "honor the Chumash peoples' enduring responsibility to care for Mother Earth." Dahill also points out, "Ventura County [where CLU is located] represents ground zero on numerous interlocking measures of climate change already affecting the university's functioning—a nexus of

---

25 Letter from Lisa Dahill to the CLU Faculty Senate, "CLU General Education: Centering in Climate Justice and a Livable Future for All," June 30, 2021. Dahill is currently Miriam Therese Winter Professor of Transformative Leadership and Spirituality at Hartford International University for Religion and Peace in Hartford, CT.
26 Letter from Lisa Dahill, "CLU General Education."

wildfire and temperature threats, desertification, economic impacts, and human suffering—presenting a microcosm of global destabilization conducive to study these phenomena."[27] Developing a liberal arts education on unceded Chumash lands begins by modeling itself on an Indigenous education responsible to and protective of its land communities, and by honoring Indigenous knowledge and stewardship, past, present, and future.

Related endeavors at Pacific Lutheran University (PLU) in Tacoma, WA, can also contribute to decolonizing liberal arts education. PLU's mission "to educate for lives of thoughtful inquiry, service, leadership, and care of others, their communities and the earth" explicitly includes environmental stewardship in a way that CLU's current mission ("to educate leaders for a global society who are committed to service and justice") does not. The position of associate vice president for Diversity, Justice, and Sustainability at PLU also puts this value of environmental stewardship as equal to the values of justice and diversity. These three values—diversity, justice, and sustainability—together shape the university's curriculum and practices, according to PLU's planning documents from 2010–20. What is more, PLU's environmental studies program puts these three values into practice. The online reading list for an intersectional environmentalism and environmental justice collaborative intends to provide PLU students, staff, and faculty with resources "to engage with and take part in the kind of in-depth critical reflection, dialogue and, ideally, transformation that antiracism and the climate change crisis call for and that our institutional commitment to diversity, justice, and sustainability, and our mission of care ask of us."[28] Another instance of PLU's diversity, justice, and sustainability (DJS) values in action is the Environmental and Social Justice Floor in DJS Community in Ordal Hall, a community that "seeks to create a safe, supportive, and diverse environment that challenges students

---

27 Letter from Lisa Dahill, "CLU General Education."
28 See PLU's Intersectional Environmentalism and Environmental Justice Collaborative Reading List: https://www.plu.edu/environmental-studies/wp-content/uploads/sites/103/2020/06/reading-list_-instersectional-environmentalism_environmental-justice_june-2020.pdf.

to explore social and environmental justice issues and begin the work towards equity as engaged citizens on both local and global levels."[29]

It remains to be seen whether CLU will reform its liberal arts education along climate justice lines and transcend the specific campus and broader cultural disconnects and competitive perceptions that make pursuing racial justice on the one hand, and climate justice on the other, a zero-sum game. In the meantime, key elements of Lutheran higher education set out in *Rooted and Open* can help Lutheran college and university faculty, staff, and students hold the two together.

Social and Ecological Embeddedness

Rooted and Open presents the common calling of NECU schools— "to equip graduates who are called and empowered to serve their neighbors so that all may flourish"—as a calling in which they are to find their identity. Since "neighbors" is inclusive of both human and other-than-human species, and since "all" means all life, the vision is comprehensive of the social and the ecological. According to *Rooted and Open*, "To be a neighbor means to seek to understand and serve people, communities and their needs. In the global and local communities in which our students move, they care for the people, space and ecology of a neighborhood; they work toward a common good."[30] Lutheran educational communities are *rooted*, an ecological metaphor, in Lutheran intellectual traditions, and thus *open to*, instead of being threatened by, engaging other religious and secular traditions. *Rooted and Open* is further rooted in ecology and service directed to climate justice, given the Lutheran conception of God's generous concern for creation:

> A common calling (*vocare*) creates advocacy (*ad+vocare*) for the sake of the neighbor to reduce suffering, build up the neighborhood and befriend the earth. Because these institutions affirm the connectedness of all forms and aspects of life in the world, they invite

---

29 See PLU's themed learning communities: https://www.plu.edu/residential-life/themed-learning-communities/djs/esj/.

30 NECU, *Rooted and Open*, 5.

students to see themselves as parts of larger wholes. They encourage them to weigh the impact of their actions on other creatures, both human and non-human.[31]

Two other key parts of *Rooted and Open* are supportive of making climate justice central to a liberal arts education, alongside vocational preparation for life, work, and democracy. First are the educational priorities based on Lutheran theological views about God coming into the world as a human animal. Second are Lutheran higher education's attention to marginalized creatures, which follows from Jesus's experience of unjust conditions, suffering, and death.

Based on the former theological conception of incarnation, Lutheran higher education treats individuals in their social and ecological embeddedness, connecting racial equity and environmental stewardship. Again from *Rooted and Open*:

> The essential relationality of Lutheran theology believes that individuals flourish only as they are embedded in larger communities, families, civic spaces and ecosystems that are also empowered to flourish. Cherishing and protecting healthy communities go hand-in-hand with cherishing and protecting the well-being of individuals. In a dominant culture where goods are increasingly privatized and fought over, graduates of Lutheran institutions can consider the whole, creatively imagine mutual benefit, and work for the health of natural and human communities.[32]

Based on the latter theological conception, Martin Luther's "theology of the cross,"[33] Lutheran higher education centers the marginalized, calling students to be "attentive to people who need them most and places that call out for healing."[34] Lutheran educational communities should be critical of the ways traditional liberal arts education can, and often does, produce and proliferate Western ethnocentrism, white supremacy, and the destruction of the natural

---

31 NECU, *Rooted and Open*, 5–6.

32 NECU, *Rooted and Open*, 7.

33 See also the chapters by Caryn D. Riswold (173–87) and Deanna A. Thompson (235–46) in the present volume.

34 NECU, *Rooted and Open*, 6.

world, positioning non-Western peoples and traditions as less developed and less important, if not pathologizing and disregarding them. Colonial liberal arts education dehumanizes human communities and degenerates natural communities. Decolonizing liberal arts education humanizes and regenerates them. Among other things, being informed by Luther's theology of the cross means a liberal arts education that involves learning marginalized Indigenous epistemologies and engaging in the hard work of reparation and repatriation.

Conclusion

The AAC&U is right to be concerned about democracy alongside life and work. It is dysfunctional and desperately needs our attention. Their guide for liberal arts education notes,

> Today . . . a new American factionalism has emerged at the heart of the democratic process itself: where once party affiliation was based on provisional acceptance of a broad political philosophy and the policy ideas that flow from it, political parties now command factious allegiance. Impervious to reasoned argument, scornful of truth and dissenting views, and allergic to compromise, this new politics plays out simultaneously as internecine warfare and media spectacle and traffics in misinformation and incivility.[35]

A liberal arts education, according to the AAC&U, should "form the habits of heart and mind that liberate them and that equip them for, and dispose them to, civic involvement and the creation of a more just and inclusive society."[36] A more just and inclusive society necessarily means working for climate justice, however daunting current climate and political realities might be.[37] A liberal

---

35 AAC&U, "What Liberal Education Looks Like," 4. For more on Lutheran education in a politically divisive culture, see the chapters by Samuel Torvend (31–43) and Martha E. Stortz (57–71) in the present volume.

36 AAC&U, "Liberal Education," 4.

37 Jafry, Mikulewicz, and Helwig explain the political dimensions of climate justice well. "Climate change brings with it shifts in material and power balances, and a 'business-as-usual' scenario will entrench or further deepen inequalities and exacerbate environmental damage. It is not unreasonable to expect that

arts education should prepare students for vocations pertaining to life, work, democracy, *and Earth's ecosystems*, with all of these domains informed by BIPOC climate justice activists calling for the dismantling of white supremacy and the implementation of just transitions. The guiding principles of Lutheran higher education make this abundantly clear.

For Further Study

Dahill, Lisa E. and James B. Martin-Schramm, eds. *Eco-Reformation: Grace and Hope for a Planet in Peril*. Eugene, OR: Cascade, 2016.

Eisenstein, Charles. *Climate: A New Story*. Berkeley, CA: North Atlantic, 2018.

Gardiner, Beth. "Unequal Impact: The Deep Links Between Racism and Climate Change." *Yale Environment 360*, June 9, 2020. https://e360.yale.edu/features/unequal-impact-the-deep-links-between-inequality-and-climate-change.

Gilio-Whitaker, Dina. *As Long as Grass Grows: The Indigenous Fight for Environmental Justice, from Colonization to Standing Rock*. Boston: Beacon, 2020.

Hawken, Paul. *Regeneration: Ending the Climate Crisis in One Generation*. New York: Penguin, 2021.

Johnson, Ayana Elizabeth and Katharine K. Wilkinson, eds. *All We Can Save: Truth, Courage, and Solutions for the Climate Crisis*. New York: One World, 2021.

---

those who are materially and political disadvantaged will bear the brunt of climate impacts, while those at the top of the sociopolitical ladder steer their lives toward a more climate-proof future. Issues ranging from water access and food security, to health-related impacts of chronic and acute climate events, to the political exclusion from making decisions on how to address climate change impacts and from sharing the benefits of these decisions are only some of the problems that may be in store for many countries, cities, communities and individuals over the next few decades." "Introduction: Justice in the Era of Climate Change," 1.

15

Vocation, Deep Sadness, and Hope in a Virtual Real World

Deanna A. Thompson, St. Olaf College

On April 21, 2021, just minutes after Derek Chauvin was convicted of murdering George Floyd, I logged on to Zoom with a small group of St. Olaf staff and faculty convened by Dr. María Pabón, vice president for Equity and Inclusion. The purpose of the meeting was to decide how St. Olaf would respond to the Chauvin verdict and the potential aftermath. Bracing for a not-guilty verdict in their meeting earlier that day, the St. Olaf's president's leadership team had tentatively planned to declare a "Day of Healing" for the day following the verdict.

The sense of relief over the verdict was palpable from everyone on the call. Colleagues of color expressed shock that Chauvin was found guilty of murdering Floyd. Even though the initial hour after the verdict was announced was calm, Pabón led us to the decision that the campus needed a collective pause. For the first time in memory, St. Olaf canceled all classes and events for the coming day.

A Bouquet of Humanity

The following day on campus was a quiet one. Students I talked to took the day off from homework. Most attendees at Wednesday's chapel service of prayer were virtual, and associate college pastor Katie Fick began the service with the acknowledgement that healing cannot take place in a single day. The service focused on prayers of thanksgiving, prayers for healing, and prayers of our individual and collective hopes.[1]

After chapel, over one hundred staff and faculty met over Zoom to talk about the verdict and the trauma of the previous year—the relentless challenges of the pandemic and the toll it had taken on all of us across the campus. We talked about the trauma—especially for Black, Brown, Asian, and Indigenous people—brought on by Derek Chauvin's kneeling on the neck of George Floyd for 9 minutes and 29 seconds and the retraumatizing effects of how often the video was shown again during the trial. Staff and faculty expressed appreciation for the college's decision to create space to mourn, to breathe, to pause from this year like no other.

St. Olaf's Flaten Art Museum invited students to channel their emotions and energy into creating a thirty-foot mural with the words "Bouquet of Humanity" at its center, a phrase Minnesota attorney general Keith Ellison borrowed from attorney Jerry Blackwell to refer to the many courageous witnesses who testified at the trial.[2] From Darnella Frazier, the seventeen-year old who filmed Floyd's murder on her cell phone and shared it with the world, to Minneapolis Chief of Police, Medaria Arradondo, who broke the blue code of silence when he testified that Chauvin's actions were outside the bounds of acceptable police action, Blackwell and Ellison pointed to the courageous actions of a bouquet of people leading to the conviction that held Chauvin responsible for the unjust taking of the life of George Floyd.

Blackwell's image also gestured toward "the more" of the moment—a glimpse into the humanity of many who refused to let Floyd's death have the last word. The mural students created embodied the paradox of the awfulness of the previous year—Floyd's murder and other forms of racism (one AAPI student wove the words

---

1 Boe Memorial Chapel, *A Service of Prayer* (2021), St. Olaf College, https://www.stolaf.edu/multimedia/play/?c=3513.

2 Annalisa Merelli, "Chauvin Prosecutor Keith Ellison Makes a Powerful Call for 'the Work of our Generation,'" *Quartz*, April 20, 2021, https://qz.com/1999381/keith-ellison-after-chauvin-is-found-guilty-of-murdering-george-floyd/.

"I am many things but I am not a virus" into the mural)—together with a bold, beautiful witness to a "bouquet of humanity" that gifts us with glimpses of hope for a world transformed.

During the time of pandemics, we have faced unimaginable challenges that reveal new insights about our identity and mission in the landscape of twenty-first-century higher education. Using the day of healing at St. Olaf as a touchstone, this chapter will propose that explorations of vocation at Lutheran institutions be linked more intentionally to the sadness and trauma within our individual and collective lives. This chapter also suggests we become more conscientious of how the Lutheran vocational calling to neighbor love can and must encompass our relatedness in virtual as well as physical spaces in service of the hard work of inclusion and our ongoing commitment to the flourishing of all.

Pandemics, Vocation, and Deep Sadness

One of the hallmarks of Lutheran higher education is a commitment to providing students opportunities to explore meaningful vocation, as the St. Olaf's mission states. Writing in the early 2000s, St. Olaf Lutheran ethicist Doug Schuurman expressed concern about trends in higher education toward conflating vocation with career and the resulting narrowing of the ethical frame that is crucial to any Lutheran understanding of vocation. Schuurman urged Lutheran institutions to ensure that our framing of vocation is always on behalf of the neighbor.[3]

The ethical dimensions of vocation beyond paid work are helpfully articulated by Lutheran ethicist and St. Olaf faculty member Kiara Jorgenson in her recent book, *Ecology of Vocation: Recasting Calling in a New Planetary Era*. She proposes that vocation "speaks less about doing the right thing or being the right thing and more about relating in a right or appropriate fashion. For this reason, vocation must be recast as something far greater than work, as even 'ethical' forms of work . . . underestimate the complex interrelationality

---

3 Douglas Schuurman, *Vocation: Discerning Our Callings in Life* (Grand Rapids, MI: Eerdmans, 2004).

of one's inhabited roles."[4] It's the ethical dimensions of our ecologies of vocation that Lutheran-affiliated institutions are called to keep front and center.

Frederick Buechner's famous definition of vocation also goes beyond narrow conceptions of career and makes space for our inter-relatedness. Buechner defines vocation as "the place where your deep gladness and the world's deep hunger meet."[5] While many students have been animated by thinking about their gladness intersecting with the world's deep need, a number of people at Lutheran-affiliated institutions have also been critical of Buechner's definition of voca-tion. Capital University pastor Rev. Drew Tucker suggests that "glad-ness is not something that should solely define the central purposes of our lives."[6] Caring for the needs of the neighbor may involve more toil and suffering than it does joy or gladness, Tucker insists. Lutheran theologian Kathryn Kleinhans also points out that the call to care for the neighbor is for their own sake rather than for the purposes of contributing to our gladness.[7] Our gladness cannot and should not be primary when it comes to the ethical dimension of the vocation to serve the neighbor in love.

Especially after several years of struggling through the pandem-ics of COVID-19 and ongoing struggles against systemic racism, all of us who work with students on vocational reflection cannot ignore the deep sadness that has pervaded many of their lives. A hallmark of Martin Luther's theology is a commitment not to shy away from the hardship that makes up human life. Luther called himself a "theo-logian of the cross" over against a "theologian of glory," because he viewed sin, suffering, and death as our dominant this-worldly reali-ty.[8] Wartburg College theologian Caryn D. Riswold suggests that, in

---

4 Kiara Jorgenson, *Ecology of Vocation: Recasting Calling in a New Planetary Era* (Minneapolis: Fortress, 2020), 53.

5 Frederick Buechner, *Wishful Thinking: A Seeker's ABCs* (New York: Harper-One, 1993), 118.

6 Drew Tucker, "(Re)Defining Vocation: Gladly Challenging a Vocational Giant," *Intersections* 53 (Fall 2021): 3.

7 Kathryn Kleinhans, "Distinctive Lutheran Contributions to the Conversation about Vocation," *Intersections* 43 (Fall 2016): 5.

8 Martin Luther, "Heidelberg Disputation (1518)," in *Martin Luther's Basic Theolog-ical Writings*, 2nd ed., ed. Timothy F. Lull (Fortress, 2005), 57 (theses 19 and 20).

Luther's view, none of us has to seek suffering and despair because "it comes to us all, unbidden. For [Luther], the good news was that in the midst of that despair is precisely where God is present, known, and revealed. It makes no sense. And it is the only thing that can make sense."[9]

Living during the plague, Luther watched helplessly as two of his daughters died before his own eyes. Time and again he witnessed senseless suffering pervade his life and the lives of his neighbors, a reality that carries particular resonance in this time of emerging from the pandemic of COVID-19 and of continuing to address the pandemic of systemic racism. Reflections on who we are and what to make of our current context need to include our deep sadness, for when we do so, we are better able to identify the sadness in the neighbor.

Returning to the illustration of St. Olaf's Day of Healing in April 2021, we see that that day offered students, faculty, and staff opportunities to lament ways they and others in our communities have been wounded. The day also made space for the creation of collective expressions of hope through virtual gatherings and a vibrant work of art.

In the reflection session for staff in which I participated during the day of healing, we used the language of trauma in reference to the pandemics with which we had been living. Theologian Shelly Rambo defines trauma as "the suffering that remains."[10] Trauma is most often caused by an event—war, forced migration, natural disaster, sexual assault, racial violence; now we can add "living through a pandemic," an ongoing event that has altered virtually every aspect of college life and has claimed millions of lives worldwide. The stress of a traumatic event is often so great "that it cannot be defended against, coped with, or managed well. The event stunts and often immobilizes. Coping skills are frozen; defense mechanisms fail.

9 Caryn D. Riswold, "Called to a Pedagogy of the Cross," *Vocation Matters* (blog), April 8, 2020, https://vocationmatters.org/2020/04/08/called-to-a-pedagogy-of-the-cross/.

10 Shelly Rambo, *Spirit and Trauma: A Theology of Remaining* (Louisville, KY: Westminster John Knox, 2010), 15.

When a person experiences a traumatic event, the survival response is triggered, causing the person to fight, flee or freeze."[11]

Traumatic experiences can rob people of the ability to talk about what they've been through and how bodies respond in divergent ways to traumatic events. We can feel numb, sad, depressed, exhausted. People living with trauma often try to hide these emotions, retreating from relationships in attempts to protect themselves. Lutheran womanist theologian Beverly Wallace notes that "trauma affects our brains, but it has a lasting effect on our bodies."[12]

Living through a global pandemic has upped the urgency that we make space for deep sadness in our conversations about vocation with our students and one another. Many of us in higher education had never taught online before, or run programs, departments, offices, even entire institutions while working remotely. While there has been great innovation and "pivoting" by all involved, it is also important to acknowledge and name the losses—that graduations were postponed or done virtually; that family rituals and gatherings were not able to happen; that we lost family members, colleagues, friends, even students, and were unable to come together to mourn and to bury our dead with the rituals and rites that give shape to our grieving.

Some experts are using the language of trauma to talk about what so many have experienced during the pandemic. Those who study trauma and its effects note that the pandemic brought on "extreme distress, children and adults alike report worry, fear, hurt, and anger along with symptoms and reactions such as anxiety, depression, fatigue, difficulty focusing, problematic behavior, and the use of at-risk coping skills such as substance abuse. There is grief over what has been lost, and uncertainty about how to navigate daily life and concerns about what the future holds."[13] Talking about trauma as

---

11 Beverly Wallace, "Bible Study: 'She Had to Keep Him Hidden'—Experiences of Trauma in the Lineage of Moses," June 30, 2020, https://connectjournalorg. wordpress.com/2020/06/30/bible-study-she-had-to-keep-him-hidden-experiences-of-trauma-in-the-lineage-of-moses/.

12 Wallace, "Bible Study."

13 Dr. Caelan Soma, "Post-COVID Stress Disorder and Pandemic Trauma and Stress Experience," *Starr Commonwealth Newsletter*, February 19, 2021,

"the suffering that remains" gives a way to name some of the dimensions of this experience that we may not be as able to talk about yet.

Teaching virtually during the pandemic has also led Lutheran theologian Caryn D. Riswold to develop what she calls "a pedagogy of the cross":

> Teaching at the foot of the cross where forces beyond our control inflict pain, suffering, and anguish. Teaching in the shadow of the cross where failures to adhere to scientific wisdom lead to unjust and inequitable trauma. Advising while facing the cross where job opportunities vanish and graduate school funding evaporates. It is a moment that calls for maximum grace, compassion, and space to hear the litanies of grief that are just below the surface if they are not right out in the open in front of us.[14]

Riswold's pedagogy of the cross communicates a distinctive Lutheran approach to making space for the sadnesses while also naming the moments of grace and hope.

A couple weeks prior to the day of healing, St. Olaf hosted a virtual panel of alumni to talk about how their faith traditions influenced their vocational path at St. Olaf and beyond. The alumni spoke eloquently and thoughtfully about their navigation of faith commitments and their ever-evolving understandings of their vocational journeys and identities. One of the panelists, Dr. Branden Grimmett, Associate Provost at Loyola Marymount University, encouraged the students with this advice: "You all have a pandemic story, and whatever step you take next is going to be interested in that story—how you used this time, how the pandemic has changed you."[15] Students attending the panel resonated with that suggestion as they know they've been through something where the implications have yet to be fully explored. As we practice and encourage the telling of our pandemic stories and how they relate to our vocational discernment, I hope we will also encourage space for lament, and understand how

---

https://starr.org/2021/post-covid-stress-disorder-and-pandemic-trauma-and-stress-experience/.

14 Riswold, "Called to a Pedagogy of the Cross."

15 Virtual Seminar, *Interfaith Perspectives on Vocation* (2021), St. Olaf College, https://www.stolaf.edu/multimedia/play/?e=3433.

this and other challenging situations might help us better identify the deep needs of the world.

But the ways we humans are in relationship to one another has been upended and rearranged through our many months of pandemic. As the description of St. Olaf's Day of Healing suggests, much of our interaction with one another was done virtually. As we anticipate chapters of life postpandemic, we have opportunities to use virtual tools to make more space for lament, sadness, and care of neighbor for the flourishing of all.

Virtual Embodied Acts of Neighbor Love for the Sake of the Flourishing of All

It is the case that our ecologies of vocation look different on Zoom than they do face-to-face. While virtual interactions differ from in-person interactions, the pandemic has revealed to many that virtual interactions are indeed real. Digital scholar T.V. Reed talks about the distinction between virtual and in-person realms this way:

> It is important to take that illusion of virtuality [of the virtual world] seriously; it is to some degree a new kind of experience. But it is also not wholly new (whenever we read a novel we also enter a virtual world, just not a digitally delivered one). Part of studying virtual worlds should be to remind users that they are never just in a virtual world, but always in a real one too.[16]

Living through a pandemic has forced us to spend more time than ever before in virtual spaces. Those experiences of virtuality invite us to consider how and in what ways our ecologies of vocation can be formed and sustained virtually. Online experiences throughout the pandemic have hopefully moved us, as theologian Kathryn Reklis suggests, beyond "seeing the real versus virtual divide in terms of embodied versus disembodied," to thinking creatively about "the

---

16 T.V. Reed, *Digitized Lives: Culture, Power, and Social Change in the Internet Era* (New York: Routledge 2014), 21.

new permutations of digital and virtual technology informing our lives as particular ways we are embodied."[17]

New ways of providing student services also emerged during the pandemic, and we are learning how virtual resources can be created that meet students where they are while also encouraging them to address some of the ways deep sadness affects their mental and physical well-being. One excellent illustration of this is how William Iavarone, director of counseling at Augustana College (Rock Island, IL), has utilized virtual spaces to develop the STEP CARE counseling resources for their students. These resources begin with an invitation to students to complete an online mental health assessment screening. Upon completion of the screening, students are directed toward a "Navigating Resources" page that directs them to resources and actions based on their levels of risk. Possible actions include exploring groups and activities on campus to help foster connections, developing a plan to increase health and wellness through exercise and nutrition, and attending community support groups on depression or other stressors. Augustana's Counseling Center still offers counseling sessions to students, but the online tools and resources now available are directing and equipping more Augustana students to discern how they should best navigate living with the particular challenges they face.

While the cherished tradition of Advent and Christmas Festivals at NECU institutions could not be held in person in 2020, virtual versions of these programs were created that spoke to the embodied realities of COVID-19 and the ways George Floyd's murder laid bare the persistence of systemic racism. Augsburg University's annual Advent Vespers virtual service revolved around the theme, "Come Now Breath of God," and began with pastor Babette Chatman linking Floyd's inability to breathe under the knee of Derek Chauvin to the struggle to breathe by those diagnosed with COVID-19. Rev. Chatman's words were heavy with grief and lament. "Yet into this breathless moment," Chatman recited, "a young pregnant woman

---

17 Kathryn Reklis, "X-Reality and the Incarnation," New Media Project at Union Theological Seminary, http://kineticslive.com/2012/06/19/new-resources-now-available-to-advance-theological-thinking-about-new-media/.

breathes in anticipation of a child's advent." Chatman pointed to the promise borne by Mary, "the promise of God taking flesh among us," and invited viewers to join the Augsburg community in their "communal waiting of the coming of the breath of God" into the midst of the pandemics of COVID-19 and systemic racism.

The loss of the ability to sing together was expressed by Augsburg's Schwartz Professor of Choral Leadership Kristina Boerger: "At a time when we need healing more than ever, it's been determined that breathing and singing together is one of the most dangerous things we can do." And yet, she noted, "it's still possible to create meaning with our voices, and we'll do it any way we can." Her words gave way to choir members' *a cappella* offering of "Beautiful Star," a piece that expresses hope that the "star of Bethlehem" will shine down "until glory dawns." For participants and viewers alike, Augsburg's virtual "Come Now, Breath of God" elicited embodied engagement through digital means.

Back at St. Olaf College, the pandemic upended the work of a group of dedicated St. Olaf students, faculty, and staff working together to bring the Hostile Terrain 94 (HT94) project to campus. A participatory art project sponsored and organized by the Undocumented Migration Project (UMP),[18] HT94 culminates in an exhibition of over 3,200 handwritten toe tags representing migrants who have died crossing the Sonoran Desert of Arizona.

The St. Olaf HT94 group's plan to install the thirty-foot map with toe tags in the fall of 2020 was thwarted by the pandemic. Rather than putting the project on hold, the HT94 student members worked together to create virtual toe tag sessions so people could fill out toe tags online. As they hosted virtual toe tags sessions throughout the summer of 2020, the group continued to refine how the sessions were conducted. Scripts for the virtual sessions provided increased guidance for participants on how to deal with potentially intense bodily reactions to filling out the toe tags with the precise location where the body was found, the condition of the body, whether the body had been identified with a name and an age at the time of death. St. Olaf student Tyreis Hunt, one of the student leaders of the project,

---

18 See https://www.undocumentedmigrationproject.org/.

notes that the act of filling out toe tags is a "process of rehumanization of the individuals who have died. We have students on campus with varying relationships to immigration, and this brings everyone together to commemorate the lives that have been lost."[19]

St. Olaf's HT94's transition to virtual toe tag events caught the attention of the national HT94 staff. St. Olaf began offering training sessions on how to host virtual toe tag events for HT94 teams across the country. My involvement with St. Olaf's HT94 team over the past two years has allowed me to witness a "bouquet of humanity" that embodies neighbor love in ways that make space for deep sadness in the promotion of justice for the flourishing of all.

Conclusion

The intense experiences related to twin pandemics sheds light on the ways in which Lutheran colleges and universities are leaning into broader definitions of vocation that speak to the realities facing students, faculty, and staff in our current context. It is also becoming clear that now is the time to harvest the many insights about how our ecologies of vocation are forged, strengthened, and sustained through virtual as well as in-person interactions. May we continue to pay close attention to how the Spirit is at work, even amidst those times of apparent God-forsakenness. When we name and acknowledge the trauma that exists for people within and beyond our campuses, we make it more possible for the work of justice and healing to emerge.

For Further Study

Mahn, Jason A. *Neighbor Love through Fearful Days: Finding Purpose and Meaning in a Time of Crisis.* Minneapolis: Fortress, 2021.

Rambo, Shelly. *Spirit and Trauma: A Theology of Remaining.* Louisville: Westminster John Knox, 2014.

---

19 Harrison Clark, "Students Prepare Exhibit to Raise Awareness about Deaths on Southern Border," *St. Olaf College News*, November 20, 2020: https://wp.stolaf. edu/news/students-prepare-exhibit-to-raise-awareness-about-deaths-on-u-s-southern-border.

Schuurman, Doug. *Vocation: Discerning Our Callings in Life*. Grand Rapids, MI: Eerdmans, 2003.

Thompson, Deanna A. *The Virtual Body of Christ in a Suffering World*. Nashville: Abingdon, 2016.

Wallace, Beverly. "'She Had to Keep Him Hidden': Experiences of Trauma in the Lineage of Moses." June 30, 2020. https://connectjournalorg. wordpress.com/2020/06/30/bible-study-she-had-to-keep-him-hidden-experiences-of-trauma-in-the-lineage-of-moses/.

Epilogue: This Very Moment

Darrel D. Colson, Wartburg College

Never has the need for Lutheran higher education been greater; never has the gift on offer from our colleges and universities better met the needs of the moment.

As we look around ourselves, we see a country in crisis. In *crises* might be more accurate. It has become trite to talk of ourselves as polarized, to speak of our separation into "tribes." Yet who can deny the evidence before us? We consume our "news" in echo chambers of the like-minded; we aggregate into zip codes with our political bedfellows; we feel hostility, sometimes even hatred, for those who believe differently on a vast range of issues, some of them once thought trivial.

In his classic study of the American character, *Democracy in America*, Alexis de Tocqueville highlighted our *individualism*, an attitude quite different from what he knew in aristocratic France. People, he says, "living in aristocratic ages are . . . closely attached to something placed out of their own sphere" and are "often disposed to forget themselves," whereas people living in democratic times will find the "bond of human affection . . . relaxed."[1]

The tendency he identified in Americans was to "acquire the habit of always considering themselves as standing alone," each one "confine[d] . . . entirely within the solitude of [his or her] own heart."[2] Yet he also discerned that no one can actually remain thus isolated, inventing *all* of his or her own opinions; rather, each individual casts about

---

1 Alexis de Tocqueville, *Democracy in America*, trans. Henry Reeve, ed. Isaak Kramnick (New York: W. W. Norton, 2007), Vol. II: 447.

2 Tocqueville, *Democracy in America*, Vol. II: 447–48.

for guidance, falling prey to the whims of "common opinion,"[3] whether based on evidence or, more likely, based on supposition or prejudice.

Within Lutheran education, we approach life differently—indeed, so differently as to be countercultural. We respect the individual, of course, for we stand on ground prepared by the Reformation, reflecting the crucial Protestant insight that faith appeals to, and abides within, the individual conscience. Indeed, we see each individual as a precious neighbor, worthy of respect, entitled to justice.

Additionally and crucially, however, we cherish and proclaim another insight birthed by the Reformation, which is that each of us is nested within a community of neighbors, or, better said, within an overlapping variety of such communities; and each of us is called to serve the precious individuals with whom we are in community. Whether relatives, friends, or strangers, all of them are neighbors.

Our schools practice radical hospitality, appreciating the diversity of faiths and opinions that students can bring, encouraging the discourse they stimulate, and pursuing the self-examination they inspire. Far from expecting our students to embrace the faith that grounds our approach, we welcome the challenge they might bring. Whether students come with religious or secular commitments, we offer them education with humility, acknowledging the many mysteries in creation and the limitations of human knowing. Critically engaging with one another in a climate of free inquiry, together we learn from one another, deepening our wisdom.

We do ask, however, that our students embrace one Reformation insight that we hold dear, and that is their call to service. On this we stand firm. Martin Luther contended that faith confers freedom, but freedom understood paradoxically—"freedom *from* the need to shore up a right relationship with God and . . . freedom *for* good and meaningful work in God's world. It is both a freedom *from* false ideas about earning one's own worthiness and a freedom *for* a life of service to and with the neighbor."[4]

---

3 Tocqueville, *Democracy in America,* Vol. II: 383.
4 NECU, *Rooted and Open: The Common Calling of the Network of ELCA Colleges and Universities,* 4. https://download.elca.org/ELCA%20Resource%20 Repository/Rooted_and_Open.pdf.

Whether our students are Protestants or Catholics, Christians or Muslims, people of faith or not, we believe they are called to our colleges and universities so that they might discern their vocations while strengthening their minds, bodies, and spirits. We insist that they will flourish by cherishing, protecting, and improving the communities we prepare them to join.

When I was a very new president walking to my first commencement, a student shared a thought that has stuck with me: "Wartburg has made me," he said, "a better Hindu." He had learned how to flourish. Upon graduation, he attended law school and now works in health care, seeking to broaden the quality of options available to the elderly so that they might flourish too.

How transformative it would be if everyone thought as he does. How utterly revolutionary if everyone—those with whom we agree as well as those with whom we don't, the pro-whatevers and the anti-whatevers—thought not about whom and what they oppose, but rather about how they might serve one another, reducing what suffering they can and enhancing lives where they can.

Simply said, such is the goal of Lutheran higher education. It is the task and opportunity of each of our colleges and universities to impart this gift, this disposition and drive for service, to the students who cross our thresholds. Our hope, our prayer is that they might, in turn, offer this very gift to everyone they meet.

Ambitious, yes; optimistic, certainly; impossible, perhaps—and yet, who can deny that our times cry out for what we offer, that our dire need in this very moment is for young people called, inspired, and prepared to serve their neighbors, our neighbors?

Appendices

List of Institutions in the Network of ELCA Colleges and Universities

Augsburg University—Minneapolis, MN
Augustana College—Rock Island, IL
Augustana University—Sioux Falls, SD
Bethany College—Lindsborg, KS
California Lutheran University—Thousand Oaks, CA
Capital University—Columbus, OH
Carthage College—Kenosha, WI
Concordia College—Moorhead, MN
Finlandia University—Hancock, MI
Gettysburg College—Gettysburg, PA
Grand View University—Des Moines, IA
Gustavus Adolphus College—St. Peter, MN
Lenoir-Rhyne University—Hickory, NC
Luther College—Decorah, IA
Luther College, University of Regina—Regina, SK
Midland University—Fremont, NE
Muhlenberg College—Allentown, PA
Newberry College—Newberry, SC
Pacific Lutheran University—Tacoma, WA
Roanoke College—Salem, VA
St. Olaf College—Northfield, MN
Susquehanna University—Selinsgrove, PA
Texas Lutheran University—Seguin, TX
Thiel College—Greenville, PA
Wagner College—Staten Island, NY
Wartburg College—Waverly, IA
Wittenberg University—Springfield, OH

List of Contributors

Anton E. Armstrong, DMA
Harry R. and Thora H. Tosdal Professor of Music
Conductor of the St. Olaf Choir
St. Olaf College (Northfield, MN)

Anthony Bateza, PhD
Associate Professor of Religion
Chair of the Department of Race, Ethnic, Gender and Sexuality Studies
St. Olaf College (Northfield, MN)

Marcia J. Bunge, PhD
Professor of Religion
The Rev. Drell and Adeline Bernhardson Distinguished Chair
    of Lutheran Studies
Gustavus Adolphus College (St. Peter, MN)
Extraordinary Research Professor
North-West University (South Africa)

Darrel D. Colson, PhD
President (2009–22)
Wartburg College (Waverly, IA)

Krista E. Hughes, PhD
Associate Professor of Religion
Director of the Muller Center
Newberry College (Newberry, SC)

Jason A. Mahn, PhD
Professor of Religion
The Conrad Bergendoff Chair in the Humanities
Director of the Presidential Center for Faith and Learning
Augustana College (Rock Island, IL)

Mindy Makant, PhD
Associate Professor of Religious Studies
Director of the Living Well Center for Vocation and Purpose
Dean of the College of Humanities and Social Sciences
Lenoir-Rhyne University (Hickory, NC)

James B. Martin-Schramm, PhD
Professor Emeritus
Director of the Center for Sustainable Communities (2019–21)
Luther College (Decorah, IA)

Ann Milliken Pederson, PhD
Professor of Religion
Medical Humanities and Society Program Director
Augustana University (Sioux Falls, SD)
Adjunct Professor in the Section of Ethics and Humanities
    at the Sanford School of Medicine
University of South Dakota (Sioux Falls, SD)

Caryn D. Riswold, PhD
Professor of Religion
The Mike and Marge McCoy Family Distinguished Chair
    in Lutheran Heritage and Mission
Wartburg College (Waverly, IA)

Martha E. Stortz, PhD
Professor Emerita
Bernhard M. Christensen Professor of Religion and Vocation
    (2010–20)
Augsburg University (Minneapolis, MN)

Vic Thasiah, PhD
Professor of Religion
Affiliated Faculty in the Environmental Studies Program
California Lutheran University (Thousand Oaks, CA)

Deanna A. Thompson, PhD
Director of the Lutheran Center for Faith, Values, and Community
Martin E. Marty Regents Chair in Religion and the Academy
St. Olaf College (Northfield, MN)

Samuel Torvend, PhD
Professor of Religion
Director of External Relations in the Wild Hope Center for Vocation
Pacific Lutheran University (Tacoma, WA)

Marit Trelstad, PhD
Professor of Religion
Endowed Chair in Lutheran Studies
Pacific Lutheran University (Tacoma, WA)

Courtney Wilder, PhD
Professor of Religion
Midland University (Fremont, NE)

Mark Wilhelm, PhD
Executive Director
Network of ELCA Colleges and Universities
Evangelical Lutheran Church in America (Chicago, IL)

ELCA Social Statements and Selected Resolutions

ELCA social statements are teaching documents that provide broad frameworks to assist the ELCA in reflecting on and discussing social issues. They are not understood as "doctrines" but rather aim to help ELCA communities and individuals to deliberate and to engage thoughtfully with contemporary challenges. They result from an extensive process of participation and deliberation and are adopted by a two-thirds vote of an ELCA Churchwide Assembly.

The ELCA's social statements as well as various policy statements, resolutions, and declarations guide its advocacy and work as a publicly engaged church. The following is a list of current ELCA social statements and selected resolutions, beginning with the most recent. You are able to access these and other documents on the ELCA's website: www.elca.org/socialstatements.

A Declaration to the Muslim Community (2022)

A Declaration to American Indian and Alaska Native People (2021)

A Declaration of Inter-Religious Commitment: A Policy Statement of the Evangelical Lutheran Church in America (2019)

Repudiation of the Doctrine of Discovery (Social Policy Resolution, 2016)

The Church and Criminal Justice: Hearing the Cries (Social Statement, 2013)

Genetics, Faith and Responsibility (Social Statement, 2011)

Human Sexuality: Gift and Trust (Social Statement, 2009)

Our Calling in Education (Social Statement, 2007)

Caring for Health: Our Shared Endeavor (Social Statement, 2003)

Sufficient, Sustainable Livelihood for All (Social Statement, 1999)

For Peace in God's World (Social Statement, 1995)

A Declaration of the Evangelical Lutheran Church in America to the Jewish Community (1994)

Caring for Creation: Vision, Hope, and Justice (Social Statement, 1993)

Freed in Christ: Race, Ethnicity, and Culture (Social Statement, 1993)

Abortion (Social Statement, 1991)

Church in Society: A Lutheran Perspective (Social Statement, 1991)

The Death Penalty (Social Statement, 1991)

The Church in Society: A Lutheran Perspective (Social Statement, 1991)

A Declaration of Ecumenical Commitment: A Policy Statement of the Evangelical Lutheran Church in America (1991)